Creative glass blowing

James E. Hammesfahr

Clair L. Stong

with a Foreword by Charles H. Greene
State University of New York, College of Ceramics at Alfred University

Color plates courtesy of Bernard Armuller

W. H. Freeman and Company *San Francisco*

OR

4/70

In memory of Herman Hammesfahr,
master glass blower and German immigrant, who in 1862
first brought to these shores many techniques of glass working
now disclosed in this volume—techniques preserved
by three generations of his grateful progeny.

Foreword

Not many people take up glass blowing, either for fun or as a vocation. In an industrially advanced nation such as the United States where modern technology and its fruit—the good life—depend so heavily on blown glass, it seems strange that not more than one in 10,000, including even the many craftsmen who make neon signs, practices the art of shaping molten glass by hand.

Most commercial glassware is now made by machine, of course. Readymade bulbs, tubes, vessels, rods, and sheets, as well as complete laboratory apparatus, are available at modest cost in an impressive range of sizes. But if you are in need of the services of a glass blower to assemble the parts, or to repair an apparatus, and you do not have a glass blower on your payroll, you face a problem with few solutions. One solution is to let the job out on contract to a specialty shop and wait in line for the finished work; this may take days or weeks, depending upon the shop. Alternatively, you may attempt to lure a glass blower away from his present employer, a common practice that does not always win friends. Or, if you are influential, you may import a glass blower from abroad, where the supply is more plentiful: in West Germany, Italy, and Japan accomplished artisans are still held in such popular esteem that youngsters compete for apprenticeships. But perhaps the best solution is to take up the art and do the job yourself.

Few glass blowers are trained in the United States. One reason is that almost none of our high schools or vocational schools offer courses in glass blowing—although they teach the elements of wood and metal work to millions. It is true, of course, that very little information about the techniques of glass blowing has been published. A number of small manuals explain *what* to do in glass blowing, but none has treated the *hows* clearly, or in detail.

This book fills that important need. I would have found it invaluable in my own graduate work in chemistry. It describes and explains many techniques that I learned the hard way, by sad experience. In addition, it contains some previously unpublished hints and suggestions that we have tried in our laboratory practice and found useful. I think the book will be essential for any graduate students of chemistry and physics who have frequent occasion to build or repair glass apparatus.

This book is not limited to those in the sciences. It introduces a new hobby: glass blowing for diversion. That the fascinations of the art have universal appeal is attested by the constant presence of onlookers that surround the itinerant glass blowers who turn out model sailing ships, miniature birds, and similar trinkets at amusement centers. Most performances that are interesting to watch are even more fun to do, and glass blowing is no exception. Moreover, glass affords at least as much latitude for creative expression as do ceramics and similar crafts that have attracted large numbers of enthusiasts.

The authors have kept the amateur very much in mind. They explain in detail how to create colorful knick knacks by techniques so simple that children younger than 12 years of age have made costume jewelry of glass on a first try with no other than written instructions. They provide descriptions of how to construct, adjust, and operate inexpensive tools for working glass by hand, and they have included a list of sources of materials.

Indeed, the book is addressed to beginners, and its explanations are confined to operations that require little more than enthusiasm, reasonable patience, some glass tubing, and a gas fire. There is no reference to the manufacture of glass pieces by machines, or with the more complex tools, such as lathes, that are commonly used to supplement hand operations during the commercial manufacture of laboratory glassware; nor is the ancient method of blowing molten glass at the end of a four-foot iron pipe emphasized. The authors assume that these operations will be deferred until the beginner has acquired some experience in constructing small glass pieces by hand.

So, I introduce this book with enthusiasm. May it acquaint many students and laymen with the satisfactions that come with the mastery of an art. A good antidote for the stress of modern living is a quiet avocation. An effective one is the manipulation of molten glass. I hope that you come to know its joys.

Charles H. Greene

Alfred, New York
December, 1967

Preface

Glass working, like the working of most basic materials, encompasses arts and sciences that vastly exceed the limitations of a single volume or even a single mind. For this reason we do not presume to suggest that the following pages cover the whole field of glass work, or even a substantial part of it. We have addressed ourselves primarily to those readers who are interested in learning how to make, from plain glass tubing and rod, laboratory glassware or small objects such as costume jewelry, miniature birds, animals, and so on. This art is known in the trade as "lampwork," a term that dates from an era when heat for softening glass rod and tubing was developed by blowing air through the flame of a wick lamp.

Essentially, we have endeavored to compile a primer for use by those who want to learn the essentials of lampwork but do not know where or how to start. The book explains the rudimentary hows and whys so that with a reasonable amount of practice the novice can master all of the basic operations. Thus equipped, he will find that the fabrication of complex shapes becomes not only easy, but fun. Moreover, a thorough knowledge of the hows and whys will prevent him from drifting into bad habits of procedure that invariably occur during hit-or-miss learning. Without this understanding, practice tends to perpetuate errors as readily as to correct procedures.

There is a correct and an incorrect way to use any book, including this one. The substance of this primer has been arranged sequentially. We suggest that you read it through before touching a piece of glass. Decide how deeply you wish to become involved. Then make a thorough study of Section II, in which tools and facilities are discussed. Acquire a full set of the tools that you will need for the kind of work that you will undertake. Don't skimp on tools. Good tools can make the difference between success and failure for a beginner. Finally, complete every basic exercise discussed in Sections III and IV before moving on. Keep the book within easy reach during practice sessions and refer to it when an operation goes out of control.

For centuries the lore of glass blowing was a closely held secret, passed down from father to son and from friend to friend. The hard-won techniques that are presented in this volume were painstakingly developed by a succession of these nameless, unsung craftsmen. To them we now pay tribute.

We are also grateful to a number of modern industrial organizations who have opened their doors, as well as their files, to us—particularly the Corning Glass Works, the General Electric Company, the Westinghouse Electric Corporation, the Driver-Harris Company, the B. F. Drakenfeld & Company, and the American Gas Furnace Company. Permission to reproduce data from their literature is hereby gratefully acknowledged.

We also thank the Editors of *Scientific American* for permission to reprint certain material that appeared originally in that esteemed periodical and for numerous helpful suggestions and editorial assistance.

It gives us pleasure, too, to acknowledge the work of Wayne Gallup whose illustrations adorn these pages. His contribution in helping us to explain the technical procedures of glass working extended far beyond the execution of attractive drawings.

Special mention must be made of the generous help that we received from Professor Charles H. Greene who, as chairman of the Glass Science Department of the State University of New York, College of Ceramics at Alfred University, not only reviewed the manuscript and made numerous helpful suggestions but throughout the project gave to us unstintingly of his time, knowledge, and warm encouragement.

Our debt of gratitude could not be retired without mention of John E. Paggioli, one of New York City's brighter and more zestful attorneys, who, in the role of social catalyst, initiated our collaboration—and gave it an occasional nudge.

Finally, it is with greatest pleasure that we acknowledge the splendid assistance of Irene Schmitt, an accomplished writer and artist, who not only combed our efforts for misspelled words and affronts to the accepted mores of the English language, but typed the final manuscript. To her we extend our sincerest appreciation.

James E. Hammesfahr
Clair L. Stong

April, 1968

ontents

Glass: Its origin, uses, and nature

Anyone can learn to blow glass. Proficiency in the art comes rather easily with practice, particularly to the artisan who is steeped in the lore of the material. How did glass come into being? What properties explain its behavior? How does it react to manipulation? To what ends may it appropriately be applied? The glass blower who dismisses such questions lightly is in the position of the cabinet maker who cannot distinguish oak from pine—knowledge essential for the expression of his skill. So, we begin at the beginning. Who invented glass?

The full story of manufactured glass, like that of metallurgy, predates recorded history. Primitive tools chipped from natural, volcanic glass appear to have been used throughout most of the past 500 centuries. Objects of manufactured glass have been dated as old as 3,000 years. The circumstances that surrounded the invention of glass are obscure. One early account was written some 2,000 years ago by the Roman encyclopedist, Pliny the Elder.

Volume XXXVI of Pliny's *Natural History* relates how a caravan of traders in minerals once camped on the white sands of the Belus River in Phoenicia. Finding no rocks at hand, the traders made a fireplace for cooking their evening meal by piling on the sand a circle of lumps of soda from their cargo. On arising the next morning they found among the dead coals a translucent substance that shattered into fragments with razor-sharp edges. Thus, according to Pliny, did men chance upon the recipe for making glass.

Historians confess that Pliny did not hesitate to use his facile imagination when spinning a tale. In this instance, however, he enjoys some measure of support from modern glass technology. Although sand resists the

Figure 1-1.
A chunk of obsidian
(a natural glass) and an
arrow head chipped from
obsidian. Tools of such
glass predate recorded
history. [Courtesy
photomedia department,
Corning Glass Works.]

heat of an open fire, soda melts even in the flame of a candle. Moreover, sand dissolves in melted soda much as salt dissolves in water. Soda is a good flux, or dissolving agent, for sand. The ingredients must be well mixed, of course, if one expects to produce glass lumps of substantial size —a detail that Pliny overlooked. He also neglected to mention one essential ingredient of glass: a substance such as lime that imparts chemical stability to the product.

In the absence of lime the fused mixture of soda and sand dissolves in water. Indeed, if the proportion of soda to sand is large the product becomes *water glass,* the familiar cement and a favorite preservative for eggs. The introduction of a small proportion of lime drastically alters the properties of the fused mixture. It then resists attack, not only by water, but by most other fluids and gases including acids. Perhaps the Phoenician

traders dined on seafood, discarding the bones and shells in the fire. Such rubbish would have provided the essential lime and could possibly have turned the trick. With the addition of this lime, the formula reported by Pliny would match that used for making most of the glass used today. Somehow, the ancients hit on a good recipe. The authors of this volume have no wish to spoil the good story told by Pliny.

Whatever the circumstances surrounding the invention of glass, the material itself made little impact on technology for some 3,000 years. A few glass utensils from the early period, consisting mostly of rude bottles, urns, and goblets, have been turned up by archaeologists, but ancient potters remained loyal to their clay, and architects continued to design structures with unglazed windows.

Then, at about the time Pliny wrote his history, an individual about whom nothing whatever is known thrust the end of an iron pipe into a heated mixture of soda, lime, and sand, and from the adhering mass he blew a bubble of glass—seemingly a trivial event. Yet, few strokes of genius have more profoundly altered the course of human affairs.

That shimmering sphere contained the seed of miracles. From it, in one form or another, have come answers to riddles as diverse as the nature of disease, the structure of the universe, the nature of the atom, and the dynamics of the living cell. Without vessels of blown glass chemists could not have compounded the wonder drugs. Eliminate the bulb of blown glass and the global network of telephones would fall silent, as would radio and televi-

Figure 1-2.

An ewer dating back to
the Roman Empire,
probably Syria or Italy,
first century A.D. The
mold is blown of amber
glass and signed by
Ennion. [Courtesy
photomedia department,
Corning Glass Works.]

Figure 1-3.

A rose vase of lead
crystal. [Courtesy
Steuben Glass.]

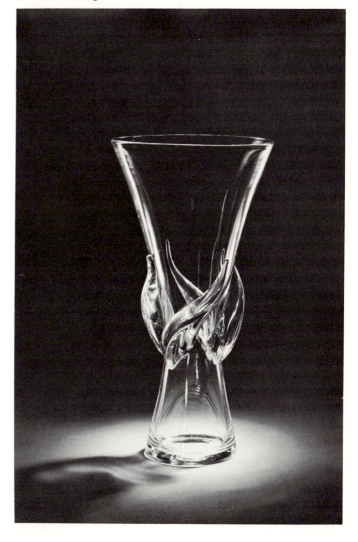

sion. Without glass bulbs man could
not make his way among the clouds,
much less probe the depths of space.
In short, glass implements almost
every facet of science and technology;
it lights man's dwelling place, his
way, and his future.

Equally distinguished contributions
to our aesthetic heritage have come
from glass. Generations of artists and
artificers have found creative expression through glass in masterworks
that range from the stained glass
windows of medieval cathedrals and
the royal banquet settings of crystal,
to the glittering baubels that adorn
milady.

The variety of uses that have been found for glass is a tribute to man's ingenuity. In industrially developed nations we are rarely farther than a few inches from some object of glass —whether it be the spectacles on the nose, the crystal in the watch, or the windshield of our motor car. Yet, curiously, despite all our vaunted cleverness and concentrated effort, we have failed to hit upon an adequate substitute for this versatile product of the ancients.

Until the latter half of the seventeenth century the term glass designated the material described by Pliny. Efforts toward the improvement of glass centered chiefly on the search for pure raw materials, and on manufacturing procedures for making a clear, colorless product. Most sand contains some iron. Even a slight trace of this element in the melt imparts a greenish cast to glass.

Glassmakers learned how to neutralize this stain by adding controlled amounts of manganese, which was in effect a bleaching agent, to the melt. Conversely, craftsmen observed that the selective addition of metallic oxides to the basic formula resulted in strongly colored glass. In one of its several chemical states iron stains glass green; in another it yields a yellow tint. Cobalt imparts a bluish hue; copper, a deep red, blue, or even green; charcoal, yellow-brown; manganese dioxide, violet. A mixture of stannic and arsenious acids produces white. Milky white glass can be made by increasing the proportion of calcium fluoride.

Color can also be developed by introducing finely divided particles of metal or metallic compounds into the melt. The suspended particles selectively reflect or scatter light of one color. Selenium combined with cadmium sulfide in the batch produces particles in the glass that scatter all wavelengths except red. The result is ruby glass, formerly made by adding particles of pure gold to the mixture.

Glass so colored or bleached is not basically altered. It remains the product of the ancients. The first significant innovation in glass making came in 1673 when the Worshipful Company of Glass Sellers, a group that dominated the glass industry of England, grew dissatisfied with the soda-lime glass then being imported from Venice. They commissioned a British experimenter, George Ravencroft, to compound a glass of native materials in the hope of freeing Britain from dependence on foreign sources. Substituting lead oxide (litharge) for soda and altering the proportions of other ingredients in lime glass, Ravencroft achieved spectacular success within three years. The resulting "lead" glass was not only as clear as lime glass, but it bent light much more strongly than the old glass, as it had a higher index of refraction. Moreover, it was characterized by a much higher dispersive power—the property of transparent substances to bend light rays of some colors more than rays of other colors. As a result, lead glass had a sparkling brilliance that rivaled rock crystal. For this reason lead glass was soon being widely used for the production of fine dinner ware and objects of art, applications for which it remains unsurpassed, even today.

The next significant advance in glass making came two centuries la-

Figure 1-4.
Arrays of laboratory
glassware form the
indispensable base of
modern technological
advances. [Courtesy
photomedia department,
Corning Glass Works.]

ter. The German physicist, Ernst Abbe, became interested in improving the microscope, and in 1876 he concluded that any striking advance had to await the development of glasses with controllable refractive index and dispersion. The lens makers had reached a dead end. In 1884 he joined with Otto Schott and Karl Zeiss to form the Jena glassworks of Schott and Sons. Within two years the firm made new glasses from one or more of 28 chemical compounds, including such exotic elements as beryllium, cerium, niobium, erbium, and uranium, as well as boron, cadmium, and tin. Abbe solved his problem and, incidentally, opened the modern era of glass making.

Early in the present century experimenters at the Corning Glass Works, Corning, New York embarked on an organized program of scientific research to explore the full potentials of glass. Similar efforts were soon undertaken by other members of the industry. The first results appeared in 1912 with the introduction by Corning of the borosilicate glasses, a group of materials that exhibit remarkable resistance to thermal shock.

Products made of these glasses are marketed by Corning under the brand name "Pyrex." Borosilicate glasses expand only about a third as much when heated as soda-lime or lead glass. For this reason they can be subjected without damage to temperature changes that would shatter the older glasses. Borosilicate glasses are also relatively inert chemically. Boron oxide is the principal ingredient of the flux.

Following the development of the borosilicate glasses qualified chemists entered the field of glass making in increasing numbers. The term "glass" no longer designated the product of the ancients but became a generic term. New glasses appeared by the hundreds. Some modern foam glasses are as light as feathers. Other special compositions are as heavy as iron. Some, in the form of fibers, are as soft as wool. Others are as hard as gem stones. Still others are so flexible that they make good springs. Some are as stiff and strong as steel. Normally, glass at room temperature is considered an excellent electrical insulator, but now fairly good conductors are also made of glass. Most glasses soften when heated to redness and shatter if suddenly chilled. Some new ones make splendid crucibles for retaining molten metals, and even when white hot can be plunged into ice water without damage!

Silica remains the primary ingredient of most of the new glasses. It is the flux that distinguishes one kind of glass from another. The fluxes are mostly the oxides of metals. Their combinations are seemingly myriad. Thousands of different glasses can be found in the marketplace. Diverse as the new glasses are, however, it is possible to group them into six major families.

The largest family, the one that accounts for the lion's share of all glass currently manufactured, is still the product of the ancients—soda lime glass. The formula is varied slightly by each manufacturer, but the product remains essentially unchanged. Similar minor modifications of Ravencroft's lead glass make up the second family. Lead glasses soften at a relatively low temperature and remain plastic through a broad range of temperatures. Hence, lead glasses are convenient to work. For this reason, neon signs are usually made of this material. The high density of the flux accounts for the high index of refraction of the lead glasses. Lead glasses also strongly absorb ultraviolet rays and X-rays; this property has been exploited for making special windows that shield observers from the hazards of radiation.

The resistance of all glasses to thermal shock increases with the proportion of silica in the melt because silica tends to retain its dimensions when heated. Moreover, silica is highly stable chemically. The reason silica exhibits little expansion with increased temperature is not fully understood, although theoretical explanations have been advanced.

When any compound is heated, the vibrations of its constituent atoms increase in intensity. The atoms then need more room in which to vibrate. They spread apart just enough to accommodate the added jiggle. So, the material expands. The two modes of vibration that occur may be illustrated by a helical spring which (1) alternately stretches and contracts or (2) bows alternately from side to side. Groups of atoms are linked into molecular structures by forces of electrical attraction known as chemical bonds. Molecules of silica consist of an atom of oxygen bonded between two atoms of silicon—a structure that may be likened to a helical spring (see Fig. 1-5, *a*). A large part of the thermal vibration in heated silica is confined to the side-to-side motion of the oxygen atom (1-5, *b*). (Nature left enough room between adjacent molecules of silica to accommodate the side-to-side jiggle.) For this reason, the distance between silicon atoms increases very little when silica is heated. The addition of fluxes to silica breaks the strong silicon-oxygen-silicon bridges that vibrate from side to side. Atoms of the flux, such as sodium atoms, become linked into the structure. Vibrations of the first mode then predominate: the molecule alternately stretches and compresses (1-5, *c*). In this state the material must expand to make room for the longitudinal motion. The rate of expansion increases in proportion to the added

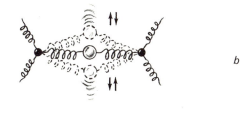

a

b

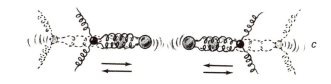

c

Figure 1-5.

● Oxygen

◎ Silicon

◉ Sodium

flux. It is for this reason that both hot lime and lead glasses shatter when thrust into ice water whereas glasses that contain larger proportions of silica emerge from the water undamaged. In borosilicate glasses, such as some Pyrex glasses, boron atoms are linked into the silica structure by silicon-oxygen-boron bonds that vibrate most strongly in the side-to-side mode. Hence these glasses have substantial resistance to thermal shock, although not as much as the high silica glasses.

Why not make glass of pure silica? In general, the manufacture of such glass is difficult. Pure silica reaches the plastic state of thick molasses at a temperature of about 3000 degrees Fahrenheit (1650°C). Bubbles of air that are naturally trapped between the grains of sand cannot escape from the sticky mass. If the temperature is raised to 4000 degrees (2310°C), the boiling point of silica, the mass, instead of becoming water-thin, evaporates! To eliminate the trapped air, the sand must be melted at high temperature under vacuum, a costly procedure. Fused silica glass may also be made by melting crushed crystals of quartz electrically, as well as by the reaction of silicon chloride and water in an oxygas flame, both expensive procedures. Pure silica glass is now routinely made by melting silica under vacuum. The product is a new family of costly glasses for special applications. Fused silica is extremely resistant to thermal shock and chemical attack. It transmits radiant energy from the ultraviolet end of the spectrum well into the infrared, with lower energy loss than any other glass. For these reasons it is of limited use for the optical parts of astro-

nomical telescopes, the bulbs of ultraviolet lamps, the windows of optical masers, and related scientific applications.

Silica is an almost perfectly elastic material. When deformed mechanically, it quickly returns to its former shape, unless it is bent so much that it breaks. Because of this property, silica in the form of fibers is an ideal material for use in suspending balances, the moving parts of electrometers, and similar instruments. Fused silica retains its shape even at white heat. Hence it is much in demand for laboratory crucibles and in the form of vessels known as ignition tubes in which substances may be burned to ash, without becoming contaminated, during chemical analysis.

Most remaining glasses are members of one or another of two additional families; the so-called 96% silica glasses and the aluminosilicate group. A few years ago experimenters at the Corning Glass Works chanced to observe that boro silicate glasses containing unusually large amounts of boron oxide were briskly attacked by dilute acid. They also noticed that the effect became more pronounced as the rate at which a formed object cooled was lowered. The acid did not dissolve the glass completely. The boron oxide and soda dissolved, but not the silica. Eventually, a procedure was developed in which a molded object is immersed, after suitable heat treatment, in hot dilute acid until the boron oxide and soda are leached away, leaving a permeable skeleton of almost pure silica. When the piece is dried and fired at a temperature of about 2200 degrees Fahrenheit the pores close, resulting in a clear transparent structure some 14% smaller than the untreated original. This glass exhibits little more thermal expansion than pure fused silica and about the same electrical properties, resistance to chemicals, and transparency to ultraviolet light. Available from the Corning Glass Works under the brand name Vycor, these glasses are used for chemical apparatus, ultraviolet lamps, and windows in space capsules.

Still another class of glasses, which makes up the sixth family, is represented by the aluminosilicate group, in which aluminum oxide and lime are chief constituents. The material combines good electrical and chemical properties with resistance to high temperature. Containing about 60% silica, this material does not require special processing and can be worked by conventional glass blowing techniques. When tempered it has good resistance to thermal shock. It is specially suited to applications that require high strength at relatively high temperatures, such as thermometers, combustion tubes, electronic vacuum tubes of the high-power type, and cooking ware used on stove burners.

A seventh classification of optical glasses can be made, although the group is scarcely a family because its members have little in common beyond the fact that all are vitreous in nature. Their atoms are locked in random array, not in the highly organized pattern of a crystal lattice. In one sense these special glasses may be thought of as fused fluxes because many of them contain little or no silica.

To compound them, glass makers have utilized more than half of the substances listed in the periodic table of chemical elements. The number of varieties runs into the thousands. Currently, one manufacturer alone compounds some 200 experimental glasses per week! Space permits the mention of only a few.

One subgroup of the optical glasses is based on the oxides of the rare earth elements, notably lanthanum and thorium. These glasses contain no silica. Superficially, they resemble ordinary lime or lead glass, and they are clear and transparent. Prisms made of them have the remarkable property of strongly and almost equally bending light of all colors, whereas conventional glasses bend blue light at a relatively sharp angle, green light somewhat less, yellow light still less, and red light least of all. Dinnerware or costume jewelry made of this material would have little appeal, and would lack luster and sparkle. On the other hand, lanthanum and thorium glasses make ideal camera lenses because with minimum correction they bring light of all colors to focus equally in the plane of the film. Their development has enabled optical engineers to design cameras of remarkably high performance.

Another glass containing silica and soda, but with the rare earth neodymium oxide instead of lime, transmits all colors except the bright yellow that is emitted by the sodium atoms from hot glass in the glass blower's flame. Known as "didymium" glass—because praesodymium, another rare earth metal, usually goes along with the neodymium—the material makes splendid goggles for glass blowers. It blocks out the dazzling yellow glare that obscures the small details when the worker is fashioning small, delicate pieces. Theatrical spotlights are also occasionally equipped with "illusion pink" didymium filters for suppressing the yellow hue emitted by incandescent electric lamps. Light so filtered imparts an attractive glow to the flesh tones of performers.

In recent years, photosensitive glass has also been developed. A small amount of cerium oxide is added to the melt in addition to controlled amounts of antimony oxide and gold. When the finished glass is exposed to light, a chemical change occurs; the cerium oxide transfers electrons to the ions of antimony and gold. The change is not at first apparent to the eye. But when the piece is subsequently heated, antimony transfers electrons to the gold centers, which grow and so color the glass a deep blue. The sensitivity extends completely throughout the piece. If the exposure is made through a photographic negative the resulting picture creates a three-dimensional effect.

Another glass, made with silver and lithium, is highly soluble in hydrofluoric acid at points of exposure to light after development by heat. This property has become the basis of a chemical machining technique. In one demonstration, 200,000 uniform holes, each smaller than the thickness of a human hair, were etched in a 12-inch square of the new glass.

One of the more recent developments to come from the laboratories of the Corning Glass Works is a composition that darkens when exposed to light and then clears when the light is removed. This "Photochromic" glass never loses its ability to change color, cycling from clear to dark and back again, without limit. In sunlight, the darkening may approach maximum intensity in a matter of seconds. The time required for regaining the original transparency ranges from minutes to hours, depending upon the composition, the previous heat treatment, and the temperature. Windows of this glass would maintain daylight of constant intensity in a room, whether the sun was shining or not. Spectacles made from photochromic glass become sunglasses in the sun and clear in the shade.

Corning has also developed a series of glasses that soften at relatively low temperatures. These contain a large proportion of lead oxide and are called "solder" glasses. They are used for joining conventional glasses that become rigid at relatively higher temperature. Although the solder glasses are more reactive chemically than lime, lead, or borosilicate materials, they are sufficiently inert for use in numerous applications, particularly in scientific apparatus such as vacuum tubes. Solder glasses are compounded to expand and contract at the same rate as the glasses to be joined. Other physical properties, such as density, viscosity, electrical resistivity, and chemical durability, may differ however.

The solders are compounded into two types. One type melts at a relatively low temperature and may be remelted at the same temperature. It solidifies as a vitreous mass. The second type also melts initially at a relatively low temperature. By appropriate heat treatment, however, the vitreous mass may be devitrified and changed to a crystalline form that melts at substantially higher temperature. Solder of this type is used for joining glass parts, such as color television tubes, that must be heated strongly following assembly.

Solder glass is distributed in the form of a fine powder. To make a soldered joint, the powder is mixed with a binder, such as collodion thinned by 99 parts of acetone, to make a creamy paste. The paste is applied to the surfaces that will be joined. The coated surfaces are pressed into contact and dried. The assembly is then heated in an oven at a temperature sufficient to melt the solder but below the softening temperature of the glass parts.

The physical properties of all glasses can be somewhat modified by heating and cooling the material at a controlled rate. Such heat treatment is known as tempering or annealing, depending upon whether internal stress in the glass is developed or relieved. The terms "annealing" and "tempering" are borrowed from the field of metallurgy and these techniques impart analogous qualities to the product; that is, they soften or harden it, respectively. Heat treatment of metals alters the crystalline structure of the substance whereas in the treatment of glass, a noncrystalline material, the effects are achieved by manipulating the patterns of internal stress.

Such internal stresses develop when two or more regions in a mass of glass are heated or cooled unequally. The surface of a molten mass cools faster than the interior, and hardens first. The interior, which is now encased by a rigid envelope, continues to cool and shrink as it stiffens. Stress develops when the shrinking interior attempts to pull away from the unyielding envelope and is expressed by a force that tends to squeeze together the molecules of the envelope. Hence, the envelope is subject to a force of compression. Conversely, the molecules of the interior undergo a pull, or tensile stress, as they are drawn simultaneously toward the center by the natural shrinkage of the mass and outward by the unyielding envelope. The pressure of this tug-of-war may amount to many tons per square inch. Internal stresses always occur to some extent when glass cools unevenly. Such stresses are relatively trivial in fused silica and the 96% silica glasses because of the low thermal coefficient of expansion of these materials.

Similar stresses also appear when a glass piece of irregular shape cools from the plastic state. The thin parts cool and shrink first, and eventually become rigid. Thicker parts solidify later. As the rigid but still hot piece continues to cool, the hotter, thick parts shrink more than the thin parts, but the glass can no longer flow and thus relieve the growing stresses. As a consequence, internal forces develop that remain in the glass when the piece cools to room temperature.

The effect of stresses so developed is easy to demonstrate. Place an irregularly shaped piece, such as a water tumbler with a thick bottom, in an oven and heat it slowly to a temperature of 300 degrees or more, and then plunge the hot glass into ice water. Doubtless it will shatter. The thin sides cool and shrink faster than the bottom. The resulting stress exceeds the breaking strength of the glass. Stresses of this magnitude can

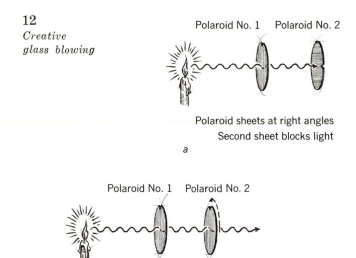

Polaroid No. 1   Polaroid No. 2

Polaroid sheets at right angles
Second sheet blocks light

a

Polaroid No. 1   Polaroid No. 2

Polaroid sheets aligned
Second sheet transmits light

b

Figure 1-6.

and examined with the aid of an easily constructed instrument that utilizes polarized light, that is, light that vibrates in a single plane. Waves of ordinary light vibrate simultaneously in all planes, vertically, sideways, and so on. Waves that vibrate in a single plane can be separated from the jumble of vibrations making up ordinary light by a special filter that consists, in effect, of a grid of fine opaque lines. A filtering material of this kind is distributed in the form of plastic sheets under the brand name "Polaroid." When a beam of ordinary light falls on a sheet of Polaroid, only polarized light is transmitted. All other light is largely absorbed. When the transmitted rays fall on a second sheet of Polaroid they are fully absorbed *if* the grid-like structure of the second sheet is at right angles to the plane in which the light vibrates (Fig. 1-6, *a*), but they are transmitted if the grid is parallel with the plane of vibration (1-6, *b*). Glass has the property of altering the plane of polarized light, depending somewhat upon the magnitude of its internal stresses. This property can be used to detect the internal stresses. A film of Polaroid is placed in front of an incandescent lamp. The observer looks at the light source through a second polarizing film and rotates the film to the point of minimum light transmission. The glass specimen is then placed between the two films. Patterns of internal stress appear as bands of light and shade, whereas unstrained glass appears uniformly clear. Detailed instructions for making and using an instrument of this type (called a polariscope) are included in Section II (see page 40).

develop in newly made pieces, which promptly crack. In occasional pieces the internal stresses fall just short of the breaking point. These may crack spontaneously days, or even years, later. Almost any external force, such as a small increase in temperature, can initiate the rupture. In this case the sequence of events is reversed. The thinner portions of the warmed glass expand more quickly than the thicker portions and so generate forces that add to the internal stresses already present. A mechanical shock, such as a gentle tap, can have the same effect. In short, the presence of internal stress, in its net effect, lowers the natural strength of the glass unless it is carefully controlled so that tensile stress does not appear in the surface of the piece. The piece gains strength, however, if the surface is under compression and the interior under tension.

Internal stresses can be detected

Although the presence of internal stress is normally undesirable, methods have been developed for utilizing it to produce glass of exceptional strength, by the technique of tempering. For example, jets of cold air are played on the surfaces of plate glass which has been heated until it is plastic. Thus chilled abruptly, the surfaces are placed in a state of compression and the interior in tension. Plates so treated may be safely loaded by tensile stresses that would break ordinary glass. The loading opposes and, in effect, cancels the built-in stress of compression. In the interior of the plate, where tensile stress is increased by tempering, the strength of the material is almost unlimited because the glass is free of imperfections. Glass so tempered is used for windows of automobiles, show cases, windows of telephone booths, scientific apparatus, kitchen ware for use on stove surfaces, and numerous similar constructions that require great strength combined with transparency.

The fascinating glass novelties known as Prince Rupert's drops provide a dramatic demonstration of the tempering effect. These small teardrop-shaped objects are made by dropping bits of molten glass into cold water. Prepare them by melting the tip of a rod of lime glass about 2 millimeters in diameter in a gas flame. Let a drop about 1/8 inch in diameter fall a distance of 4 or 5 inches into a container of warm water 10 or more inches deep. Many of the drops will break but some will survive. Fish out a chilled drop by its tip and examine it with the polariscope. The internal stresses will appear as a dazzling pattern of rainbow colors. Next,

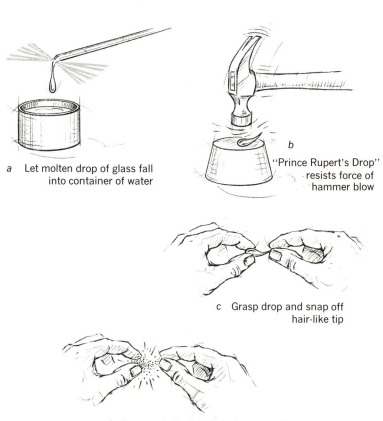

a   Let molten drop of glass fall
into container of water

b   "Prince Rupert's Drop"
resists force of
hammer blow

c   Grasp drop and snap off
hair-like tip

d   Drop explodes into harmless granules

Figure 1-7.

place the body of the drop flat on a smooth anvil and, while holding it by the tip, strike the body sharply with a hammer. If all has gone well the hammer will bounce off the undamaged glass.

Next, shield your eyes from the drop and snap off the slender thread of glass attached to the small end. The

entire drop will explode into minute fragments (Fig. 1-7)! The particles have dull edges and will not cut you even if you rub them between your forefinger and thumb. In effect, the broken tip acts as an imperfection from which myriad fractures are propagated through the entire piece in response to the imprisoned stresses. All tempered glass reacts in the same way to surface damage. A tempered sheet of plate glass can withstand astonishing loads, but when even a small area is chipped, the sheet bursts into fragments.

Internal stresses are relieved by just the opposite technique. The glass is heated slowly to the so-called annealing "point," the temperature at which the molecular arrangement is so altered within a reasonable period of time that the internal stresses disappear. Actually, there is no "point" at which glass softens. Only crystalline substances have melting points. (Glass —like tar, pitch, and other amorphous substances—is a fluid that becomes more or less viscous depending upon its temperature. Even at room temperature, glass must be regarded as a supercooled fluid.)

After the internal stresses have been relieved by heating the glass to, say, the consistency of cold pine pitch, the temperature is gradually lowered —so slowly that all regions of the mass are at practically uniform temperature during the cooling. The mass shrinks uniformly and no strains develop. The treated piece is said to be "annealed."

Although glasses, particularly the varieties that contain a large proportion of silica, are relatively inert under ordinary conditions, they are attacked by certain substances, notably fluorine and hydrofluoric acid, and, to a lesser extent, caustic alkalies such as sodium or potassium hydroxide. These reagents, particularly hydrofluoric acid, are commonly used for etching glass. The surface to be etched is coated with an inert varnish, such as one that has an asphaltum base, through which the desired design is cut, and exposed to the reagent. If the fluid is placed in contact with the glass, a polished groove will be etched. Exposure to the fumes will make a matt impression. In addition, etching baths that contain potassium or ammonium fluorides precipitate insoluble silica fluorides on the glass surface and so produce a matt surface.

An effective etching solution for glass of all kinds consists of 10 parts (by weight) of ammonium fluoride, 4 parts of distilled water, and 1 part each of sulfuric acid and hydrofluoric acid. Mix the ammonium fluoride and water in a plastic container, then add the sulfuric acid *slowly* to prevent the temperature of the solution from rising above 140 degrees Fahrenheit, and finally add the hydrofluoric acid. By adding two parts of gum arabic in solution, the preparation can be converted into an etching ink for application by an ordinary pen. Store in a tightly capped plastic bottle. *Warning: Do not breathe the fumes or let the solution come in contact with the skin. Hydrofluoric acid is extremely caustic. In case of accidental contact, wash off the fluid immediately in running water and call a physician.* The acid penetrates the skin so that the effects may not be apparent until hours after contact with the acid.

Most glass dissolves only slightly in water. Nonetheless, the so-called soft glasses, such as soda-lime and lead types, are impaired to some extent by prolonged exposure to humid air, particularly in the smoggy atmospheres of metropolitan centers. Flux appears to dissolve from the surface and to react with carbon dioxide and other contaminating substances in the air to form carbonates that collect on the surface as a whitish or light gray film. Such aging spoils the glass. Glass tubing or rod that has been stored under unfavorable conditions for 10 years or more may be difficult to work, may tend to shatter upon exposure to heat more readily than new glass, and, unless cleaned, may not seal effectively or have normal strength when blown or otherwise formed into desired shape. Stocks of glass should be limited to a five-year supply. Corroded and otherwise soiled glass may be cleaned by soaking for several days in a 10% solution (by weight) of chromium trioxide, followed by a thorough rinse in distilled water. This treatment will remove foreign matter from the surface. Actually, the aged surface of the glass should be removed. This can be dissolved away with hydrofluoric acid or a solution of ammonium difluoride. Glass so treated should be immersed for a few minutes in a 5% solution of sodium hydroxide, to neutralize the acid, and then rinsed with distilled water. Obviously, such treatment is warranted only in the case of rare or costly glass. No treatment is a substitute for clean, fresh stock.

Tubing and rod are supplied by manufacturers in standard lengths of 4 feet. Diameter and wall thickness are specified in millimeters. (There are 25.4 millimeters in 1 inch.) Most manufacturers produce tubing in three weights, or wall thicknesses: thin, standard, and heavy. Glass is sold by the pound. When ordering glass, specify the amount in pounds, the diameter in millimeters, the weight of the wall (thin, standard, or heavy), and the kind of glass desired (lime, lead, borosilicate, and so on).

Stocks should be stored flat on shelves in a dust proof cabinet. Each kind of glass should be kept in a separate compartment clearly marked with its type. Cold, clear glass of all types looks much alike, and feels much alike. It is easy (and distressing) to mix the several varieties. Soft glasses cannot successfully be joined to the hard varieties (the borosilicates) nor can the hard glasses be joined to the high silica types. Should the stock become mixed, tests are available for identifying the several families.

Lead glass scratches easily and will turn black and opaque when heated to softness in a fire that is rich in gas and lean in air, such as the flame of a propane blow torch. The burning fuel has greater affinity for oxygen than the lead oxide. Hence the lead oxide gives up its oxygen to the fuel and is thereby reduced to metallic lead, which stains the glass. There is no convenient test for identifying lime glass, but if one is working with only lead, lime, and borosilicate, a test is not needed for lime because borosilicate (Pyrex) can, like lead, be identified easily. First, borosilicate softens at a much higher temperature than either lime or lead glasses. It must be worked in a fire enriched by oxygen, so try a suspected piece in the heat of an air-gas flame. If it refuses to soften enough for convenient working, it is borosilicate. Pyrex brand No. 7740 glass, a popular kind of Pyrex, can be positively distinguished from all other glasses, including quartz and high silica types, by a simple test. This test is based on the property of glass to bend light at a characteristic angle that is expressed numerically as the "refractive index." Glass, when immersed in a fluid of matching refractive index, becomes practically invisible. Pyrex brand No. 7740 glass has a refractive index of 1.474. So does a solution consisting of 16 parts (by volume) of methyl alcohol and 84 parts of benzene. The solution is made up in a wide-mouthed jar equipped with a close fitting screw top. The solution may be kept for many years. To make the test, simply immerse the suspected glass in the solution. If it disappears, it is Pyrex. (A faint, varicolored outline may be detected if the specimen is viewed against a light.) The submerged portion of a length of tubing that is anything other than 7740 glass (including lime and lead glasses as well as the high silica types) remains plainly visible. Lime glass will similarly disappear in chlorobenzene. *Warning: Benzene is highly toxic. Avoid breathing the fumes. Open the container only in a well ventilated room, preferably under a fume hood.*

Not all soft glasses expand and contract at the same rate when worked in the fire. This is particularly true of colored glasses in which the various hues are imparted by the addition of metallic oxides in varying amounts and by related modifications in the flux. Some quickly become butter-soft in the fire, while others at the same temperature remain stiff. The glass that becomes plastic at the lower temperature is said to be the "softer" of the two. It is somewhat difficult to make a smooth joint between glasses of differing softness. Moreover, if the difference in the softening temperatures is great the joint may crack when the piece cools because internal stresses tend to develop as the glasses solidify and shrink at differing rates.

When working with glasses of differing softness, it always pays to make a "sealing" test before constructing an object, to learn in advance if the joints—or "seals," as they are commonly known—will break when they are cooled. The compatibility of unknown glasses can be determined experimentally. For example, the ends of unfamiliar tubes may be heated to the plastic state and simply pushed together so that they fuse. If the resulting joint does not crack when cooled in the air, the materials are likely to be compatible. A more effective and interesting test is employed by glass manufacturers. Draw the materials to be tested into slender rods about 6 inches long and 6 millimeters in diameter. (See page 58 for the technique of drawing.) Next, simultaneously heat about ½ inch of one end of each rod to the plastic state, and place the molten portions in overlapping contact (Fig. 1-8). Squeeze the overlapped portions lightly between the jaws of a pair of tweezers to assure a good joint. Then, without twisting the softened region, bring the center of the joint to yellow heat, remove from the fire, and quickly stretch the molten glass into a thread about 30 inches long. The smaller the diameter of the thread after drawing, the more sensitive the test. Thus it is well to stretch the rods a little where they have been pressed together with the tweezers prior to the final heating and drawing. Be sure to hold the thread straight until it is cold and rigid. Only then may it be released so that you may observe the curvature. If the glasses are compatible (i.e., if they shrink at the same rate when cooled), the thread will remain straight when you release it. Such glasses can be sealed successfully. On the other hand, if, when released, the thread curls into loops smaller than about 10 inches in diameter, the glasses are incompatible and seals made between them will almost certainly crack upon cooling. (The curling is caused by the uneven shrinkage of the two components of the thread.) The glass with the greater coefficient of expansion will be on the inside of the curve. Threads of lead glass and lime glass will remain relatively straight. Those made from lead glass or lime glass and borosilicate will form coils an inch or so in diameter. Neither lead nor lime can be sealed to borosilicate.

For all but the most exceptional applications, the glass blower works with either lime, lead, or borosilicate glasses. In descriptions of the techniques of glass blowing it will be assumed in the following sections of this book that the reader will use one or another of these three materials. Beginners are urged to practice first with lead glass. As previously mentioned, it has the broadest range of working temperature, remaining soft longer than does lime or borosilicate when it is removed from the fire. All

three of these glasses, particularly lead and lime, must be annealed after they have been worked. Lead and lime must be kept hot when being worked. If permitted to cool, they tend to crack when abruptly reheated. Borosilicate, on the other hand, can usually be abruptly reheated without cracking. Even so, such rough treatment is not

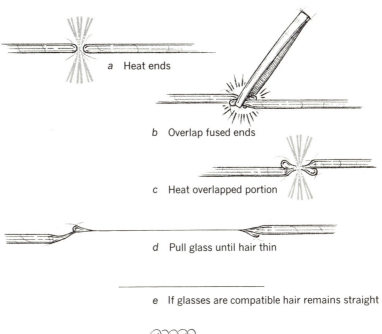

a   Heat ends

b   Overlap fused ends

c   Heat overlapped portion

d   Pull glass until hair thin

e   If glasses are compatible hair remains straight

f   If glasses are incompatible hair will curl

Figure 1-8.

Characteristics of representative Corning glasses

Expansion (number of parts in 10 million per degree C)	Corning Glass Works code number	Strain point (degrees C)	Annealing temperature (degrees C)	Softening temperature (degrees C)
8	7900	820	910	1500
21	7240	515	580	840
32	7740*	510	550	820
36	7720	495	525	755
40	3320	500	535	785
46	7050	460	495	700
50	7060	460	495	690
62	7520	530	565	750
70	7530	530	560	730
77	7550	515	545	715
85	7560	500	535	700
89	0120***	400	433	630
90	0010**	390	425	625
92	0080**	475	510	695
99	0250**	433	465	650

* Pyrex   ** Soft glasses   *** electrical lead glass (bulbs, etc.)

Note: The glasses in this table are listed in the order of increasing thermal coefficient of expansion. Each glass will seal directly to its immediate neighbors and to any other in the series through a graded seal that includes all intermediate glasses. Exceptions are 0010, 0080, and 0120, which may be regarded as having the same coefficient.

good practice. All glass should be warmed gradually, even material that is well annealed. This is one good reason for practicing with lead and lime glasses. Of necessity, the worker acquires the habit of heating the material slowly and of protecting it from drafts of cold air when it cools. The habit sticks when he graduates to borosilicate materials.

The accompanying table lists the characteristics of the more commonly used glasses. Study the data carefully before proceeding to Section II.

The glass blower also has occasion to work with another class of glasslike materials, known as colored enamels, that are used for making colored designs on glass. In general, enamels are compounded much as are conventional glasses, but, for use, they are ground to a fine powder that is mixed with an oil for application to a glass object. The decorated piece is fired in an oven. The heat burns the oily medium away and fuses the enamel to the glass. The characteristics and colors of enamels, and the techniques of applying them are discussed in Section VI.

The *T*ools of the glass blower

The essential tools of the glass blower are few in number, primitive in design, and relatively inexpensive. A complete set may be purchased for about $125, and the essential items for less than $50. (A list of suppliers will be found in *Sources of Tools and Materials* at the end of the book.) Aside from the gas burners, most of the tools can be improvised from commonly available materials. Instructions for making, adjusting, and using them are presented in the following pages.

Glass fires

Fires used for glass work differ from those of ordinary gas burners in three major respects. First, the flame of a glass fire has a sharp boundary; the heat is concentrated where it is wanted and the temperature is relatively high. Secondly, the fuel mixture, which consists of either gas and air, or gas and air enriched by oxygen, can be adjusted to meet the special requirements of the kind of glass being worked; it can be made "rich" or "lean" in the proportion of gas to air as desired. The necessity for this adjustment arises from the chemical properties of the metallic oxides making up the glasses. A flame rich in gas tends to rob the oxides of oxygen, thereby reducing them to metal. The resulting metal discolors the glass. The prolonged heating of some glasses may cause some of the ingredients to separate and crystallize. Glass so transformed is said to be "devitrified." It loses its transparency, luster, and strength. For these reasons glass fires must be considered chemical agents as well as sources of heat. Thirdly, glass fires are designed to soften the material at about the pace at which the artisan works—not so quickly that the glass melts out of control nor slowly enough to waste time. Of course

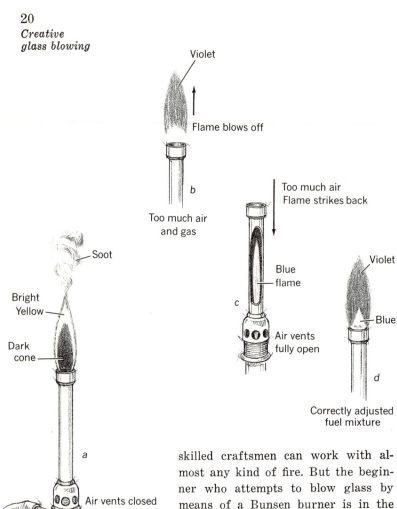

Figure 2-1.

inward. Simultaneously, convection carries the hot gases upward. As a consequence of these two motions, the flame assumes the shape of a hollow cone. The interior of the cone is composed of relatively cold fuel, a complex mixture of hydrocarbon molecules. Most of the heat is liberated by the combustion of hydrogen that splits off from the molecules. The light comes from the residue, particles of carbon brought to incandescence in the heat of the burning hydrogen. The carbon fails to burn because of insufficient oxygen. The glowing particles cool and escape from the flame as soot. The soot is wasted fuel (Fig. 2-1, *a*). The production of heat can be greatly increased by supplying the fire with enough oxygen to burn the carbon particles. When this is done, the flame turns from bright yellow to blue; the carbon liberates heat instead of light.

To burn the carbon, air can be mixed with the gas before it flows from the end of the pipe. The operation of bunsen burners and propane torches is based on this scheme. A small jet of gas is admitted to the bottom of a short pipe that has perforated sides. Air, entrained by the jet, flows into the pipe through the perforations. The mixture is ignited as it flows from the upper end of the pipe. The speed at which the flame travels through the gas, as well as the rate at which heat is liberated, increases as the ratio of fuel to air decreases. If the rate at which the mixture flows from the top of the pipe exceeds the speed at which the flame travels downward, the flame is blown from the end of the pipe and the fire goes out (2-1, *b*). Conversely, if the velocity of

skilled craftsmen can work with almost any kind of fire. But the beginner who attempts to blow glass by means of a Bunsen burner is in the awkward plight of the piano student who wears mittens. Don't handicap yourself with a poor fire.

What accounts for the unique properties of glass fires? How are the burners adjusted and used? Consider, first, how a column of propane or illuminating gas burns in air. When gas that is flowing from an open pipe is ignited, it burns only at the boundary, where the air and gas meet. Sufficient oxygen for supporting combustion is unavailable except at the interface. The combustion reaction travels

the combustion front exceeds the rate of gas flow, the flame darts into the pipe and burns inside. The fire is said to "strike back" (2-1, *c*). When the mixture contains almost but not quite enough air for complete combustion and the rate of gas flow just exceeds by a little the velocity of the combustion front, the flame rests on the top of the pipe in the form of two cones, a relatively cool inner cone of bluish green surrounded by a larger, hotter flame of light transparent blue (2-1, *d*). Most Bunsen burners include a loose-fitting sleeve that may be slid up and down the outside of the pipe for regulating the amount of air that enters the perforations, and a needle valve for regulating the rate of gas flow. These two controls are manipulated experimentally to produce the desired stable flame. Propane blow torches are based on the same principle but usually have no provision for regulating the flow of air. As mentioned, either burner can be used for glass work although they are not recommended for beginners. Both will blacken lead glass.

To achieve a somewhat higher temperature, blow a jet of compressed air, positioned coaxially inside the pipe near the open end, into the cone of cold gas as it flows from the burner pipe. The flow of both gas and air is controlled by petcocks. The size, shape, and temperature of the resulting flame depends on the ratio of gas to air, the rate of gas injection, the effective length of the pipe, and the diameter of the air jet. Blast burners of this type, which are also known as "cannon fires," are usually fitted with a sliding sleeve for altering the length of the pipe, and a set of noz-

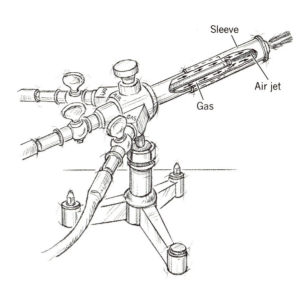

zles graduated in diameter for creating the air jet (Fig. 2-2). Needle flames about ⅛ inch in diameter and 1 inch long can be developed by setting the pipe at minimum length and using an air jet of the smallest diameter. The flame is made longer and bushier by extending the length of the pipe and using larger air jets. The bushy flames are turbulent and noisy.

Most commercial blast burners include a third gas inlet for admitting oxygen to the mixture. The addition of oxygen causes the fire to burn at higher temperature by reducing the proportion of nitrogen in the fuel mixture. Nitrogen, which composes four-fifths of the atmosphere, makes no contribution to the heat liberated by an ordinary fire. On the contrary, this relatively inert gas absorbs heat that would otherwise raise the temperature of the flame.

Temperatures intermediate between those of an air-gas fire and a fire en-

Figure 2-2.

A burner of this type, in one form, consists of three parts: a pinion gear, a perforated bushing, and a straight pipe. The gear and bushing fit snugly against the inner wall of the pipe, near one end of the pipe. The openings in the bushing admit a fairly large amount of fuel to the central hole of the gear and less fuel to the spaces between the gear teeth. The central hole of the gear is the nozzle for the central flame, and the spaces between the gear teeth are nozzles for the pilot flames (Fig. 2-3). The dimensions of the openings are so proportioned that the relative velocity of the gas mixture is correct at only one critical pressure. The proportion of gas to air in the fuel mixture is equally critical because this ratio determines in part the speed at which the flame travels through the mixture. When the fuel is correctly adjusted, a burner of this type develops an intensely hot needle flame consisting of two slender coaxial cones. The flow of gas is laminar, not turbulent. A typical flame measures about ¼ inch in diameter at the base, comes to a sharp point at a distance of 3½ inches, and emits a gentle hiss, the sign of correct operation.

Such burners are known in the trade as "glass fires." They can be mounted in various arrays. In one arrangement, two or more are mounted side by side and directed to a common focal point. A companion set directs flame to the same focal point from the opposite side. This arrangement creates a so-called "crossfire." Such crossfires are used almost exclusively by itinerant glass blowers who stage exhibitions of glass blowing in schools and at recreation centers (Fig. 2-5).

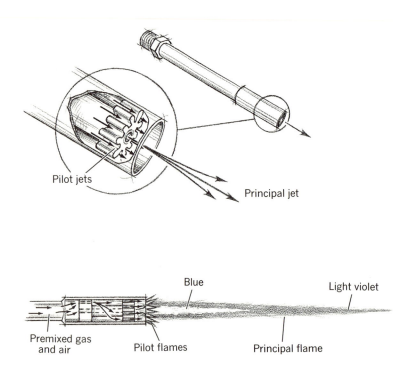

Pilot jets

Principal jet

Blue

Light violet

Premixed gas
and air

Pilot flames

Principal flame

Figure 2-3.

riched by oxygen are developed by mixing air and gas in almost explosive proportions (adding almost enough air to the gas for complete combustion) and forcing the compressed mixture through a nozzle at a velocity slightly in excess of that at which the flame travels through the fuel mixture. Under these conditions one would expect the flame to be blown off the end of the burner. This is prevented by surrounding the nozzle with pilot fires that continuously ignite the mixture. In effect the pilot fires stabilize the central flame by anchoring it to the tip of the burner.

The crossfire

The crossfire has no peer as a tool for the beginner. It heats the work on two sides simultaneously, thus making a minimum demand on manipulative skill. The rate at which a crossfire softens glass varies approximately in proportion to the number of flames. The beginner can start with one or two burners on each side and increase the number as skill is acquired. The burners can be directed to a common focal point or spread to converge on a line; this enables the beginner to distribute the heat as desired, without shifting the work in the fire.

Burners of this type were developed late in the nineteenth century by prolonged trial and error. Doubtless they could be made at home by a clever and persistent mechanic. On the other hand, commercial burners are currently priced at about $1.70 each; this is less than the retail price of the required stock brass. We use the No. 3151JC New Style Glass Fire, manufactured by American Gas Furnace Company, Elizabeth, New Jersey. A single fire of this type, when mounted in an appropriate handle, can be used as a hand torch that develops a needle flame, or several fires may be combined by means of appropriate manifolds to form a crossfire. Figure 2-4 depicts the structural details of a serviceable hand torch which has a single glass fire, and Figure 2-5 illustrates one possible scheme for assembling a crossfire comprising two glass fires on each side supported by standard ⅛-inch pipe fittings. A professional crossfire, manufactured by American Gas Furnace Company, that employs as many as five glass fires

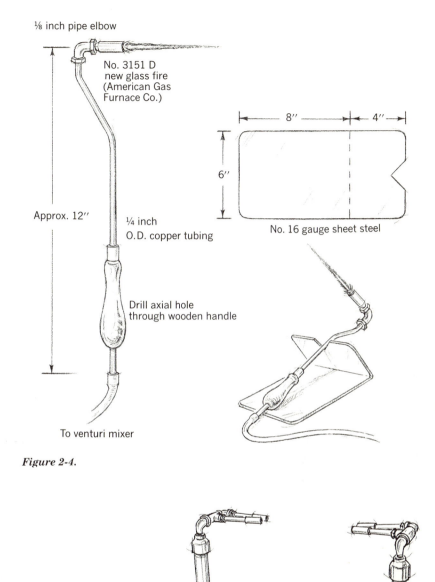

⅛ inch pipe elbow

No. 3151 D
new glass fire
(American Gas
Furnace Co.)

Approx. 12″

¼ inch
O.D. copper tubing

Drill axial hole
through wooden handle

To venturi mixer

8″   4″

6″

No. 16 gauge sheet steel

Figure 2-4.

Figure 2-5.

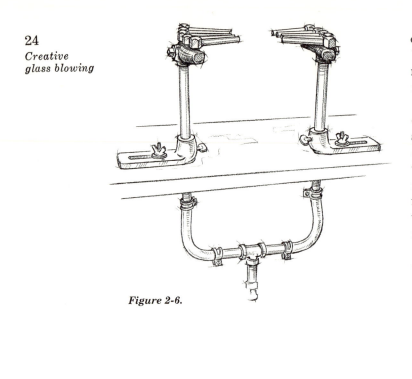

Figure 2-6.

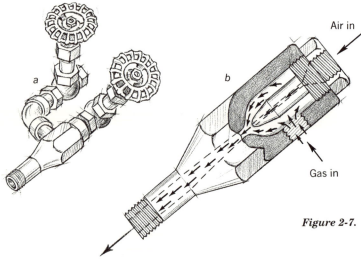

Air in

Gas in

Figure 2-7.

Fuel mixture out

on each side, is shown in Figure 2-6. We recommend a crossfire of not more than two glass fires on each side for beginners.

Gas and air must be supplied to the crossfire through a carburetor, the size of which varies with the number of glass fires. A crossfire employing a total of four No. 3151JC glass fires may be supplied with the required fuel mixture through a No. 12-40-31 venturi mixer, complete with needle valves, manufactured by the American Gas Furnace Company. The same mixer can be used, if desired, for supplying fuel to a hand torch equipped with a single No. 315JC glass fire (Fig. 2-7).

The venturi mixer

The venturi mixer acts both as a carburetor and as a pump for increasing the flow of illuminating gas from the supply main. Normally, illuminating gas enters residences at a pressure of only a few ounces per square inch, inadequate for supplying fuel to the high velocity jets. In essence, the venturi mixer acts as an aspirator. A jet of compressed air flowing through a constricted tube creates a region of low pressure. Gas, admitted to this region, is entrained by the jet and subsequently compressed as illustrated (Fig. 2-7, *b*). The ratio of gas to air in the resulting mixture can be altered by needle valves that control both the gas and the air. Propane may be substituted for illuminating gas if the pressure is appropriately lowered by means of an automatic regulator. Incidentally, a check valve should be installed in the gas line (see page 30).

The essential supply of compressed air can be provided most inexpensively by one or more compressors from old electric refrigerators. Many dealers in refrigerators give away such compressors for the asking. At the most, they are priced at $5 or so. New compressors of adequate capacity are currently priced at $25 and up.

If a refrigerator compressor is used, avoid damaging the copper tubing that serves as the inlet and exhaust lines. Saw off the excess, leaving nipples about 2 inches long. If necessary, improvise a wooden base for supporting the compressor upright in the position occupied by the unit in the refrigerator. Splice an appropriate extension cord to the power terminals of the motor and fit the other end of the cord with a three-terminal plug. Use the third terminal for making a ground connection to the case of the compressor. Start the machine and identify the air outlet.

Connect the outlet to the air inlet of the venturi mixer by an appropriate length of rubber tubing. If either the volume of the air or the pressure is excessive, insert a T fitting for bleeding off the excess. Slip a short length of rubber tubing over the leg of the T and partially close the tubing with a pinch clamp. The exact adjustment of the pinch clamp for the proper pressure must be determined experimentally. The No. 3151JC glass fire requires approximately 0.45 cubic foot of air per minute at a pressure of about 1 pound per square inch. (Pressure can be measured inexpensively by means of a water manometer. A pressure of 1 pound supports a column

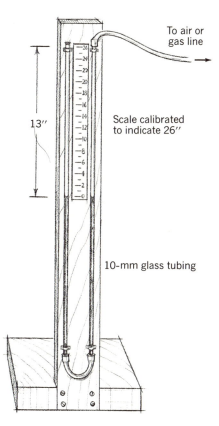

Figure 2-8.

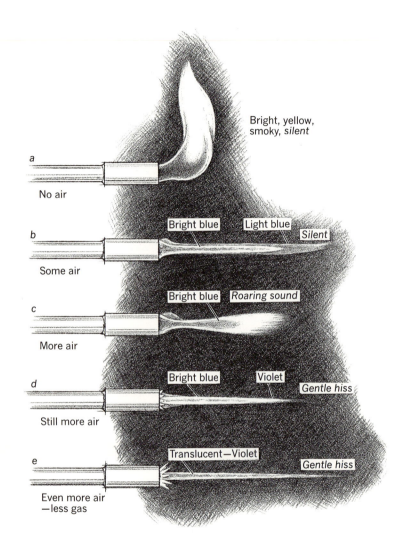

a

No air

b

Bright blue   Light blue   *Silent*

Some air

c

Bright blue   *Roaring sound*

More air

d

Bright blue   Violet   *Gentle hiss*

Still more air

e

Translucent—Violet   *Gentle hiss*

Even more air
—less gas

Bright, yellow,
smoky, *silent*

Figure 2-9.

of water approximately 28 inches in height. See Figure 2-8.)

Adjusting the glass fire

To put the 3151JC glass fire into operation, first close both needle valves of the venturi mixer, start the compressor, and turn on the gas. Open the needle valve that controls the gas and light the fire. Adjust the yellow flame to a height of approximately 4 inches (Fig. 2-9, *a*). Then slowly open the needle valve that controls the air. The length of the flame will increase for a few seconds, perhaps to as high as 10 inches. It will then turn yellowish blue and shorten to about 5 inches. Continue opening the air valve. The flame will gradually turn solid blue and a bright greenish-blue central cone, surrounded by an envelope of lighter blue, somewhat resembling the flame of a Bunsen burner, will develop (2-9, *b*). The gas will burn silently. Admit still more air. The inner cone will now shorten to a length of about 1½ inches, develop a brush-like appearance at the tip, and generate a pronounced roar (2-9, *c*). The flow of gas has become turbulent. Up to this point all combustion has occurred beyond the end of the burner despite the fact that the nozzles are recessed approximately ⅛ inch. Open the air slightly more, perhaps a half turn of the needle valve. Suddenly, the roar will change to a gentle hiss as laminar flow is restored (2-9, *d*). Satellite pilot flames will form inside the recess at the end of the burner and the principal flame will assume the shape of a slender blue cone approximately ⅛ inch in diameter at the base and 3 inches long, enveloped by a second violet cone of about twice the base diameter and an inch longer. This is the ideal fire for working lime glass.

Finally, open the air valve an additional quarter turn. The inner cone will now change from blue to transparent violet. This is the proper adjustment for working lead glass (2-9, *e*). The outer cone will become almost invisible even when viewed against a black background in a dimly lighted room. Incidentally, the workbench should be painted flat black. (A piece of plywood about 3 feet square may be painted flat black and set up behind the fire for the background, if desired.) When the Venturi Mixer is properly adjusted, the combined gas and air pressure in the manifold of a hand torch or crossfire equipped with 3151JC glass fires measures 3.5 ounces, which is equivalent to a water column 6 inches high. Once the needle valves have been adjusted, you need not disturb them except for altering the mixture when you are shifting from one type of glass to another. Increase the proportion of gas in the mixture when working lime glass.

Hand torches

Substantially all novelty items, including miniature vases, birds, animals, and so on, can be made in the crossfire by procedures that will be described in Sections III, IV, and V. Much laboratory glassware can also be made in the crossfire. Until the beginner acquires some dexterity in manipulating softened glass, however, he should acquire a pair of hand torches: one equipped with a single glass fire that develops a needle flame; the second, with a crossfire consisting of a pair of

so-called "fishtail" burners. Fishtail burners develop flames in the shapes of thin ribbons approximately 1/16 inch thick and 3/4 inch wide (in the case of the type 81-WNS burners manufactured by the American Gas Furnace Company). We use them in the No. 658-N hand torch also made by this firm (Fig. 2-10).

A hand torch of this general type is indispensable for connecting stationary configurations of glass tubing, such as vacuum systems and similar apparatus that cannot be readily moved to the workbench. Beginners will discover that, in general, it is much simpler to make T seals and similar forms with the hand torch than with the crossfire, because the torch is so easy to manipulate.

The fishtail hand torch may be operated from the same venturi mixer used with the crossfire, although the performance of the torch will be improved by a special mixer designed for its lower fuel requirement. A separate mixer will also elimi-

Figure 2-10.

The adjustment of blast burners is largely a matter of experiment and depends upon the size and character of the desired fire. Gas is admitted first and lighted. Air is then added gradually. Relatively low air pressure creates a needle flame; a higher pressure yields a turbulent, noisy, bushy flame. Small fires require the use of small air nozzles and big fires, nozzles of larger diameters. The pipe or "barrel" of the burner is extended or shortened by altering the position of the sleeve to produce a flame of maximum stability. Blast burners can be used for softening large areas of glass, such as the bottoms of flasks, or lengths of glass tubing up to about 3 inches as may be required when making bends of substantial radius.

A more convenient apparatus for softening glass tubing, however, is the ribbon burner (Fig. 2-11). This device delivers a flame approximately 1 inch in width and up to 36 inches long depending upon the size of the burner. It operates on pressurized premixed fuel and requires a special venturi mixer. Ribbon burners of current design are equipped with an adjustable strip of sheet metal for altering the length of the fire. The same effect can be achieved with burners of older design by covering a desired length of the unit with a strip of wet asbestos paper.

Figure 2-11. nate the inconvenience of readjusting the needle valves when you are shifting from the crossfires to the hand torch. The procedure for adjusting the fuel mixture for this torch is similar to that for adjusting the fuel mixture for the crossfire. First, turn on the gas and regulate to produce a yellow flame about 1½ inches high. Then open the air valve until the flame becomes light blue and burns with a barely audible hiss. In operating fires that use premixed gas and air, always turn the gas on first when lighting the burner and off first when shutting down. Glass fires are designed for a specific rate of fuel consumption. Attempts to increase the heat beyond the designed limit by employing higher fuel pressure or enriching the mixture by an increase of the proportion of gas fail. The fire simply blows off and goes out.

The oxygen-gas fire

Most professional glass blowers who specialize in the fabrication of laboratory glassware prefer to work with a single gas-oxygen jet burner. The pressurized mixture is fed to a nozzle that consists of a copper tube with heavy walls of the general type used in oxy-acetylene welding torches. The size and character of the flame is controlled by altering the pressure of the fuel and diameter of the nozzle.

Some burners of this type feature a rotary turret that carries a series of nozzles in graduated sizes, and a pilot flame which burns continuously and ignites the fuel automatically (Fig. 2-12). To select a fire of desired size the worker merely rotates the turret. One flame goes out and the next appears. The burner is attached to its heavy base through a ball and socket joint that permits the flame to be pointed in any direction. The artisan has instant access to flames that range in size and character from a needle point to a large, bushy form.

Oxygen may be added to the fuel supply of all burners designed for compressed air and gas. Simply insert a T fitting into the air line and couple the oxygen hose to the leg of the T. The tank of compressed oxygen must be equipped with an automatic pressure regulator and a needle valve for releasing the gas into the air line at the appropriate rate: about 10% oxygen to 90% air.

If oxygen is to be used routinely, as for making laboratory glassware of Pyrex or other borosilicate glasses, it is both more economical and more convenient to substitute a special venturi mixer for the T fitting. This device consists of a pair of venturi mixers connected in tandem. The first section combines the oxygen and air in the optimum ratio of 7 to 10 parts of air to 1 part of oxygen (by volume).

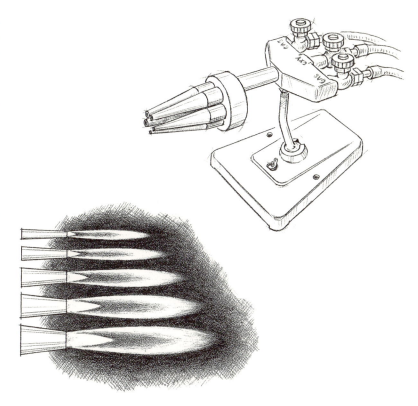

Figure 2-12.

The second similarly adds gas in optimum ratio to the oxidizing mixture. As a safety measure, it is advisable to insert a check valve between the mixer and the gas line. Check valves permit the gas to flow in only one direction. The device prevents oxygen from backing up in the gas line and forming an explosive mixture. Once the needle valves of the mixers have been adjusted, the apparatus requires no further attention.

To make the adjustment, first turn on and ignite the gas. Then add air to produce the correct fire for working soft glass by the procedure described previously (see page 26). Next open the gas adjustment slightly. Then gradually open the needle valve that admits oxygen. Continue adding oxygen until the flames shrink to about half of their former length. Next, add gas until the length of the flame has grown about 50%. Finally, add oxygen to restore the flame to its former length.

A properly adjusted flame to which oxygen has been added consists of a brilliant bluish-green inner cone surrounded by an almost invisible outer cone of violet. In a crossfire, the sharp purplish tips of the flames should meet at the center focal point. Venturi mixers for combining oxygen with the air-gas fuel mixture must be designed to meet the special fuel requirement of each burner. They are manufactured to order by the American Gas Furnace Company.

Although a wide selection of burners is thus available, we urge the beginner to start with a crossfire. It may be operated on either household gas or propane. After mastering the basic operations of glass blowing you may wish to add oxygen for working the borosilicate glasses. Under no circumstances should the beginner attempt to work the borosilicate glasses during initial practice sessions. Habits can be formed that almost certainly will be painful to break.

The workbench

Among the glass blower's facilities, next in importance to the fires are the work place, the bench, the supplies and tools, in that order. Any space that would be suitable for a kitchen stove can be used for the workplace. The glass fires are no more hazardous to either the building or the worker than a conventional gas stove. The room should be normally ventilated and lighted. Any sturdy bench or table with the top at least 30 inches square can be used for supporting the fires (Fig. 2-13). The top should be covered by a hard sheet of compressed asbestos approximately $\frac{1}{4}$ inch thick, such as Transite, which may be purchased at most lumber yards or from other suppliers of building materials. Do not cover the bench with sheet metal. Hot glass may crack when laid on a cold metal surface. As previously mentioned, the background should be painted flat black. The fires are all but invisible when viewed against a light background. At least, the burners should be mounted on a black baseboard.

Glass storage

Glass tubing and rod should be stored flat on a convenient shelf that is divided into labeled compartments for the various sizes and kinds of glass. Do not store tubing vertically unless the tops are covered to prevent dust from settling on the inner wall.

Miscellaneous supplies

Of first importance among the additional materials is a supply of asbestos paper and an assortment of corks in a range of sizes that fit the glass tubing. The asbestos paper comes in rolls approximately 36 inches wide and in various weights. We prefer the weight and quality of paper used by manufacturers of neon signs. This material is more flexible and porous than the kind usually sold by hardware stores. Sign makers draw lettering full scale in reverse on the paper to guide the glass blower in bending the glass tubing. Usually it is possible to purchase such used paper inexpensively. Full rolls of new paper can be procured from distributors of neon sign supplies. The paper is used by glass blowers in innumerable ways: as covering to protect hot glass from cold drafts of air, as shields to protect the hands from heat, as small rolls in the form of plugs to support glass rods and tubes coaxially inside larger tubes, and so on. Corks are used to plug the ends of tubing for blowing bulbs and other forms. Handy fixtures for supporting short lengths of tub-

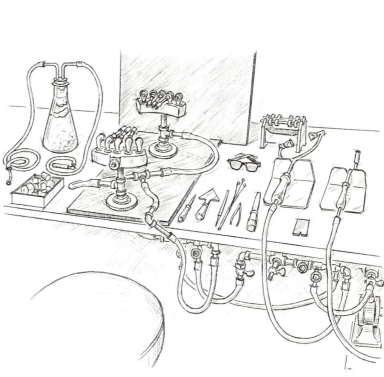

ing in the fire can also be made of corks. To make one of these fixtures, first burn a center hole axially through the cork, which fits snugly the short length of rod or tubing. A cork borer makes a cleaner hole, and it is more convenient to use, of course. When the cork is inserted into the work piece the small rod or tube serves as a handle (Fig. 2-14).

In addition to the corks, an assortment of stoppers (whimsically called "policemen") should be made of rubber tubing in sizes to fit glass tubing

Figure 2-13.

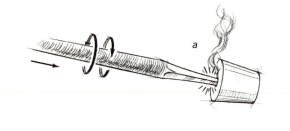

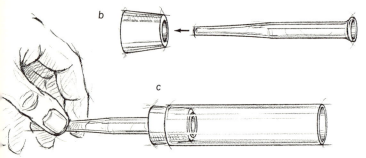

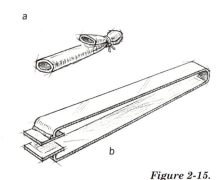

Figure 2-15.

Figure 2-14.

from 6 to 15 millimeters in diameter. Cut the rubber tubing into 2-inch lengths, fold over a ¼-inch length of one end, and wire it in place, as illustrated (Fig. 2-15, *a*). Policemen are handier than corks for closing tubes of small diameter. Keep the supply of corks and policemen in a shallow box on the bench. The supply should also include an assortment of paper clips and a dozen small spring clips of the kind girls and women use for making pin curls. The clips are handy for clamping the edges of asbestos paper that has been looped around hot tubing for protection against drafts.

Tweezers

Other essential tools include at least one pair of tweezers about 8 inches long. Tweezers are easy to make from 14-gauge sheet steel. Cut a strip of the metal about 1 inch wide and 17

inches long, taper the ends as desired, and fold the piece into a slender U, so the tapered jaws are separated by about ¾ inch. The jaws of tweezers can be fitted with small plates of various forms for shaping molten glass. A pair of tweezers fitted with small flat jaws is handy for squashing a sphere of soft glass into a disk, for example, as is a pair with curving jaws for making irregular shapes. The jaws are cut from the sheet metal and brazed to the tips of the tweezers (Fig. 2-15, *b*). Brazing is easy to do with the small hand torch. Just support the pieces to be joined on a block of charcoal, coat the joint with a paste made of household borax and rubbing alcohol, apply the heat by means of the hand torch, dip the tip of a rod of brazing brass into the borax paste, and feed it into the work as though it were solder. Brazing rod can be purchased for pennies from most automobile repair shops.

The blowing hose

A blowing hose equipped with a swivel connector and glass mouthpiece is handy for blowing some types of novelty glasswork and essential for blowing many kinds of laboratory glassware. The rubber tubing should be of the best quality of gum rubber, ³⁄₁₆ inch in diameter, and of the heavy-wall type. (Thick walls of good rubber are unlikely to kink during a crucial operation and shut off the air.) Such tubing may be procured from distributors of neon sign supplies. One end of the hose should be equipped with a glass mouthpiece that is flanged for resting behind the teeth (see page 98). The other end of the hose slides onto a right-angled swivel, the outlet of which is equipped with a short length of rubber tubing appropriate in size for the work at hand. The swivel permits the work to be rotated continuously in one direction without twisting the blowing hose.

In addition to the blowing hose and swivel, the artisan who fashions laboratory glassware will need an apparatus for drying the blown air. Moisture from the breath can contaminate many types of scientific apparatus. The air dryer can be a 1-liter flask filled with a chemical, such as calcium sulfate, that absorbs moisture. (The chemical is available in the form of a commercial product, Drierite, that changes from blue when dry to pink when moist, and vice versa. The moist chemical can be dried by baking it for an hour in a kitchen oven. Baking also reverses the color.) Air is blown into the bottom of the flask through a 6-millimeter

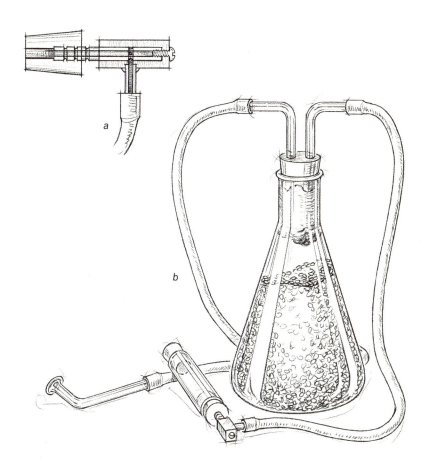

Figure 2-16.

glass tube, and from the flask into the work by a second tube that leads from the top of the flask through the perforated stopper. It is advisable to cover the top of the chemical by a tuft of absorbent cotton. The cotton serves as a filter to prevent the air from carrying small particles of the chemical into the work (Fig. 2-16).

Glass holders

Frequently it becomes necessary to support a small object in the fire. This is accomplished by means of various clamps known as "holders." In general, holders are not available on the market. We make them of iron wire, mostly BS gauge No. 14, that is known to hardware dealers as galvanized tie-wire. The completed tool consists of a bundle of three wires, each about 1 foot long, bound together at one end and looped at the other. The loops serve as jaws. A helical coil of the same wire slides over the bundle to bring the jaws into clamping contact with the work as illustrated (Fig. 2-17, *a*). The helical coil may be made by winding the wire around a steel welding rod, about ⅛ inch in diameter, that serves as a mandrel. The job can be done by improvising a fixture from half of a door hinge, the welding rod, and a wooden clamp that is made by fastening two 12-inch lengths of ¾- by 1½-inch soft pine at the ends. The door hinge is screwed to the corner of the workbench so the edge of the hinge that is normally occupied by the bolt extends slightly beyond the bench. The bolt hole becomes a bearing for the welding rod. A crank, having a throw of about 6 inches, is bent in one end of the welding rod. The rod is slipped into the bolt hole so that the crank extends away from the bench. The end of the wire to be coiled is fastened to the throw of the crank. Just wrap the end of the wire around the rod. Two or three turns is enough. Then, by rotating the crank, twist the wire onto the straight portion of the rod, an inch or so beyond the crank. Now grip the rod and wire in the wooden clamp at the point where the wire leads away from the rod. Turn the crank and adjust the wooden clamp at an angle that causes the wire to wind into a closely spaced helix (Fig. 2-17, *a*). Make the helix about 1 foot long. The helix can then be cut into 1-inch lengths (by means of a hacksaw) for use in making up several holders.

Next, cut three 14-inch lengths of straight wire. (Wire may be straightened by clamping one end in a vise, gripping the other in a pair of pliers, and stretching the material about 1% of its length. Alternatively, the free end of the wire may be attached to a lever, such as a broomstick, for stretching if you are not strong enough to do the job by hand.) Form loops in one end of each length of wire by wrapping the ends of the wires around a mandrel, such as a ⅜-inch metal rod or a glass tube (2-17, *b*, *c*). Bend the loop so that it is centered on the straight portion of the wire, as illustrated (2-17, *d*). Next, slip the three wires into a length of the helical coil and place a small sphere such as a glass marble between the three loops (2-17, *e*). The marble will be held securely if the loops are spaced evenly around its circumference. Push the helical coil toward the loops until they grip the marble snugly. Now wrap a short length of adhesive tape around the bundle about midway between the helical coil and the free ends of the wires. The tape binds the wires so that they remain parallel to each other. Finally, slip an additional coil over the free ends and solder it in place, as illustrated (2-17, *e*). The wire loops will now retain their relative positions when the adhesive tape

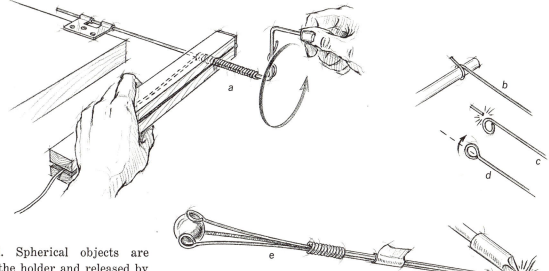

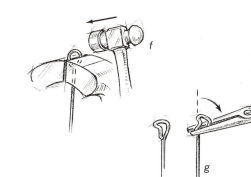

is removed. Spherical objects are clamped in the holder and released by sliding the movable coil.

A special holder of the same type can be made for manipulating disks, such as the bottoms of miniature vases, wine glasses, and the like. Make up three wires with loops, as described above. Next, clamp the loops, one at a time, in a vise so that half of the loop extends above the jaws and the straight part of the wire is vertical. With a hammer, bend the exposed portion of the loop over to make a sharp right angle with the clamped portion (2-17, *f*). Remove the wire from the vise and, with a pair of pliers, bend the straight portion to an angle of 45 degrees at the point where it joins the loop (2-17, *g*). The distant side of the loop is now in line with the axis of the straight wire as illustrated. Finally, assemble the three wires into a bundle, slip a helical coil over the bundle, and grasp a disk,

about the size of a five-cent coin, between the facing loops. Tape the assembly as in the previously made holder, and slide the wires relative to each other until the disk spins true when the bundle is rotated between the thumb and forefinger. Finally, slip an additional helical coil over the free ends and solder in place. Remove the tape and disk (2-17, *h*).

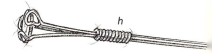

Figure 2-17.

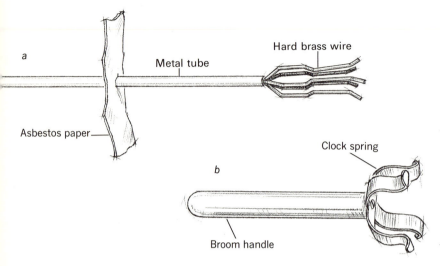

Figure 2-18.

Holders of two other types are occasionally useful, particularly for making laboratory glassware. One consists of a brass tube about $\frac{3}{16}$ inch in diameter and 6 inches long, into one end of which a bundle of 5 wires is inserted and soldered. The wires are spread at an angle of about 20 degrees as they emerge from the handle and then extend parallel to the axis of the handle, as illustrated (Fig. 2-18, *a*). Holders of this type are used for supporting short lengths of glass tubing in the fire, such as electrode assemblies, and are called electrode holders. They may be purchased from distributors of neon sign supplies.

Holders that are similar in principle but larger are handy for manipulating spherical bulbs. They consist of a wooden handle, such as an 8-inch length of broomstick, the end of which supports a pair of spring steel strips bent in the form of open C's assembled at right angles to each other (Fig. 2-18, *b*). Holders of this type can be purchased from dealers in scientific supplies.

The bucks

When making beads or glass fibers, the glass blower draws molten material from the tip of a glass rod that is supported in the fire. The rod rests on a pair of improvised supports known as "bucks" (Fig. 2-19). Bucks can be made of two 6-inch lengths of pipe, one of which telescopes inside

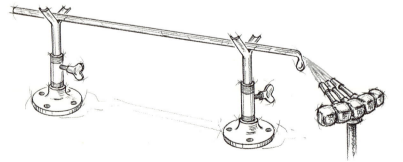

Figure 2-19.

the other. We use ⅜- and ½-inch pipes.
The ½-inch pipe is threaded on one end
and is screwed into a pipe flange that
serves as a base for the tool. A tapped
lateral hole takes a thumb screw for
clamping the inner ⅜-inch pipe. The
upper end of the ⅜-inch pipe is
split and spread to form a V about 1½
inches wide at the top, as illustrated
(Fig. 2-19).

Flaring tools

A set of flaring tools in a range of
sizes is essential. They are used for
expanding glass tubing into funnel
shapes and opening glass bulbs into
hemispheres, as explained in Section
IV. The smallest may consist of the
well rounded tine of a rattail file
about 8 inches long. (Fig. 2-20, *a*).
File the rough corners from the tine.
Then round it off and polish it with
successively finer grades of emery
cloth, finishing with crocus cloth.
Larger flaring tools are made
from strap iron about ⅛ inch
thick and as much as 1 inch wide. The
flaring blade, which resembles a burn-
ishing tool, is made by tapering the
metal at one end and shaping a tine at
the other end for insertion in a
wooden handle that can be purchased
from a hardware store (2-20, *b*). Flaring blades should be about 3 or 4
inches long, rounded and polished
with crocus cloth. A flaring tool in the
shape of an arrow head (about 1½
inches per side) made of 16-gauge
sheet steel is occasionally convenient
for shaping glass objects 3 inches or
larger in diameter (2-20, *c*). This
tool is available from dealers in scientific supplies.

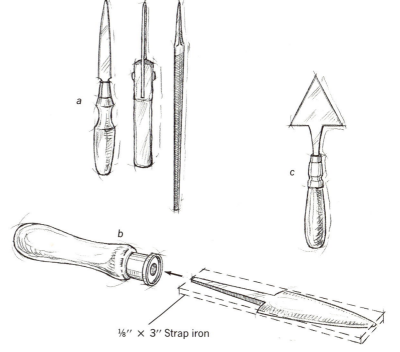

⅛" × 3" Strap iron

Figure 2-20.

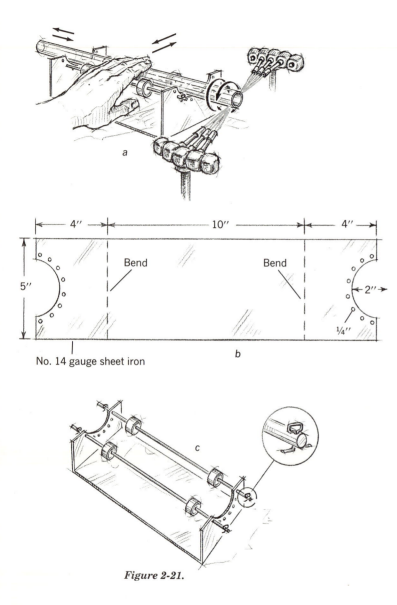

No. 14 gauge sheet iron

Figure 2-21.

The glass roller

To make a flare, the glass tubing must be rotated at a uniform rate, an operation that becomes progressively difficult as the size of the tubing increases beyond 15 millimeters. The procedure can be greatly simplified by the use of free-turning rollers for supporting the work. The tubing is placed on the rollers and stroked back and forth by the palm of one hand. By simultaneously exerting a slight pressure toward one side or the other, the tubing can be slid into and out of a fire placed close to one end, as illustrated (Fig. 2-21, *a*).

A set of rollers can be improvised from a rectangle of 16-gauge sheet metal, a pair of ¼-inch steel rods, the wheels from a roller skate, and four cotter pins. First cut the sheet metal into a strip 6 inches wide and 18 inches long. From the ends, cut out semicircular pieces having a radius of 2½ inches. Around the edge of the openings, drill a series of ¼-inch holes spaced approximately ¾ inch apart (2-21, *b*). Bend up the ends to a right angle, 4 inches from each end of the sheet (2-21, *c*). Cut the rods to a length of 11 inches, and, approximately ½ inch from each end of each rod, drill a ³⁄₃₂-inch hole (crossways) for the cotter pins. Slide a pair of roller skate wheels onto each rod, insert the ends of the rod in corresponding holes of the sheet metal base, and insert cotter pins in each end of the rod. The spacing between the wheels (of the two rods) may be adjusted by shifting the rods to appropriate holes in the base. The rollers will accommodate tubing that ranges in diameter from about 10 to 100 millimeters.

Glass cutters

The well equipped small glass shop will have at least three tools for cutting glass. The most essential is an ordinary flat 6-inch file. We prefer the Nicholsen Warding Bastard. The technique of using the file for cutting rod and tubing is described in Section III. Eventually the file will become dull. It may be sharpened by grinding the edges on a carborundum wheel; and it can be resharpened until the metal becomes so thin that it snaps under the pressure of ordinary use. A wheel cutter should also be acquired for use on sheet glass.

Tubing larger than 25 millimeters may be cut with a hot wire. Our device consists of a base of Transite about ½ inch thick that supports a pair of brass rods near the ends, as illustrated (Fig. 2-22). Axial holes are drilled in both ends of the ¼-inch rods and threaded to take 8/32 machine screws. The transite base is drilled for the screws. The holes are countersunk on the bottom side of the Transite. Flathead screws are used for attaching the rods to the base. The heads are subsequently coated with a thick layer of epoxy cement that serves as electrical insulation. Holes about 1/16 inch in diameter are drilled through the rods at a point that intersects the bottom of the axial holes at the top. Nichrome wire, threaded through these holes, is clamped by roundheaded 8/32 machine screws that occupy the axial holes at the top. Iron washers soldered to heads serve as finger grips for turning these screws. The wire may be heated by current supplied by a variable voltage transformer, such as a Variac. The Variac controls the tem-

perature of the wire. Connection between the Variac and the brass rods is made by a pair of leads equipped with alligator clips. The length of the wire may be adjusted as desired by releasing the clamping screws.

Alternatively, the temperature of the wire may be controlled by inserting a resistance in series with one of the leads from the 110-volt power source. A convenient resistance may be made by connecting eight porcelain lamp sockets in parallel. The sockets may be mounted on any convenient base. Connect one lead of an extension cord to one terminal of the sockets. The other lead of the extension cord connects directly to one brass rod of the hot wire fixture. From the opposite terminal of the sockets connect a lead to the remaining brass rod of the fixture. The temperature of the wire is controlled by screwing more or fewer 100-watt lamps into the sockets.

As explained in Section III, soft glass tubing larger than 25 millimeters in diameter is cut first by filing a nick all around the tube at the point where the glass is to be parted. The nick is then touched to the hot wire. It is cracked by thermal shock. The procedure for cutting borosilicate glass is similar. These harder glasses are not as sensitive to heat, however. If the borosilicate glass fails to part after it has been in contact with the hot wire for, say, 20 seconds, lift the tube from the fixture and touch the heated nick with a narrow strip of cloth moistened with cold water (such as a lamp wick) and promptly pull the ends of the tubing apart. Usually, the tubing parts as a clean break, but now and then the edge may be somewhat jagged. These

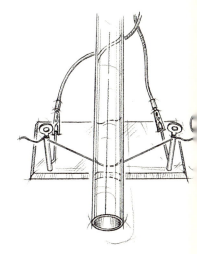

Figure 2-22.

The polariscope

Glass that has been heated to the softening point and cooled unevenly develops patterns of internal stress, as discussed in Section I. Stressed and unstressed glasses appear identical to the unaided eye. The stresses show up clearly, however, when the glasses are examined through a polariscope, an inexpensive and easily constructed instrument. One simple form of the polariscope consists of a light box, closed by a sheet of Polaroid (a special plastic), and a pair of Polaroid sunglasses (Fig. 2-24, *a, b*). Light that comes through the sheet of Polaroid is said to be "polarized," because the sheet absorbs, increasingly, all light waves except those that vibrate in a single plane. During use, the light box is turned to a position that favors the transmission of waves that vibrate in the vertical plane. Polaroid sunglasses, on the other hand, are designed to favor the transmission of waves that vibrate in the horizontal plane. For this reason, the lighted box appears dark when viewed through the sunglasses. Glass that is stressed gains the power to rotate the plane in which light waves vibrate, the amount of such rotation depending upon the amount of the stresses. Hence, when stressed glass is held in front of the light box and viewed through the sunglasses, the stressed regions rotate the plane of the vertically polarized waves just enough so that some of the light can make its way through the sunglasses. As a consequence, the distribution and intensity of the stresses become visible as patterns of light and shade (2-24, *c*). Unstressed glass displays no patterns (Fig. 2-24, *d*). To

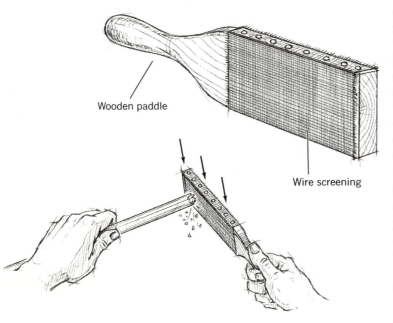

Wooden paddle

Wire screening

Figure 2-23.

small points may be broken off by striking the cut end diagonally with a piece of heavy screening (about .1-inch mesh made of No. 18 steel wire) tacked to the face of a wooden paddle (Figure 2-23). Larger irregularities may be nibbled away by repeatedly gripping the glass edge forcefully between the jaws of tweezers and "bending" the tweezers back and forth, or they may be filed off with a *wet* file.

construct the instrument, make a box of ¼-inch plywood that measures 6 inches in height, width, and length. Drill two ½-inch holes near the center of each side, for ventilation. Install a porcelain socket and a 60-watt incandescent lamp equipped with a connecting cord and plug in the bottom. Just above the lamp install a 6-inch square of frosted or milky glass. The glass may be secured in place by strips that are tacked and glued to the sides. Complete the unit by similarly installing the Polaroid sheet, sandwiched between two sheets of window glass, in the top of the box.

The design may be improved at slight cost in terms of additional work. For example, the sunglasses may be supported in the normal viewing position by an extension bracket attached to the box. The position of the glasses will then remain fixed when the operator tilts his head from side to side. A binocular eyepiece equipped with HN 22 Polaroid may be substituted for the sunglasses. HN 22 Polaroid is a more effective polarizing agent than the material used in sunglasses and, accordingly, produces a sharper image of higher contrast.

The addition of another optical element to the polariscope will transform the black-and-white images of the stresses into colored images. The colors enable the observer to distinguish between the stresses of compression and tension, an important distinction in cases in which tension appears in the surface of glass where it may induce fracture. The additional optical element may consist of a sheet of either mica or cellophane approximately .005 inch thick. Mica works somewhat better than cellophane, and

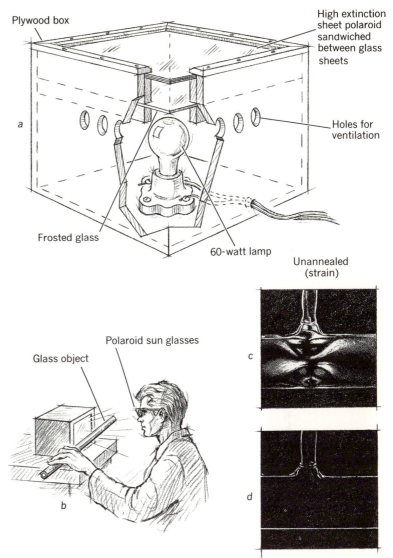

Figure 2-24.

it does not age and thus depreciate in quality with the passing of time. Mica is sold in presplit blocks several times thicker than required, and their cost increases disproportionately with size. Thick sheets may be split to the required thickness by inserting a sharp knife into the edge of the block. A bubble of air will enter the material at this point. A piece of hard wood that has been sharpened to a knife-edge is then placed between the sheets and the bubble pushed across the block. Place the sheet, so split, flat against the Polaroid of the light box and examine it through the sunglasses or the eyepiece. The mica will appear either dark, clear, or colored. Now rotate the sheet slowly, while keeping it flat against the Polaroid. The mica will now glow with all of the colors of the rainbow, one at a time. Next, turn the sheet to the position at which a red color is seen, not a bright red like a fire engine but a deep rose. Hold a thin strip of unstressed lime glass in front of the rose color and, using both hands, exert a bending force on the glass—not enough to break it. A pattern of stress will appear in color: blue on the outside edge of the bowed strip where the glass is in tension and yellow on the inner edge where it is in compression. Other rainbow colors will appear in the middle, where the glass is unstressed. In lead glass the colors will be reversed: blue in regions of compression and yellow in regions of tension. Stresses in clear plastics take on the colors of those in lead glass.

The sheet of mica may be inserted between the glass sheets that protect the Polaroid. It must be rotated to the position at which the rose color appears, and installed in contact with the outer glass cover. Alternatively, two small squares of mica (similarly oriented) may be cemented by the corners to the outer surface of the sunglasses.

The thickness of the mica sheet is critical and must be determined experimentally. If the colors fail to appear, or seem pale and dilute, try a thicker or thinner sheet (.005 inch is only approximate).

Clear cellophane of the kind used for wrapping gifts may be substituted for the mica. Cellophane is available from novelty stores and from dealers in artist's supplies. It comes in sheets approximately .001 inch thick. Cut a strip approximately 6 inches wide and 36 inches long. Divide the strip into six equal squares. Without rotating the squares (relative to their position in the sheet) pile them into a stack. Place the stack on the light box, just as though it were a sheet of mica, and repeat the procedure discussed above. If colors fail to appear, or seem weak or faded, remove one or more sheets of cellophane until the hues are most vivid. Then adjust the position of the stack for the deep rose hue and assemble it in the instrument. A detailed discussion of why the colors appear is beyond the scope of this volume but, in a word, certain materials in proper combination polarize light of some colors more strongly than they polarize light of other colors and thus give rise to the observed effect.

Didymium goggles

Another optical device of considerable convenience when working borosilicate glasses is a pair of goggles fitted with lenses of didymium glass. When the glass is heated in an oxygas flame the intense yellow glare, known as "flare-off," almost totally obscures the work. The glasses are relatively opaque to the glare, but all other colors are seen clearly and appear unaltered.

The annealing oven

Strained glass must be annealed, that is, heated slowly until the strain is relieved by plastic flow, and then cooled slowly and uniformly. Several procedures for annealing small glass parts have been devised. They will be discussed in the sections that explain the basic operations of glass blowing. Complex pieces are most conveniently annealed in special ovens that can be heated to at least 800 degrees Fahrenheit (426°C) and maintained at any temperature. We use ovens of two types, a small one that can be heated over the burner of a kitchen stove, and a larger one equipped for electrical heating. The cabinets of both ovens are made of Transite.

The smaller oven consists of a box 8 inches on each side that has a 4-inch circular opening in the bottom. This hole, which is centered over the flame of the gas burner, is covered by a 6-inch square of Transite spaced about ¾ inch above the opening by ⅛-in

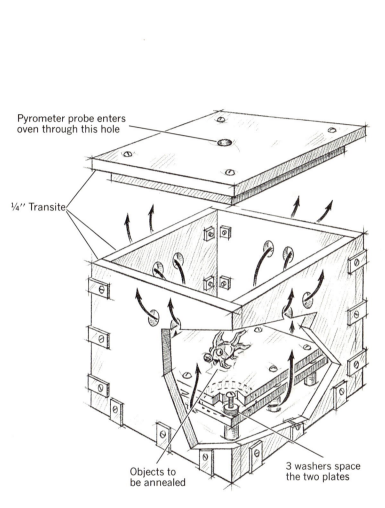

Pyrometer probe enters
oven through this hole

¼″ Transite

Objects to
be annealed

3 washers space
the two plates

Figure 2-25.

pipe nipples, as illustrated (Fig. 2-25). Eight nipples provide three points of support on each side of the square. (Multiple attachment is necessary because Transite tends to crack after protracted heating.) The square acts as a shield to prevent flame from coming into direct contact with glass objects.

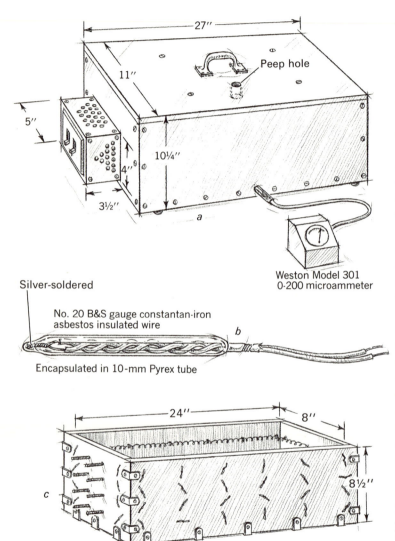

Peep hole

27″

11″

5″

10¼″

4″

3½″

a

Weston Model 301
0-200 microammeter

Silver-soldered

No. 20 B&S gauge constantan-iron
asbestos insulated wire

b

Encapsulated in 10-mm Pyrex tube

24″

8″

8½″

c

Figure 2-26.

A second square of Transite of the same size is spaced approximately ⅛ inch above the first square by iron washers. Both of the squares are attached to the bottom of the oven by stove bolts. The second platform serves as the bottom of the oven. A cover for closing the oven at the top is made of two squares of Transite bolted together, the bottom section fits the inside of the oven, and the top extends over the edge of the sidewalls. A hole 10 millimeters in diameter is drilled through the center of the cover for admitting the probe of the Pyrometer that measures the oven temperature. The perforated sides and the bottom of the oven are assembled by means of angle brackets. All cracks where sections of Transite meet are calked by a paste of crude talcum powder and water glass (sodium silicate). Any equivalent refractory cement may be used, of course.

The large, electrically heated oven consists of a pair of Transite boxes nested to form a 2-inch space for insulation that consists of an inner sheet of aluminum foil backed by either glass or asbestos wool. The inside dimensions of our oven are 6 inches in depth, 8 inches in height, and 24 inches in length. The heating elements consist of four coils of Nichrome wire that were removed from the replacement units of radiant heaters. The replacement units were purchased at a local hardware store. Two are of 1-kilowatt capacity, and two of 600 watts each. The coiled wire was stretched enough to extend around the walls of the oven and fastened to the Transite inner wall by cotter pins that fit holes in the Transite, as illustrated (Fig. 2-26).

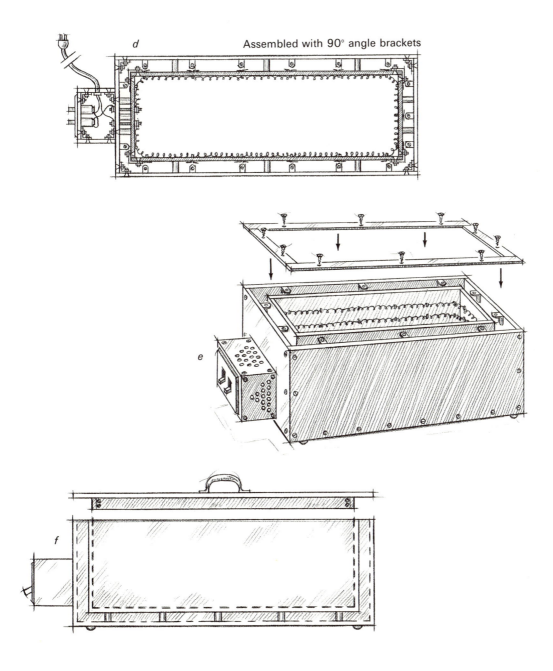

d Assembled with 90° angle brackets

e

f

The ends of each coil attach, between nuts, to brass stud bolts that extend through one end of the oven. Each 1-kilowatt coil is connected in parallel with a 600-watt coil. The pair can be turned off and on by a toggle switch mounted in a small box at the outer end of the oven. All coils are turned on to heat the oven to the annealing temperature of soft glass (800 degrees Fahrenheit). This temperature is reached in about 20 minutes. One set of coils is then turned off. The remaining coils usually maintain the annealing temperature to within a few degrees, their output compensating for loss of heat through the walls of the oven. With all coils operating, the temperature rises to approximately 1200 degrees Fahrenheit (650°C), beyond the annealing temperature of the borosilicate glasses.

The pyrometer

The pyrometer is also homemade. It consists of a pair of iron-constantan thermocouples connected in series, and a microammeter that indicates from 0 to 200 microamperes.

The thermocouple wire comes as a twisted pair insulated by an asbestos covering. Two lengths, each 3 feet long, are required. Approximately one half inch of the insulation is stripped from all ends. The wires on one end of each pair are twisted together as a

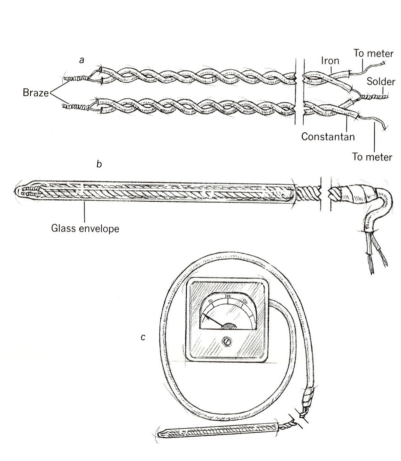

Figure 2-27.

pigtail splice and brazed. These two splices make up the thermocouple junctions (Fig. 2-27, *a*). At the other end of the wires the iron member of one pair is similarly spliced and brazed to the constantan member of the other pair. The two remaining ends are spliced to a convenient length of copper extension cord. A 4-inch length of 8-millimeter soft glass tubing is slipped over the junction end of the pairs and softened in the fire until the glass shrinks into contact with the asbestos insulation (2-27, *b*). The glass envelope merely protects the asbestos from abrasion. The free end of the extension cord is connected to the terminals of the microammeter (2-27, *c*).

The instrument may be calibrated in either of two ways. First, hold the thermocouple junctions in the fire and note which way the pointer of the meter moves. If it moves backward reverse the connections. Next, place the junctions in the annealing oven, along with a 12-inch length of 4-millimeter rod of lime glass supported near the ends about an inch above the bottom of the oven by blocks of Transite. With the cover of the oven in place, switch on the power and let the unit heat until the meter indicates a current of 60 microamperes. Hold this current reading for 5 minutes by switching one set of heating coils off and on as required, then turn off all heating units, and let the oven cool.

Examine the glass rod. If it has not sagged at this temperature, repeat the procedure. This time let the temperature rise until the meter reads 65 microamperes. If the rod still remains straight try again at 70 microamperes. The objective is to determine the temperature at which the rod becomes sufficiently plastic to sag perceptibly in 5 minutes. In our oven, this occurs at a current indication of 75 microamperes. We then assume the annealing temperature to have been reached at a current about 10% lower, or, in our oven, at 67.5 microamperes. At this temperature we anneal glass for 3 minutes per millimeter of glass thickness. A similar procedure is followed for determining the annealing temperature (in terms of meter current) of other glasses, such as the borosilicates.

The pyrometer can also be calibrated in degrees. We did this by procuring a conventional mercury thermometer calibrated to 400 degrees Centigrade (752°F). The bulb of the thermometer was inserted into the oven along with the pyrometer probe. As the temperature rose a tabulation was made: the indicated current was listed in one column and the corresponding thermometer indication in the adjacent column.

Next we procured a small alundum crucible together with 2 pounds of zinc and 2 pounds of lead. These metals freeze at characteristic temperato detect. The temperature remains constant for several minutes as the metal freezes, and then falls.

The zinc was remelted to release the thermocouple, which had become embedded in the frozen metal, and replaced by lead. Lead freezes at 589.6 degrees Fahrenheit (327.4°C). The current indication at this lower temperature was determined by the procedure used for zinc. These two temperatures, together with their equivalent current indications, were entered on the table. A graph was then drawn by plotting the current in microamperes against temperature (Fig. 2-28).

Still other tools are occasionally improvised for special applications. An example is a pair of tweezers with angular jaws and a slender rod that runs midway between the jaws from its point of attachment at the bend of the U. The rod is inserted into the softened mouth of a small bottle; the jaws form the neck as the bottle is rotated. Another example is a set of dies attached to the inner surfaces of a gate hinge. This tool is used as a mold for pressing special shapes, such as leaves, simulated seashells, items of costume jewelry, and the like, from softened glass. The list continues without limit. All tools are convenient on occasion. In the strictest sense, however, to the glass blower only two facilities are indispensable: a good fire and a pair of dexterous hands.

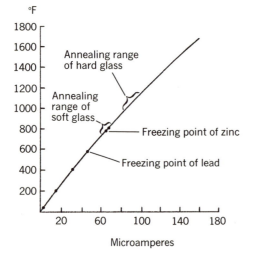

Figure 2-28.

tures, which we used for calibrating our pyrometer. The zinc was placed in the crucible and melted. The thermocouple junctions were immersed in the molten metal. The current, as indicated by the meter, dropped continuously. As the metal started to freeze, the current remained constant for a time. The current, at this temperature, was recorded. When the metal had frozen completely, the pointer of the meter resumed its descent. Zinc freezes at 787.1 degrees Fahrenheit (419.5°C). The freezing point is easy

Solid glass: Basic operations

Operations that involve no blowing of air demand much of the glass blower's time and skill. Solid glass in the form of sheet or rod is heated to softness and then stretched, bent, pressed, fused, and otherwise forced into the desired shape. The glass blower utilizes such natural forces as surface tension, which tends to pull the plastic mass into a round ball, and gravity, which causes the mass to sag. Examples of objects made of solid glass include the stems of wine glasses, the handles of pitchers, beads and similar baubles, stirring rods, stoppers, glass fibers, the hooks and bracing of laboratory apparatus, and so on.

In general, the techniques employed for altering the form of solid glass are somewhat easier to master than those that require blowing. For this reason, beginners are urged to accumulate a few hours of experience in manipulating solid glass as a prelude to work with tubing. The "feel" for the molten material so acquired will pay off handsomely when the time comes for blowing bulbs.

Cold cuts

Ordinarily, glass is shipped by the manufacturer in relatively large pieces; sheets of window glass are made in standard widths up to 6 feet and plate glass up to 15 feet. Rod stock and tubing come in 4-foot lengths. You must cut these pieces to desired size. Actually, one does not "cut" glass as wood is cut by a knife. Glass is brittle at room temperature. When sufficient pull is exerted, the material fractures. Glass always breaks under tensile stress, never under compressive stress. (Glass can be crushed, of course, but in this case it fractures as a consequence of tensile stresses that appear when the material yields under compression.) A so-called "cold cut" actually involves breaking the glass along a desired line by the application of tensile stress, a stretching force. Glass that is free of surface imperfections, such as minute cracks, exhibits astonishing strength. Specially made pieces have withstood tensile forces of as much as 400 tons per square inch. The presence of even a few microscopic cracks in the surface, however, can drastically weaken the material. The forces tend to concentrate at the bottoms of the cracks and are not relieved by plastic flow as they are in metals, such as copper, that bend easily. As a consequence, the cracks grow and spread in response to stress. Glass blowers take advantage of this for breaking the material along a desired path. To cut cold glass they first scratch the surface by means of a sharp, hard tool and then apply tensile stress across the line of surface fractures so made.

To cut sheet glass, simply lay the material on a flat support such as a clean bench top, and draw a "glass cutter" across the sheet at the place where the break is desired. This makes a line of small cracks. The tool may be a diamond point mounted in an appropriate handle, a similar point of hard metal such as tungsten carbide, or a small wheel sharpened to a V-shaped edge. In general, cutting tools of the wheel type are preferred. They work well, are inexpensive, and are available at most hardware stores. Use a straightedge, such as the side of a wooden board, to guide the tool. Cutters of the wheel type should be lubricated by dipping the wheel into kerosene just before the stroke is made. Some workers also lubricate the glass with kerosene. The fluid does not necessarily help the cutting ac-

tion, but it does catch the powdered glass fragments that are otherwise thrown into the air by the tool. The fragments can damage the lungs if inhaled.

A pressure of approximately 8 pounds should be exerted on the tool during the stroke. A lighter pressure will fail to mar the surface adequately. Greater pressure may bend and break the sheet in an undesired direction, particularly at the edge where the stroke begins. To sense the 8-pound pressure, just press the tool against the platform of a bathroom scale or equivalent balance.

Having scored the top surface by means of the cutter, move the sheet so the line of scoring is even with the front edge of the bench. Then grasp the middle of the overhanging portion and push it down abruptly. Wear a glove if you are afraid of cutting your hand. In cutting narrow sheets, use one hand to hold the glass in contact with the bench, and the other to do the pushing. When the overhanging portion is pressed down, the upper surface of the sheet is stretched on each side of the scored line, and the bottom surface is similarly compressed. Tension enlarges cracks along the scratched line until they extend completely through the sheet. The result is a clean "cut."

The same principle is used for cutting rod and tubing. For rods and tubes up to 20 millimeters in diameter, the glass is best scored by a flat file. (We use a 6-inch Warding Bastard of the type manufactured by the Nicholson File Company.) With one hand, simply brace the glass at an angle of approximately 45 degrees in a shallow notch that you have made in the edge of the bench and with the other press a corner of the file against the glass (Fig. 3-1, *a*). Holding the file at an angle of 45 degrees (3-1, *b*) and using the thumb as a guide, make a firm stroke directly across the glass as illustrated. Exert a downward force against the file of about 3 pounds for 6-millimeter rod and tubing of standard wall thickness, and of about 6 pounds for rod and tubing of larger diameters. Again, to become acquainted with the "feel" of 3 pounds and 6 pounds press the file against the platform of a spring balance. One stroke of a sharp file is usually sufficient to cut tubing of 6 millimeters or less in diameter. Larger sizes will usually require three or more strokes. The nick should extend approximately a third of the way through the wall, for tubing, and to a depth of approximately 1 millimeter, for rods larger than 8 millimeters (3-1, *c*). In addition, the nick should extend approximately one third of the distance around the circumference of the piece. Rock the file this amount as you make the stroke. The bottom of the nick should have the form of a sharp V, not rounded; the file must be sharp. Many workers wet the nick before making the break. This may prevent the inhalation of minute glass fragments that sometimes fly from the break, but, in our opinion, it does not result in a better cut. Having made the nick, grasp the rod or tubing by the hands on each side of the nick, with the thumbs extended but not touching, move the arms inward until the glass rests firmly against the stomach, and point the nick directly away from the stomach. Then pull the ends apart. *Do not deliberately bend the glass with your hands.* The inadvertent pressure exerted on the

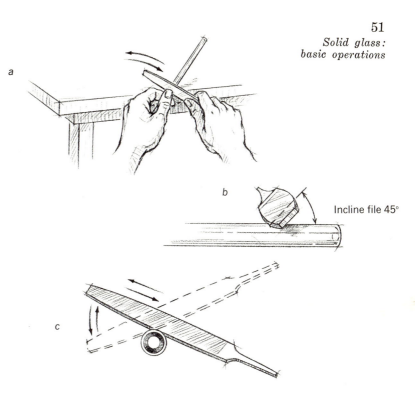

Incline file 45°

Figure 3-1.

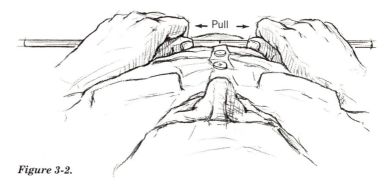

← Pull →

Figure 3-2.

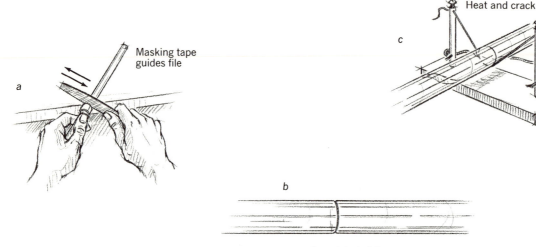

Masking tape
guides file

a

c Heat and crack

b

Completed nick

Figure 3-3.

piece by the stomach will result in some bending force. The material will part as a clean, square break (Fig. 3-2). For short pieces, 4 inches or less in length, grasp the glass through several folds of cloth to prevent an accidental cut if the glass shatters. Some experienced workers prefer to pull the glass apart by grasping the tubing with the fingers of each hand (palms down), putting the tips of the thumbs together and tightening the grip on the glass. This presses the thumbs tightly together and exerts pull on the glass. It also invites a cut should the glass shatter.

Alternatively, tubing that has been properly nicked can be parted simply by striking the glass a sharp (but not forceful) blow with an edge of the file on the side directly opposite the nick. It can also be parted by touching one end of the groove with the molten tip of a glass rod. The heat expands, and thus stretches, the glass. Indeed, al-

most any mechanical or thermal shock that, in effect, exerts tension on opposite sides of the nick will cause a clean break.

The file will become dull after making a few cuts. It is easily sharpened. Just grind the edges square on a carborundum wheel equipped with a fixture for supporting the flat side of the file at right angles to the cutting edge of the wheel.

Tubing larger than 20 millimeters in diameter can be cut most conveniently by means of a heated wire. The construction of the hot wire has been discussed in Section II. To prepare for making the cut, first file a nick completely around the piece (Fig. 3-3, *a*). To guide the file, wrap the glass with a layer or two of adhesive masking tape at the point to be cut. Place the smooth edge of the file against the tape and file the circular nick (3-3, *b*). Remove the tape, let the wire reach yellow heat and then place a portion of the nick squarely in contact with the hot wire. A crack will appear along the heated arc. Rotate the glass to bring another zone into contact with the wire (3-3, c). This will extend the crack. Usually the piece will part on the third shift. The hot wire is a particularly effective device for cutting large glass bottles and jugs.

Fire-cutting

Rods and tubing may also be parted by melting the glass. This operation is called "fire-cutting" or "burning off." As an introductory exercise, light and adjust the crossfires as explained in Section II, select a standard length of 6-millimeter glass rod, grasp the rod at convenient points of balance, and slowly warm (preheat) the material at a point about 20 inches from one end by passing the rod directly up and down through the focus of the crossfire at the rate of about one pass per second (Fig. 3-4, a). The rod should be lifted about an inch above the flame and lowered about an inch below it during each pass.

After six or eight passes, support the material steadily in the flame, but rotate the piece a full turn alternately clockwise and counterclockwise. After a few seconds the rod will soften and feel "wobbly." Note the yellow color, called "flare-off," that the hot glass imparts to the flame. While continuing to rotate the rod, stretch the ends apart about ¼ inch (3-4, b). The center of the heated portion will shrink appreciably as the rod is stretched and will quickly reach a bright yellow heat. Stretch the material another ¼ inch.

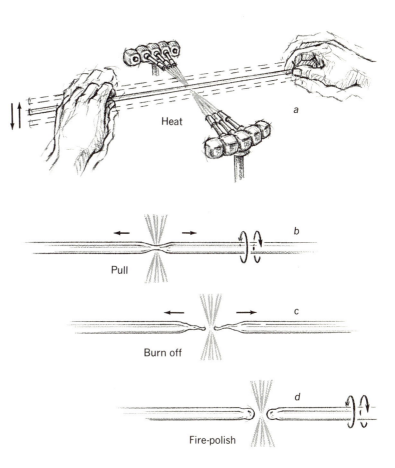

Figure 3-4.

Try to move the hands in step. Prevent the heated portion from twisting or wobbling out of shape. (No one can do it perfectly.) Within a second or two the narrowed portion will reach the fluid state and part in the middle. Continue to rotate the severed ends in the fire until the thinned tips have been drawn into molten blobs by surface tension (3-4, c, d). Then lay the glass aside on asbestos paper to cool. This completes the fire cut. When the 20-inch length has cooled, cut it in the middle by the same technique.

Fire-polishing

The edges of glass that have been separated by breaking the cold material are naturally sharp and, like all broken glass, can cut you. For safety all sharp edges should be removed, particularly those on tubing that must be put in the mouth for blowing. This can be done by melting the edges in the fire, an operation known as "fire-polishing." Surface tension then draws the softened glass into a smooth, rounded contour. Select one of the 10-inch lengths of 6-millimeter rod that you have just fire-cut and, with the file, cut off the rounded end. Nick the glass about ½ inch from the end, and brace the piece against the bench so that the nick is even with the bench top and faces away from the bench. Then make the cut by striking the tip of the rod immediately above the nick with the edge of the file (Fig. 3-5, *a*).

Preheat the cut end by passing the glass up and down through the focus of the crossfire, just as when preheating for a fire cut. Then, while rotating the rod by one hand, support the cut end steadily in the fire (3-5 *b*). Yellow flare-off will be observed almost immediately. After about 6 seconds the edges will have melted and lost their sharpness. Inspect the end. The corners will have become nicely rounded (3-5, *c*). Rods smaller than 6 millimeters will have a full polish within 4 or 5 seconds. Larger rods require proportionately more time. The edges of tubing are similarly treated. When fire-polishing a tube, however, always plug the opposite end with a cork, to prevent the flame from rushing through the piece and burning your hand.

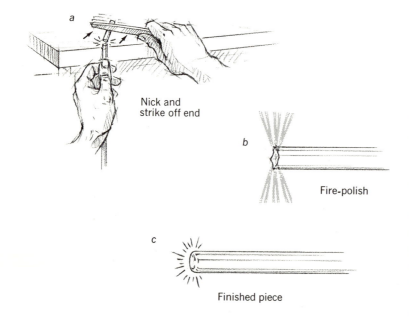

a

Nick and strike off end

b

Fire-polish

c

Finished piece

Figure 3-5.

Frequent occasion arises for rounding the end of a glass rod, either by making the form of a hemisphere, as on a stirring rod, or by making a complete sphere of a diameter substantially larger than that of the rod. The required technique is merely an elaboration of fire-polishing.

Preheat the end of the rod, bring the material to a complete fire polish, and while supporting the rod horizontally in the fire continue heating the tip of the glass. Within about 20 seconds, depending on the thickness of the rod, surface tension will draw the molten glass into a hemisphere. Unfortunately, gravity is also at work. Unless you rotate the piece uniformly, the tip will sag. You can correct the tendency to sag merely by rotating the rod so that the bent end points upward. Held still in this position, the glass will flow back into a hemisphere. But, unless the material is rotated at an appropriate rate, it will again sag out of control.

Here, then, is the first skill you must develop in the course of becoming a glass blower: the knack of rotating hot glass at a rate that precisely counteracts the force of gravity (Fig. 3-6). The trick is not difficult to master if you follow a few simple rules. First, never soften more glass than you need for making a desired form. If you intend to impart a rounded shape to the end of a rod, heat only the tip. Second, never soften the material more than necessary to accomplish your objective. Obviously, stiff glass is easier to control than runny glass. Watch the work as it softens and changes form. Alter its position

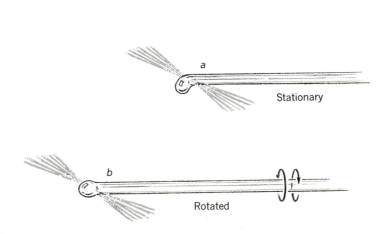

in the fire to take advantage of gravity, or to offset the effect of gravity, as the case may be. This is accomplished by rotating the work. Now, practice until you have made three rounded ends in succession. Lay them aside on asbestos paper to cool.

Next, preheat and then soften the tip of another 10-inch rod. Your object in this exercise will be to collect a mushroom-shaped lump on the end of a rod. While rotating the tip of the rod in the focus of the crossfire, gradually lower your hand so the rod slopes upward into the fire at an angle

Figure 3-6.

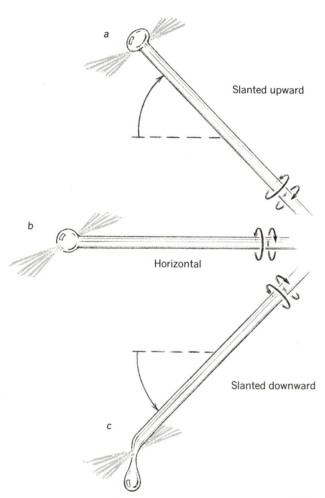

a

Slanted upward

b

Horizontal

Slanted downward

c

Figure 3-7.

of approximately 45 degrees (Fig. 3-7, *a*). When the tip has heated to yellowness, feed about ⅟₁₆ inch of additional glass into the fire. Observe that a bulge, one slightly larger in diameter than the rod, now forms at the tip. Continue feeding glass into the fire as the bulge grows. The bulge should be well centered and should turn without wobbling as you rotate the piece.

Incidentally, you may grasp the rod with the palm of the hand up or down, according to your preference, but you should make the rotation by moving your fingers and the thumb sequentially, much as a walking caterpillar moves its legs. First rotate the rod by the thumb and index finger, supporting the rest of the glass against the base of the little finger (Fig. 3-8, *a*). When the thumb and index finger have reached the limit of their travel, wrap the little finger and its neighbor over the rod and then draw them upward, a motion that continues the rotation (3-8, *b*). The glass is now supported against the inner surface of the index finger (3-8, *c*). Midway through the stroke, wrap the large middle finger around the rod and similarly stroke it upward until the index finger and thumb are again in position to resume work (3-8 *d, e, f*). The motion may be clockwise or counterclockwise, according to preference. You can, and should, practice this motion on a length of cold rod, or even a leadpencil, during odd moments until it becomes second nature. Both hands must become proficient.

Within a minute or two the growing bulge at the tip of the rod will doubtless begin to wobble. Drop the work partially out of the fire until you regain control. Your object is to turn the rod in the direction and at the rate that opposes the sag. If you rotate the piece too rapidly, the sagged portion will be carried to the top; if you rotate too slowly, it will be carried to the bottom. The whole point of the exercise is simply to learn the rate at which hot glass sags, and to develop skill in counteracting the effect. You will learn the knack of it within an hour or less. Don't let the glass become runny. If it does, move the material to a cooler part of the fire. Practice until you have accumulated a nicely centered mushroom-shaped bulge about twice the diameter of the rod. Rotate it in the air until the glass stiffens and then let the work cool on a sheet of asbestos paper. Then make five more good ones in succession.

Open your next practice session by making still another mushroom-shaped bulge of the same size. As this bulge nears completion, gradually elevate your hand to bring the rod into the horizontal position. This will greatly exaggerate the tendency of the bulge to droop. If the work starts to go out of control, move the glass out of the fire so that it stiffens a little. When the bulge has been nicely centered, resume heating the work. Do not feed additional glass into the accumulating mass. Simply rotate the piece to keep the molten portion centered on the rod. Within seconds, surface tension will convert the mushroom shape into a sphere (Fig. 3-7, *b*). When a perfect, well-centered sphere has formed, remove and cool the piece. (It is assumed that the centering rotation is continued in air until the glass has stiffened.) Make five well-centered balls before you end the session.

Figure 3-8.

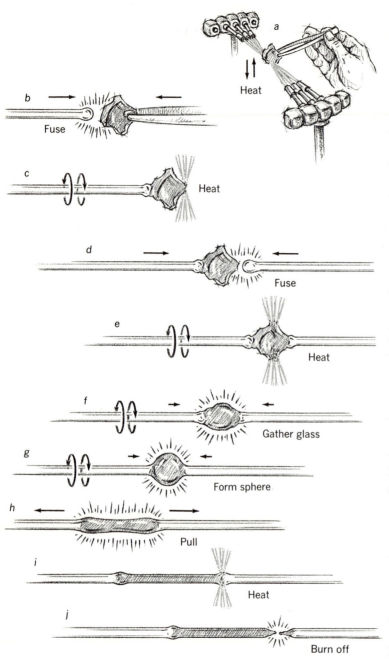

Heat

b → ╱╲ ←
Fuse

c Heat

d → ╱╲ ←
Fuse

e Heat

f → ←
Gather glass

g → ←
Form sphere

h ←
Pull

i Heat

j Burn off

Figure 3-9.

Having completed these pieces, you are prepared to make an amusing novelty. You will require at least one rod of colored glass. If you do not chance to have a stock in color, you can make your own from an old colored bottle or other colored scrap. Assume that you will make your own.

Put the colored bottle in a bag of strong paper or cloth, gather the open end of the bag around the neck of the bottle, and with a hammer blow break the glass. Take out a fragment about 1 inch square. Handle it carefully to avoid cutting yourself. If a piece of the desired size is not found, cut a larger one to size by means of the wheel-type glass cutter.

Grip the colored fragment with a tong or tweezers and preheat it slowly but fully in the crossfire (Fig. 3-9, *a*). Move the piece up and down through the focus of the flames, as when preheating rod, and shift it from side to side so the flame sweeps the surface uniformly. If the fragment is about $\frac{1}{8}$ inch thick, preheating may require up to 20 or more passes at the rate of a pass per second.

When a slight flare-off appears at the edges, hold one corner of the fragment steadily in the fire. With your other hand preheat and then soften the tip of a convenient length of 6-millimeter rod. Then place the softened tip into contact with the softened corner of the fragment (3-9, *b*). The two will fuse (3-9, *c*). Press the glasses together until the fused junction is about twice as thick as the rod. Then lift the work out of the fire just long enough for it to solidify.

When the fragment can be supported by the rod without sagging, remove the tweezer and, using the rod as a handle, commence rotating the fragment about 2 inches above the focus of the fire. This keeps the piece hot for the next operation. You will add a second handle of rod to the opposite corner (or side) of the fragment. If permitted to cool, the fragment would develop internal strain as a consequence of shrinking unevenly and it might shatter when reheated. Fuse a second handle of rod to the opposite side of the fragment by the same technique (3-9, *d*). When it has been joined, lift the work from the fire. Before the glass stiffens, pull the handles apart slightly, just enough to align the handle. If the piece wobbles when spun by the two hands, reheat the junction of the first handle until perceptibly soft, and again pull and simultaneously rotate the rods (3-9, *e*). The piece should roll true, as though it were a straight rod.

While being rotated, the fragment is now lowered into the fire and kept in alignment, without twisting, as it softens. Each hand will sense the motion of the other by the force transmitted through the plastic fragment. Do not pull the handles apart or push them together. Shift the fragment back and forth through the focus of the crossfire while maintaining the rotation. As the fragment becomes molten, surface tension will pull it

into an egg-shaped bulge (3-9, *f*). Time may be saved at this point by twisting the fragment so that it is worked into a roughly spherical ball. The handles must be permitted to drift inward just enough to supply the needed glass. The operation is not dissimilar to that of making a spherical bulge on the end of a rod, a procedure with which you are now familiar, except that now you are using both hands. Continue heating the glass and letting the handles drift inward until the molten mass has become roughly spherical (3-9, *g*).

Remove the work from the fire. Continue rotation. Just as the sphere starts to stiffen, stretch the glass into a rod by pulling the handles apart slowly (3-9, *h*). Try to time the pull so that the material stretches about 4 inches just as it solidifies. If one end of the ball starts to pull out too much, move the hands so the rod is pulled vertically, with the softer glass at the bottom. Rising air will then cool the thin end faster than the top portion of the glass, so that the end stiffens somewhat. The thicker part will then pull out into a uniform diameter. You now have a thin rod of colored glass (3-9, *i*). Let it cool. Then melt off one handle (3-9, *j*). Essentially, this is the technique employed for manufacturing all glass rod. The size of the finished piece is determined by the amount of available glass, plus the speed of the pull and the length of the stretch.

Now return to the amusing novelty.

First, seal a rod of opaque white glass to one of crystal glass, burn off, and let the mass flow into a doorknob shape (Fig. 3-10, *a*, *b*). Permit the glass to solidify but keep it hot by rotating the work about two inches above the crossfire. While thus manipulating the work with one hand fuse the tip of the colored rod (opaque white) to the center of the doorknob, stretch the molten glass to form a short rod and burn it off (3-10, *c*). Now, by rotating the work in a horizontal position let the short rod flow into a sphere (3-10, *d*). Similarly add two small spheres to opposite sides of the sphere just made (3-10, *e*, *f*). Next, select a rod of contrasting color, heat the tip to softness, and stretch it into a point that is bent to a right angle. Shift the work to a position about 2 inches beneath the fire. While holding both rods horizontally, rotate the colored rod so the tip of the point enters the lower edge of the fire. (3-10, *g*). With the glasses in this position you can easily rotate the colored rod through a half-circle to bring the molten tip quickly into contact with any part of the work (3-10, *h*).

Stop rotating the work. Hold it in a position such that the two smallest spheres are aligned horizontally. (These spheres represent the ears of the figure). Touch the upper surface of the work at a desired place with the molten tip of the colored rod. The glasses will fuse. When you pull the rod away some of the colored glass will stick to the surface. The thin thread of colored glass that forms between the sphere and the tip of the rod will be burned off if you lift the work quickly through the fire.

By this technique you can "draw"

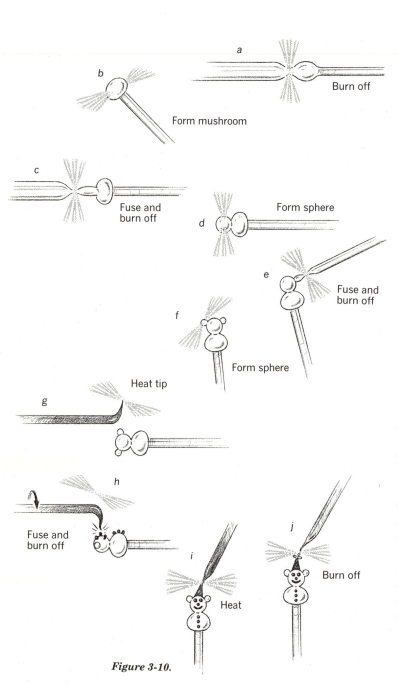

Figure 3-10.

Burn off

b
Form mushroom

c
Fuse and burn off

d
Form sphere

e
Fuse and burn off

f
Form sphere

Heat tip
g

h
Fuse and burn off

i
Heat

j
Burn off

a funny face on the sphere; make the eyes, nose, and mouth just as though you were working with crayon (3-10, *i, j*). Moreover you can draw in three dimensions; make a projecting nose easily by fusing the tip of the rod to the appropriate point on the sphere and burning it off to leave a short projection. The nose can be shaped as desired by letting the sphere stiffen, reheating the projection, and molding it with an appropriate tool. Other features—ears, eyebrows, hair, and so on—may be added in color according to your taste and talent. When applying the features, work at the edges of the flame. Having completed the face, rotate the work about an inch above the focus of the crossfire for 2 minutes and then lay it aside on asbestos paper to cool.

After the piece has cooled, make a similar sphere on the other end of the rod (Fig. 3-11, *a*). When it has completely formed, place the molten mass on a block of Transite and with a flat tool, such as a putty knife, press the sphere into a flat disk about the size of a dime (3-11, *b*). Then, with the tool covering only the disk, bend the handle upward to an angle of about 80 degrees and hold this position until the glass solidifies (3-11, *c*). Slight wrinkles may be removed by fire-polishing surfaces. You now have a unique stirring rod for mixing drinks.

Such spheres can easily be modified into pear shapes or teardrops. First, make the sphere by the technique of supporting the tip of the rod at an upward angle in the fire until a mushroom-shaped blob of glass has collected, and then support the tip horizontally until surface tension pulls it into a ball. When it reaches this form

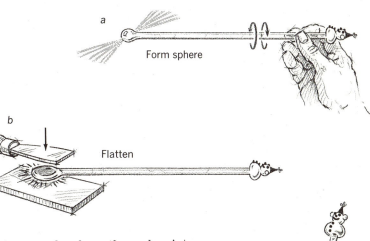

Figure 3-11.

elevate your hand so the rod points downward into the fire. Gravity will pull the mass into the teardrop form; the junction between the rod and sphere will become increasingly narrow and so thin that eventually the drop will fall, trailing a hair-like filament of glass behind (Fig. 3-7, *c*). Remove the work from the fire just *before* the neck becomes as thin as desired. (The glass continues to stretch somewhat as it cools.) The final shape of the teardrop is thus determined by the amount that you heat the material *after* pointing the rod downward and also by the initial diameter of the molten mass. You will quickly learn to judge these factors by experiment. Teardrops of appropriate proportions make attractive stoppers for miniature urns and similar novelties. Other applications are suggested in Sections V and VI.

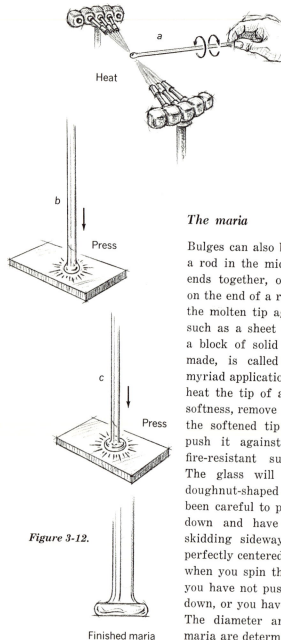

Heat

b

Press

c

Press

Figure 3-12.

Finished maria

The maria

Bulges can also be made by softening a rod in the middle and pushing the ends together, or they can be made on the end of a rod simply by pushing the molten tip against a flat surface, such as a sheet of asbestos paper or a block of solid carbon. A bulge, so made, is called a "maria." It has myriad applications. To make a maria, heat the tip of a 6-millimeter rod to softness, remove it from the fire, point the softened tip straight down, and push it against any firm, smooth, fire-resistant surface (Fig. 3-12). The glass will spread out into a doughnut-shaped disk. If you have been careful to push the rod straight down and have prevented it from skidding sideways, the disk will be perfectly centered, and it will run true when you spin the rod. If it wobbles, you have not pushed the rod straight down, or you have let it skid, or both. The diameter and thickness of the maria are determined by the length of the softened zone and by the depth to

which the molten mass is pressed. Doubtless you will succeed in making a perfect maria of the end type on your first try. Thereafter, you will quickly learn to control its proportions by experiment. Having made a good maria of this type, round off the opposite end of the rod and you have a handy muddler.

Marias are frequently required at an intermediate zone along the rod. They are not quite as easy to make as the end type because the hands must move in unison as the rod softens and is pushed inward to form the bulge. To make one, grasp a convenient length of rod by both hands near the ends and, after preheating a zone near the middle, rotate the work until it softens (Fig. 3-13, *a*). Before the piece becomes wobbly, press the ends inward. To the best of your ability keep the rod straight and well aligned. Don't let the softened zone skid sideways. Observe that the heated zone now bulges; its diameter has become larger than that of the unaltered rod (3-13, *b*). Just before it reaches red heat, the glass softens enough that the maria may be made. If heated to redness, the material becomes increasingly difficult to control; the ends that join the softened zone tend to skid and to bend out of alignment as well as to twist when the hands are rotated slightly out of step with each other. Here, again, we encounter the cardinal rule of the glass blower: *Never heat glass hotter than absolutely necessary for accomplishing your immediate objective.* This rule will be mentioned again and again in the pages that follow. Failure to observe it has discouraged more beginners than has anything else. To summarize: Using both hands, heat a zone in the middle of the glass rod. Rotate the zone continuously in the focus of the crossfire. As the zone softens, push the ends of the rod toward each other, while continuing uniform rotation. A doughnut-shaped bulge will form that is symmetrical with respect to the rod. The bulge will run true, like the wheel of an automobile, only if the ends of the rod are kept straight, in axial alignment. Don't soften the glass more than necessary. As the work is removed from the fire, pull the ends slightly, just enough to straighten the rod.

Don't be discouraged if your first marias wobble a bit. You can correct this defect. Return the work to the fire and heat the rod on one side at the point where it joins the maria. When the glass softens, bend the rod so the maria is at right angles to the rod on the side that has been softened. Let the glass solidify. Do the same on the other side of the maria. Remove the work from the fire and stretch it enough to straighten the rod. Wobbles are caused, primarily, by skidding. The softened zone becomes slightly S-shaped. Watch for the S and correct it by pushing the ends sideways, just enough to restore alignment. Marias may also become eccentric; that is, when rotated they turn like a wheel that is not centered on its axle. Eccentric marias are caused by failure to support the rod in a straight line. The rod is permitted to bend, to take the form of a broad V. When the ends are pushed together while the rod is so bent, an excess of glass is forced away from the apex of the V. The excess remains when the rods are straightened. The result is the observed eccentricity. The defect cannot be corrected.

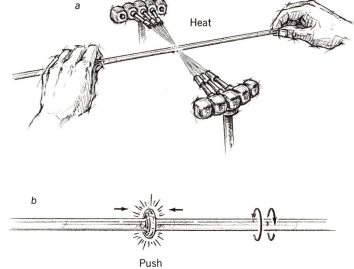

Marias of this type can be made in diameters as large as two or three times the diameter of the rod and, with practice, they can be made in rods of almost any length. The form is used in novelty glassware as the body of an animal, ornamentation on miniature candelabra, the stems of wine glasses and so on. In laboratory apparatus, marias serve as stops and supports, filter barriers, poppet valves, and similar constructions.

Figure 3-13.

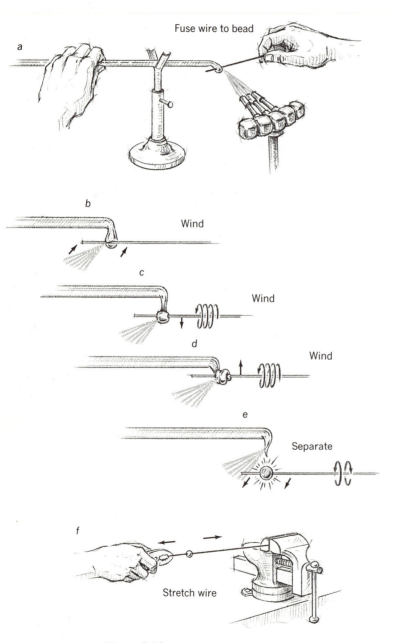

Figure 3-14.

Wire work

Many artisans specialize in so-called "wire work," the application of bits of molten glass to wire. Indeed, this operation was the first manufacturing enterprise to reach the new world from Europe when in the sixteenth century adventuring conquistadores founded a glass factory in California for making wampum. Costume jewelry of almost limitless variety can be made by this technique, even by the novice.

As an introductory exercise, make a bead of the kind used in a necklace. You will need a stock of soft glass rod, of approximately 8 millimeters in diameter, as well as a supply of *straight* wires about 10 inches long and 0.051 inch in diameter (No. 16, American Wire Gauge). Professional glass blowers prefer wire of the type known as "low" brass. (See "Sources of Tools and Materials," page 189). You will also require a pair of fixtures, or bucks, for supporting the rod in the fire (Section II, page 36). The tip of the glass rod is heated by rotating the rod. You can set up an appropriate fire by removing the rear burner of the crossfire, so the flame is directed horizontally toward the back of the bench.

Place the glass on the bucks so that one end can be slid into the fire (see Fig. 2-19). Preheat the end by sliding the rod into and out of the flame at the rate of about one pass per second. Then advance about ¼ inch of glass into the fire (Fig. 3-14, *a*). Let it soften and droop. When the glass has reached yellow heat, grasp a wire, much as you would manipulate a slender rod of glass, and preheat a zone near the outer end. About three passes through the flame will do.

Holding the wire horizontally, rotate it between the thumb and first three fingers (so the top surface moves away from you) and touch the heated zone of the wire to the region of the drooped glass—about a quarter of the distance up from the bottom of the blob (3-14, *b*). The glass will stick to the wire and wind around it as the wire turns. Pull the wire down slightly as you turn it and then move it upward, winding continuously (3-14, *c*, *d*). The relatively solid, inner region of the sagged glass will act as a wiper during the up stroke that limits the radius of the glass which accumulates on the wire. If the glass at the point of contact with the wire is heated so that it is too thin, it will not accumulate. At the top of the upstroke pull the accumulated mass away from the molten blob *through the lower region of the flame* (3-14, *e*).

If all has gone well—and you have rotated the work continuously—an almost perfect sphere of glass will have formed on the wire. Continue the rotation, reversing direction of rotation at will, until the bead solidifies. When cooled, the bead may be removed from the wire by either of two methods. Clamp one end of the wire in a vise, grasp the free end by a pair of pliers, and stretch the metal. The wire shrinks enough when thus stretched to permit the bead to slide freely (3-14, *f*). Alternatively, cut off the wire close to the glass and drop the bead into a container of nitric acid. Within a few hours the acid will have eaten the metal away. *Caution:* Nitric acid is highly toxic and corrosive. Handle it accordingly.

You may encounter three difficulties. First, the glass may not stick to the wire. This indicates that the wire is not hot enough when touched to the glass. Secondly, the glass may refuse to wind onto the wire as a smooth, nicely rounded mass. It tends to bunch up, as a misshapen blob. This means that you are lifting the wire away from the sagged mass too soon. As explained, the glass at the rear of the sagged portion is cooler and, hence, more rigid than the forward region that is in direct contact with the flame. If you lift the wire close to the sagged portion, the collected glass (which is quite runny) is smoothed to a spherical shape by the relatively solid mass. Finally, as the piece nears completion and is about to be withdrawn, the wire may melt. This can happen only if the wire is excessively exposed to the flame. Work on the region of the glass that has sagged out of the center of the flame, below the focal point of the fire.

Having made one good bead, continue. Conserve wire (after becoming proficient) by spacing several beads at ½-inch intervals. Beginners may experience difficulty when attempting to space beads closely on the wire because the heat tends to crack beads that have cooled. Speed comes with practice, however, and the trouble vanishes. As glass is consumed, advance the rod into fire with your free hand. When making beads for a necklace, do not strive for uniformity. Let chance determine the sizes. You can sort the beads later for stringing.

A bead can be made on the tip of the wire, of course. Until fashion changed, hatpins that terminated in a black bead were popular. Map tacks and similar stickpins are still so made, and by hand! It is easy to change the spherical bead at the end of a ire into a teardrop: after the sphere has formed just incline the

wire downward into the flame and rotate as though you were making a teardrop on the end of a rod (Fig. 3-15).
With practice it becomes possible to
pick up the end bead from the molten
glass and remove it from the flame at
once. By working quickly, the teardrop forms before the glass stiffens,
so that extra heat is not needed.

An end bead can also be flattened,
and converted into a maria. First,
change the sphere into a pear shape
and then push the glass straight down
against a flat surface (Fig. 3-16, *a*).
Do not push the wire so far that it
makes contact with the base material
(3-16, *b*). If the base material is
rough it may mar the outer surface of
the maria. The polish can be restored
by exposing the surface to the flame
for a few seconds (3-16, *c*). When the
work cools, cut the wire off at a point
about ½ inch from the glass and bend
it into a small loop. You now have a
button (3-16, *d*). The wire loop takes
the thread.

Buttons of this type make attractive glass eyes for toys. First, make
a maria of brown glass (or other desired color) on the end of a wire. When
it solidifies soften the end of a black
rod about 4 millimeters in diameter
and fuse it to the center of the button (Fig. 3-17, *a*). Burn off the rod
and fire-polish the surface of the maria
(3-17, *b*). The eye now has a black
pupil (3-17, *c*). Forms, such as sun-
bursts, are made by fusing colored
rod radially to the edge of the button
and stretching the material to tapered
points that are bent into zig-zags by
means of tweezers before the glass
stiffens (3-17, *d*). When making such
forms, keep the entire piece heated
until the work is finished. Damaging

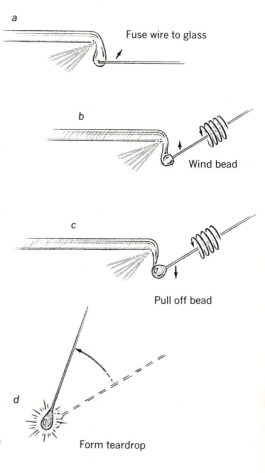

a

Fuse wire to glass

b

Wind bead

c

Pull off bead

d

Form teardrop

Figure 3-15.

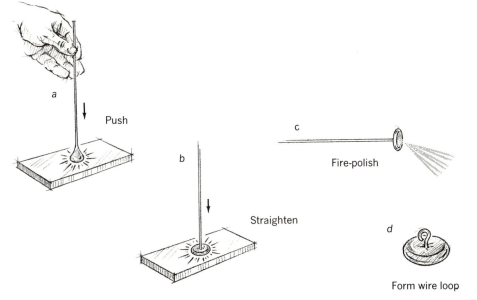

a Push

b Straighten

c Fire-polish

d Form wire loop

Figure 3-16.

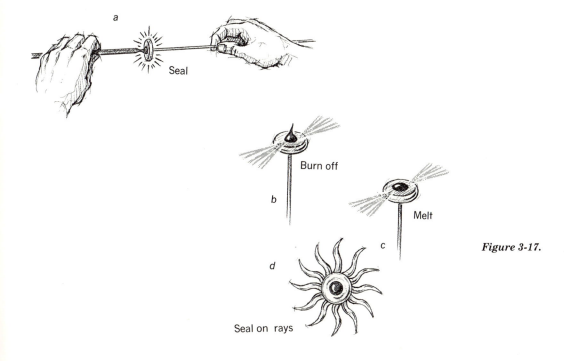

a Seal

b Burn off

c Melt

d Seal on rays

Figure 3-17.

Creative
glass blowing

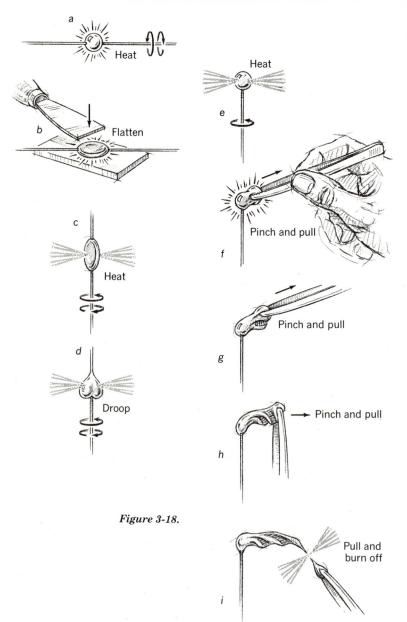

Figure 3-18.

strains will develop and the piece will almost certainly shatter if it is reheated after cooling. The variations in form that can be imparted to such pieces are limitless.

Beads also lend themselves to a variety of shapes. For example, a heart-shaped bead is easy to make. Begin by forming a conventional spherical bead near the end of a wire (Fig. 3-18, *a*). When the mass has become fully rounded, and is molten, place the glass on a flat surface and squash it into a pancake with a carbon block, a spatula, or other convenient tool (3-18, *b*). Then return the piece to the crossfire, supporting the wire vertically with your hand beneath and slightly to one side of the focus, so that the flame plays alternately on each side of the pancake as the work is rotated (3-18, *c*). The outer edges will soften and droop, pulling the glass into the form of an inverted heart (3-18, *d*).

Egg-shaped beads are wound by shifting the wire lengthwise while it is in contact with the drooped mass. This form can be converted into a rectangular shape by pressing the glass on four sides. Doorknob shapes are made by feeding excess glass onto the central zone of a bead that would otherwise become a sphere.

Multicolored beads also are easy to make. After the desired shape has solidified, add one or more colored stripes by touching the softened tip of a colored rod to the rotating piece, as when adding a pupil to the glass eye. The stripe (or polka dots, if desired) are then fired in place by rotating the bead in the flame. Interesting effects can also be achieved by crushing glass of various colors into fragments and, with a sieve, collecting particles that are about the size of granulated sugar. (The glass can be pulverized safely by placing the large pieces between two sheets of galvanized iron of the kind sold by tinsmiths, sealing the edges with adhesive tape, and pounding the sandwich with a hammer.) The molten bead is rolled in the mixture of colored fragments and then fire-polished.

The variety of interesting shapes into which spherical beads can be transformed is limited only by the imagination of the artisan. Instead of the heart shape, for example, the glass can be easily pulled into a miniature plume with a pair of tweezers. The sequence of manipulations are depicted in Figure 3-18, *e* to *j*. When combined in symmetrical patterns, such plumes make attractive elements of costume jewelry.

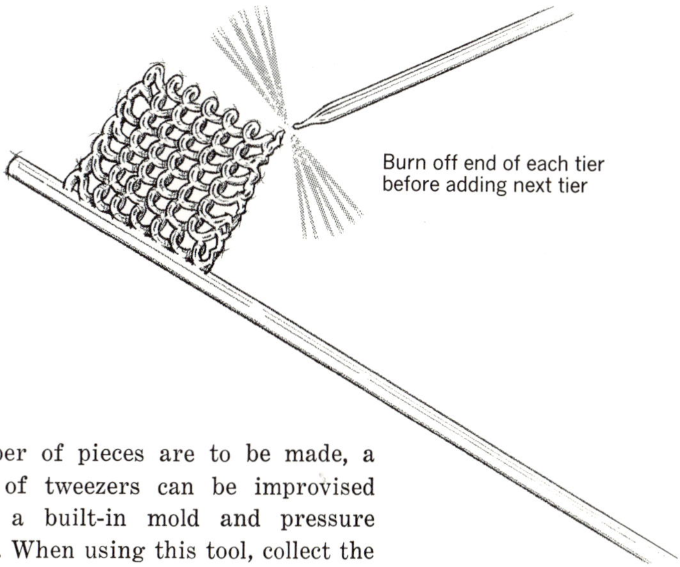

Burn off end of each tier before adding next tier

Press molding

Irregular forms, such as sculptured miniatures in bas-relief, can be molded from solid rod by a pressing technique. A plaster mold is first made of a strong, heat-resistant material such as dental stone. The open mold is placed face up on the bench. A mass of glass is then collected on the end of a rod to fill the mold. As the collected teardrop starts to fall, move the end of the rod directly over the mold and when the mass enters the cavity, press it into place immediately with a carbon block. A filament of glass will link the part to the rod. Break it off. The completed piece will contain a lot of strain and must be annealed. The edge of the finished piece to which the filament was attached may then be smoothed on a grinding wheel. If a

number of pieces are to be made, a pair of tweezers can be improvised with a built-in mold and pressure plate. When using this tool, collect the molten glass as a sphere. Pick the sphere off the end of the rod by the jaws of the tool.

The network technique

Lace-like forms appear in many glass novelties that range in variety from ship models and bird's nests to miniature bases and Christmas tree ornaments. Itinerant glass blowers usually describe the operation of making such pieces as "crocheting in glass." Actually, the finished piece consists of a network of finely spiralled glass rod, each turn of which is fused to adjacent turns of neighboring spirals, as illustrated (Fig. 3-19 and Plate 1).

Figure 3-19.

lower surface of the flames and points away from you toward the upper left (toward the ten of an imaginary clock). The position is somewhat awkward because the left hand must be placed behind the front burner of the crossfire. (Fig. 3-20). A convenient length of 4-millimeter lead glass rod is now preheated and the tip softened. This piece is manipulated by the right hand and is called the working rod. The rod is inclined downward at an angle of about 45 degrees through the left edge of the flame. The molten tip is now touched to the hot end of the base rod (Fig. 3-21, *a*). The glasses fuse. The working rod must now be rotated in the *counter-clockwise* direction and simultaneously lifted about ⅜ inch, then moved, and then swept downward through an arc until it again touches the heated rod about ⅛ inch away from the first point of contact (3-21, *b, c, d, e*). Again, the glasses fuse. The motion generates one turn of a small spiral of glass rod, the ends of which are fused to the base rod. The working rod is now rotated *clockwise* until the thumb and forefinger have been returned to their starting positions, *without lifting* the working rod from its point of contact (3-21, *f*). This motion simply prepares you to make the second spiral loop. The fact that the molten glass has been twisted is incidental. The second loop is now made, then the third, and so on. Completed loops are moved slowly away from the fire as the working rod is advanced onward, loop by loop. Thus the loops cool slowly, and are partially annealed. The working rod is gradually heated to the plastic state as it moves through the flame.

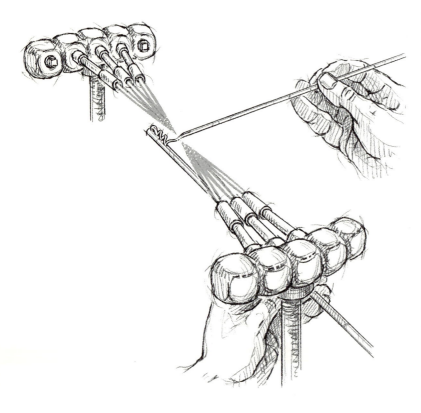

Palm faces its owner

Figure 3-20. To make a network, first preheat a 1-inch zone at the end of a 4-millimeter rod of convenient length, which is called the base rod. Then with your left hand (assuming that you are right-handed) incline the rod upward from beneath the fire so that the preheated zone just grazes the

The rate at which the working rod becomes molten is determined by the depth to which the glass is immersed in the fire. The beginner should advance the material through the edge of the fire, as directed. In this position the rod will soften at the rate of about ⅛ inch per second; a loop can be made every 3 seconds. The worker gains speed with practice. After an hour or so even a novice will find it relatively easy to make a loop per second. The rod must then be fed through an appropriately hotter region of the fire.

Having fused an inch-long spiral of loops to the base rod, burn off the working rod at its final point of contact. A second spiral is then fused to the first (Fig. 3-21, *f*). The operation is begun by fusing the molten tip to the upper center of the first loop of the first spiral, and is continued by making a loop that terminates at the upper center of the second loop of the first spiral. When the second spiral has been completed, again burn off the working rod and similarly add succeeding spirals to make a network at least one inch wide.

The charm of glass networks resides in the uniformity of their texture and contour. The "stitches" must be as alike as possible, and, in form, plane pieces should be flat and rounded pieces, free of bumpy surfaces. The loops should not vary too much in thickness. Beginners will doubtless find that the spacing between loops tends to vary at first. Evenness of spacing comes with a practiced eye.

Most workers acquire the knack within eight practice sessions of an hour each. Variation in the diameter of the loops arises from failure to ad-

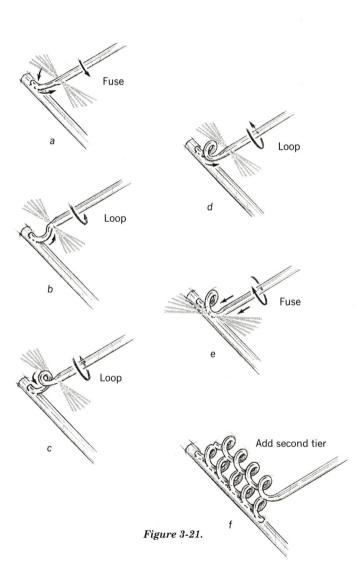

Figure 3-21.

A glass basket

In its present circular form the network may be regarded as the bottom of a small basket. Complete the piece by building up the sides, as illustrated in Figure 3-23. The direction of the working rod now lies in the plane of the network, as illustrated (Fig. 3-23, *a*). Fuse loops to the edge of the network at an angle of roughly 70 degrees and add additional tiers to make the basket about half as high as its width (3-23, *b*). To make the basket handle, fuse the tip of the rod at right angles to any point around the rim of the basket and soften about 2 inches of the rod, heating it from its point of attachment. Simply move the zone to be softened up and down through the fire. When the glass has become plastic, lift the work from the fire, invert the basket, and bend the rod into a smooth arc separated about $1\frac{1}{8}$ inches at the ends. In the course of bending the arc, bring the junction between the soft and solid portion to within about $\frac{1}{2}$ inch of the rim. Burn off the rod at this point (3-23, *d*). Slowly preheat the point at which the handle joins the rim. Do not rush this operation. Strain now exists in the glass and abrupt heating will shatter the work. Then soften the material just enough so the handle can be bent into contact with the opposite rim of the basket. When contact is made, preheat the work carefully at this point, soften the tip of the handle, and press it into fusing contact with the rim (3-23, *e*). (Cold glass is sufficiently flexible to accommodate this small movement.) Finally, cut off the 4-millimeter rod flush with the bottom of the basket. This is done by apply-

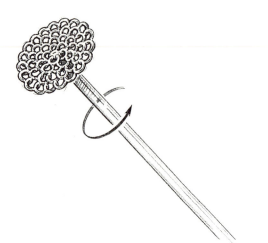

vance the rod at a uniform rate, failure to move the rod through a given region of the fire, or both. For controlling the position of the working rod in the fire, improvise an elbow rest for your right arm. It will help to steady the work.

Having made a few flat squarish networks with even stitches, try your hand at making circular ones. Make an end maria on a piece of 4-millimeter rod. Now, instead of making loops along the length of the piece, fuse loops around the end maria. Space the stitches so that the final loop meets the beginning of the first. Always burn off the rod at the end of the tier. Then add the second tier, just as though you were making a rectangular piece. You will find it necessary to squeeze in an extra stitch or so to compensate for the increased circumference of the piece. Continue until the network reaches a diameter of about 1 inch (Fig. 3-22).

Figure 3-22.

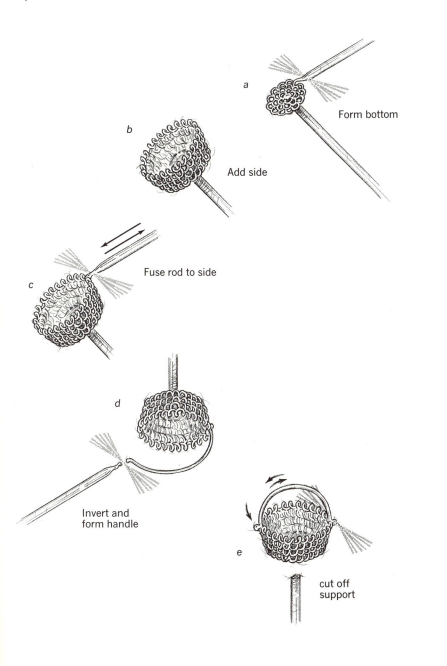

a   Form bottom

b   Add side

c   Fuse rod to side

d   Invert and
form handle

e   cut off
support

Figure 3-23.

ing the molten tip of a rod to the base rod just at the basket's bottom, then nipping lightly with cold wire cutting pliers.

A somewhat more attractive handle, one that resembles twisted rope, can be substituted for the plain rod. To make the rope, gather a spherical mass of molten glass on the end of a rod (Fig. 3-24, *a*) and immediately press it into a disk (3-24, *b*) that is approximately ¾ inch wide and perhaps ¹⁄₁₆ inch thick. Then fuse a handle of similar rod opposite to the point of attachment (3-24, *c*). You may think of this form as a maria set edgewise in a rod. Now resoften the disk, remove the work from the fire, and simultaneously stretch and rotate the handles in opposite directions (3-24, *d*). When the center portion has narrowed to the desired diameter (roughly 3 millimeters for this basket handle) maintain just enough tension to straighten the piece. Cut a 2-inch length from the central portion and install as the handle of the basket (3-24, *e*).

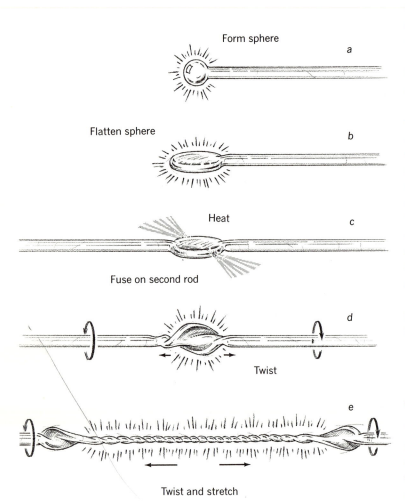

Form sphere   *a*

Flatten sphere   *b*

Heat   *c*

Fuse on second rod

d

Twist

e

Twist and stretch

Figure 3-24.

Glass icicles

The identical technique can be used for making glass "icicles" for your Christmas tree. After completing the twisting and stretching operation, cut the piece in the middle (Fig. 3-25, *a*). Then soften a narrow zone of one piece at the junction between the rod and the twist (3-25, *b*), stretch the twisted portion until it shrinks to a diameter of about 4 millimeters, and simultaneously bend a full loop approximately ¼ inch in diameter. Burn off the excess rod close to the loop.

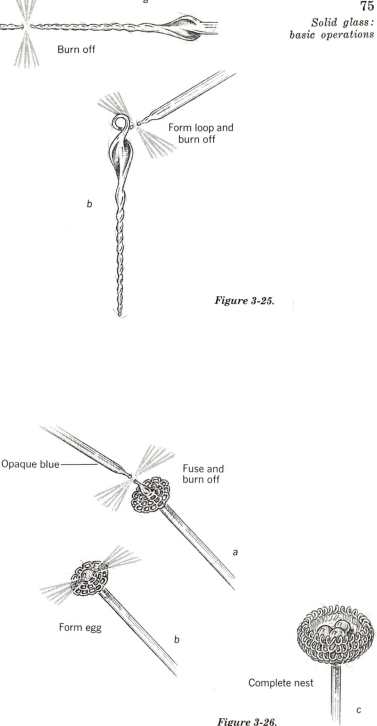

Burn off

Form loop and
burn off

a

b

Figure 3-25.

Even more attractive icicles can be made from colored scraps of sheet glass. Fuse a selected scrap to rod handles as when preparing to convert such scrap into rod (see page 58). When the material softens, pull and stretch the mass into an icicle and form the supporting loop.

A bird's nest

A somewhat more advanced application of the network technique involves the fabrication of a bird's nest, replete with the bird and colored eggs. Even if your tastes do not run to such knickknacks, you are urged to do the project as a familiarizing exercise. The skill so acquired will serve you well when you tackle more complex operations involving combinations of solid and blown forms.

Begin by making the bottom of a basket. Next, select a rod of colored stock, soften the tip, and fuse it to a point slightly away from the center of the network (Fig. 3-26, *a*). Burn off the rod slightly above the junction, say, about ⅛ inch above. Fire-polish the projection, just enough to round the end (3-26, *b*). When viewed from above, this glass resembles a miniature bird's egg. Add two more eggs, arranged as desired. Complete the nest by extending the network up and around the eggs. The operation is similar to making the sides of the basket, but now you must round the side gently and extend it up and over as a smooth curve (3-26, *c*). The nest and its eggs is now complete.

Opaque blue

Fuse and
burn off

a

Form egg

b

Complete nest

c

Figure 3-26.

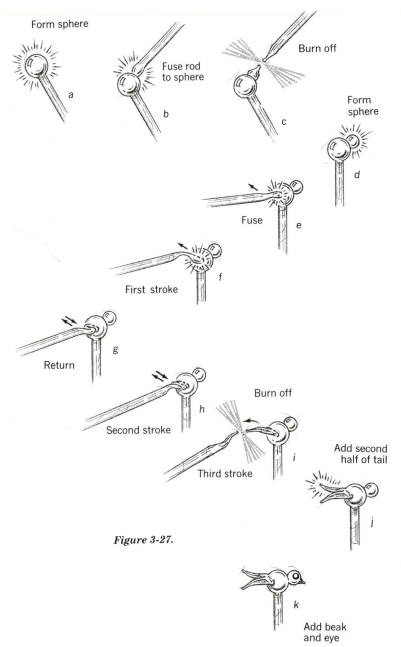

Figure 3-27.

To fashion the bird, collect a sphere of colored glass, about ⅜ inch in diameter, on the end of a 4-millimeter rod (Fig. 3-27, *a*). Let the sphere solidify, but keep it hot. Soften the tip of an identical rod and fuse it to the hot sphere. (Its position should be such that it is pointing to the two of an imaginary clock. Burn off the rod, leaving just enough glass attached to the sphere to form a ball about 3/16 inch in diameter after the stub has been rounded in the fire (3-27, *b*, *c*, *d*). This ball will become the head of the bird. Next, add the wings and tail. Proceed by softening the tip of a 4-millimeter glass rod of desired color. At a point on the body, opposite the head, at approximately the ten o'clock position, stroke the heated tip sideways against the body of the bird, much as you would stroke with a crayon. (Work close to the fire so the "crayon" does not stiffen.) Then lift the tip just enough to clear the body, return it to the beginning position, and stroke again. Lift and return. Make a total of three strokes and then lift the rod away in an arc as illustrated (3-27, *e*, *f*, *g*, *h*). The stroking action accomplishes two objectives: first, the circular cross section of the rod is altered into a ribbon shape, which is thickest on the side that points away from the work; secondly, the texture of the glass becomes ribbed, approximating the appearance of feathers (3-27, *i*). You have now made half of the bird's tail. Add the remaining half by repeating the operation in reverse on the other side. The two halves of the tail should merge at the body and diverge outward (3-27, *j*). Similarly form and attach the wings.

The eyes are made next. Soften and

make a narrow constriction in a rod
of black glass. The constriction should
be about the thickness of a common
pin. Cut the glass at its narrowest
point. Soften the tip and immediately
apply it to the eye position on the
bird's head. You must work quickly.
The tip becomes molten immediately
when exposed to the fire and it cools
as promptly. Withdraw the rod, and
burn off the resulting filament of
glass and fire-polish the portion that
remains attached to the head. Similarly, make the second eye. Finally,
soften the tip of a yellow rod, apply it
to the beak position and withdraw.
Burn off the rod, leaving the tapered
beak attached. This completes the
bird (3-27, *k*). To perch it on the edge
of the nest, cut off the rod that has
been serving as a handle and substitute a wire holder (see Fig. 2-17, Section II). Reheat the bird *slowly,* soften
the region where the rod was formerly
attached, reheat the nest *slowly,* and
fuse the bottom of the bird to the edge
of the nest (3-27, *l*).

Glass sloop

The apex of the network technique has
been reached (for the beginner) when
he completes a sailboat model. Again,
the prime objective is not the acquisi-
tion of a novelty but the manipulative
skill that develops during the construction. To make the vessel illustrated, start by making a network
circle. Add a row of loops to the top
and bottom edges of this circle (Fig.
3-28, *a*). To make the keel, heat the
end of a 4-millimeter working rod and
fuse it to the central area of the top
of the circle, stroking a few times to

Fuse bird to nest

get a good bond, and then draw out
to form one half of the keel. Repeat
this procedure in the opposite direction to finish the keel, which will be
1½ inches long (3-28, *a*).

With the keel as a base, build up
the hull of network, rounding the
structure approximately as suggested
by the drawing (Fig. 3-28, *b*). Keep
the structure hot as you work. Next,
fuse a saddle across the hull at a point
about a quarter of the hull length
from the bow, attaching the ends of
the saddle to the gunwales as illustrated (Fig. 3-28, *c*). Fuse the working rod to the saddle and draw out
past the stern of the hull to form
the boom. Fuse on and draw a flowing
line from the stern to the end of the
boom, and burn off. (Aside from being
part of the vessel, this line keeps the
boom rigid when the saddle softens
during the placing of the mast.) Install the mast by softening the end of
a 4- or 6-millimeter rod and fusing it
to the saddle in the position shown

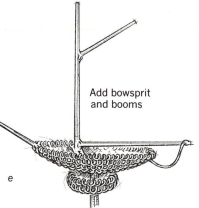

Add bowsprit
and booms

e

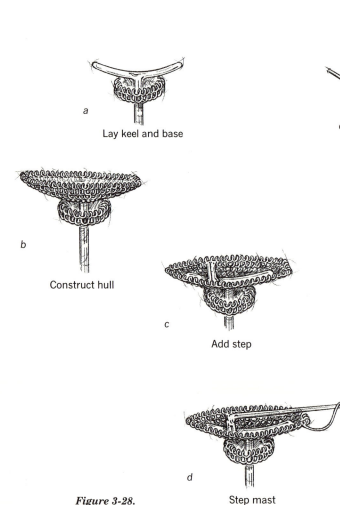

a

Lay keel and base

b

Construct hull

c

Add step

d

Step mast

Figure 3-28.

(3-28, *d*). For a realistic appearance, the mast should taper uniformly from bottom to top. In a model of this size the mast should be about 4 inches tall. Make the taper by softening a zone about ¾ inch long, beginning at the gunwale, and stretching the glass just enough to form a perceptible taper, feeding the working rod into the fire as the mast is drawn out to get additional glass. Burn off the rod at the point where the gaff (top sail support) is to be set. Now run up the *heavy* side lines that are to be part of the ladder, and any other lines you wish to terminate at this point, and burn off. Now apply the ladder rungs. Holding the working rod tip in the fire until it is runny, start at the bottom of the ladder and work up to the top, crisscrossing the ladder sides as you go. Allow the runny glass to overlap the ladder sides at each crossing. The fusing will be automatic. Try to simulate dribbling molasses. With both ladders

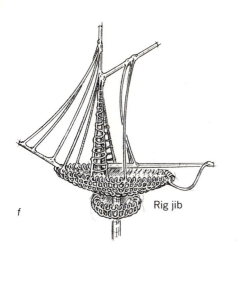

f   Rig jib

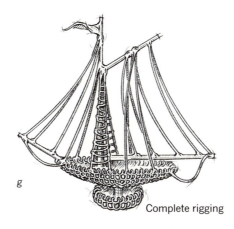

g   Complete rigging

on, fuse ¼ inch of the top juncture. To this, apply the gaff and then the rest of the mast (3-28, *e*, *f*). By the same technique, install the bowsprit (3-28, *e*). Make a practice of rotating the construction 3 or 4 inches above the focus of the crossfire during intervals when glass is not being actually applied. This keeps the work heated.

The rigging is now to be installed. For this operation the vessel is held in a horizontal position beneath the flames, and the lines are drawn out almost horizontally, from left to right. Gravity and your judgment govern the graceful flowing lines. With practice and experience, your timing will become perfected.

Soften the end of a 4-millimeter rod, and fuse it to a desired point of attachment. Support the rod parallel to the mast as it solidifies. In this position the rod can be passed back and forth through the edge of the fire to soften a length of glass that, when

stretched, will extend to the point of attachment, a projection such as the mast or bowsprit. Now, moving the hands in unison, pass the rod back and forth through the edge of the fire until it softens, then make the stretch, wind the glass around the desired point of attachment (a projection) and burn off (3-28, *f*). When the rigging is complete (3-28, *g*), attach a pennant to the tip of the mast by the technique used for making the bird's wing. Novelties utilizing the network technique range from simple furniture, and the costumes of human figures, to ships under full sail. The variety is limited only by the imagination of the artisan. To make a cat-rigged sloop (a vessel having a single sail without a gaff), leave off the gaff and the ladders, and run all lines to the mast top, fusing the top juncture, drawing to a point, and burning off. The base rod is removed the same way it is removed from a basket.

Interesting pieces can also be made of solid glass. An example is the fabrication of a miniature turtle. Collect a mass of molten glass about ⅜ inch in diameter on the end of a 4- or 6-millimeter rod of brownish color, let it assume a slight teardrop form (Fig. 3-29, *a*), and quickly lay it down on a sheet of asbestos paper. The molten mass will flow into a flat-bottomed dome approximating the shape of a turtle (3-29, *b*). With a finely pointed rod of contrasting color, apply polygonal spots to the rounded surface that suggest the characteristic markings of the tortoise shell (3-29, *c*). Dark brown rod is conventionally used for fusing the stubby head, feet, and tapered tail (3-29, *d*). Eyes are applied in the same way as they are to the bird. Realistic feet can be made by softening the tips of the legs and pinching the glass slightly upward with tweezers equipped with grooved jaws (3-29, *e*).

Miniature candlesticks are also relatively easy to make. They illustrate a common application of the maria. First, fuse and seal a 4-millimeter rod of opaque white glass to a 6-millimeter length of ruby rod. To make the seal, heat just the tips of both rods, press them together lightly, and, as they solidify, exert just enough pull to straighten and shrink the bulge that forms at the junction (Fig. 3-30, *a*). Then heat the narrowest possible zone in the ruby glass that adjoins the seal just made. When the glass softens, push the ends of the rod to form a maria about 8 millimeters in diameter (3-30, *b*). Now cut the ruby rod about ⅝ inch from the maria. Soften about ¼ inch of the end and make a maria of the end type by pushing the softened

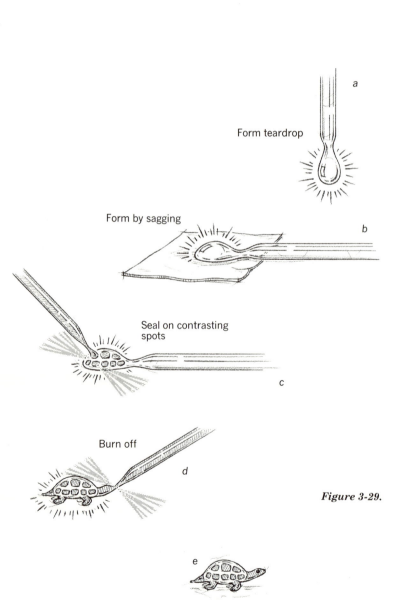

Form teardrop

Form by sagging

Seal on contrasting spots

Burn off

Figure 3-29.

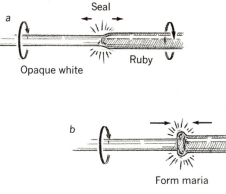

Seal
a
Opaque white
Ruby

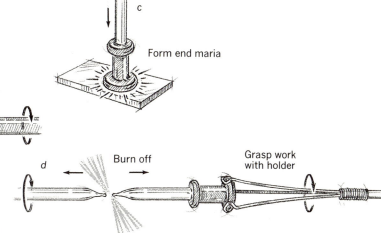

b
Form maria

c
Form end maria

d Burn off Grasp work with holder

zone straight down onto a flat surface
(3-30, *c*). When the work cools, grasp
the end maria in a wire holder. Heat a
narrow zone in the white rod about ¾
inch from its junction with the ruby
rod, stretch the glass, and burn it off
(3-30, *d*). Then heat the end of the
remaining portion of the white rod and
make the characteristic wax drippings by fusing molten stripes to the
candle. Apply the glass as though you
were making a single crayon stroke.
The effect is pleasing if three strokes
are made in differing lengths around
the candle (3-30, *e*). Finally, form
the wick by fusing a short, thin, rod
of black to the center of the top, as illustrated (3-30, *f*).

Candles somewhat more ornate can
be made by forming a shallow pan by
the network technique, fusing the
holder to the center of the pan, and
adding a wax catcher of network at
the point where the candle is sealed
to the holder. A handle attached to the
pan curves up into contact with the
wax catcher. The piece is quite light.
For this reason the top of the handle
need not be fused to the wax catcher
(Fig. 3-31).

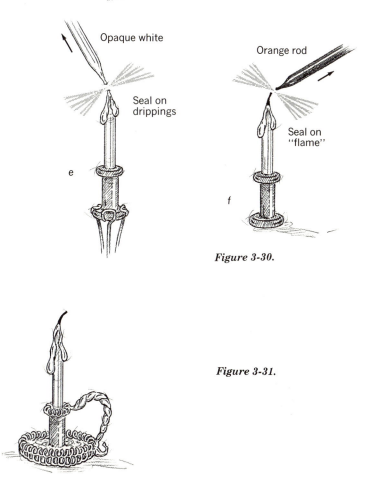

Opaque white

Seal on drippings

Orange rod

Seal on "flame"

e

f

Figure 3-30.

Figure 3-31.

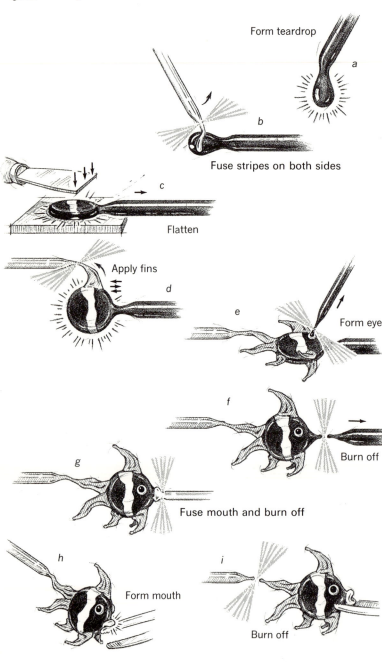

Form teardrop

a

Fuse stripes on both sides

b

Flatten

c

Apply fins

d

Form eye

e

Burn off

f

Fuse mouth and burn off

g

Form mouth

h

Burn off

i

Figure 3-32.

A useful exercise in combining glass is involved in making exotic fish. Gather a ball of glass approximately ½ inch in diameter on the end of a 10-millimeter black rod, and incline the rod to form a teardrop with a neck about 8 millimeters in diameter (Fig. 3-32, *a*). With a rod of sharply contrasting color add a thick stripe to each side of the teardrop, vertically or horizontally (3-32, *b*). Then soften the mass and press it into a disk approximately an inch in diameter. While maintaining pressure on the flattened portion, stretch the neck of the teardrop about ⅛ inch (3-32, *c*). This is the body of the fish. Fins are now to be added. While keeping the body hot, soften the end of a rod of desired color and by the technique of repeated crayon strokes make the fins just as you made the bird wings. Make a single, sweeping dorsal fin above (3-32, *d*, *e*,) and a pair of adjacent ventral fins below. These will become "legs" on which the completed fish will stand. If one fin turns out to be slightly longer than the other, soften the tip of the longer fin and pick off the surplus glass by touching it with the heated end of a rod. If the difference in length is slight, simply soften the tip of the longer fin and while holding the body vertically, press both fins against a level surface. The longer of the pair will flatten to equalize the length. Next, add a short, stubby anal fin. Finish by making the tail, just as you made the tail of the bird, but after finishing the second part of the tail fin let the glass solidify with the rod still attached to the fish. This rod will become a new handle. Next, add the eyes (3-32, *e*). Opaque yellow creates an exotic effect. Make them just as you made the eyes of the bird. After firing the eyes to a smooth, hemispherical contour, add small spots of black in the center of each eye to make the pupils. Fire the black so that it merges with the yellow. When heating the eyes, support the fish horizontally just beneath the fire so the flames play on the eyes only. Watch the work carefully to prevent the fins from softening and sagging. Burn off the black rod close to the body (3-32, *f*).

Make the mouth by softening the tip of a 6-millimeter rod of orange glass and fusing it to the point formerly occupied by the black rod handle (3-32, *g*). Burn off the orange rod, leaving about ¼ inch attached to the body. Rotate the adhering bit of orange in the fire until surface tension pulls it into a sphere. Then with a thin, flat tool, such as the jaw of a tweezers, press a horizontal groove into the softened mass (3-32, *h*). Finally, grasp the body by a pair of tweezers and burn off the rod handle attached to the tail fin. Flat designs of this type make novel brooches. To make a brooch of the fish, omit the eye and ventral fin on the rear side. A special safety pin may then be attached to the rear side with epoxy cement. Pins made for brooches of this type may be purchased from dealers in jeweler's supplies.

Amusing tops for stirring rods are fun to improvise, and require little skill. Examples of three versions appear in Figure 3-33. The difficulty of executing realistic forms varies with the talent of the artisan. As a general observation it can be said that if you can make a figure in clay you can make it in soft glass.

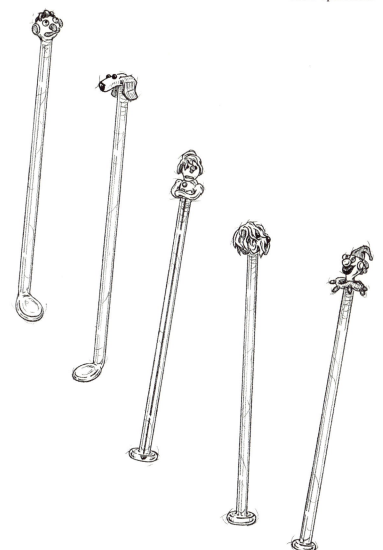

Figure 3-33.

Spun glass

So-called "spun glass" (glass that when heated to the molten state has been drawn into a continuous filament) is widely used in novelty work as well as in scientific apparatus. It can be used for the tail feathers of ornamental birds, a decorative accessory on Christmas tree balls, an effective ink eraser when it is bound as a tightly packed bundle of fibers, and an inert filter for removing unwanted particles from both gases and fluids. The material should not be confused with rock wool, the kinky, short-fibered substance used for heat insulation.

As manufactured commercially, molten glass is pulled from an appropriate container through perforations in a sheet of electrically heated platinum at speeds of a mile per minute and more. Amateurs can make a similar product with inexpensive and much less complex equipment. All that is needed (in addition to the crossfire and a pair of bucks for supporting a glass rod) is a wheel with a broad rim on which to wind the filament. The rear burner of the crossfire must be shut off, thus heating the glass on only the front side.

A wheel of any convenient diameter may be used. The wooden wheel employed by the senior author's grandfather, who introduced the process in the United States late during the last century, was 6 feet in diameter and turned at the rate of 250 revolutions per minute. Several rods of glass were heated simultaneously and were advanced through the fire by hand as the material was drawn away by the wheel. Two workers conducted the operation. One manipulated the glass rods. The other operated the wheel. To start the procedure one worker grasped the molten tip of the rod by a pair of tongs and pulled a filament to the wheel, located about 20 feet away. Water was then thrown on the surface of the wheel and the filament was pulled against the wet rim, to which it adhered. At the end of the run the wheel was stopped and the hank of "spun" glass removed by cutting the fibers by a sharp knife. Fibers of comparable diameter, but shorter in length, have been made by attaching one end of a glass rod to the arrow of a crossbow and clamping the other end to a rigid support. When a short length of the rod has been softened to the fluid state, the crossbow is fired. An extremely fine thread of glass trails behind the flying arrow.

Plates

Plate 1.
a ship's model

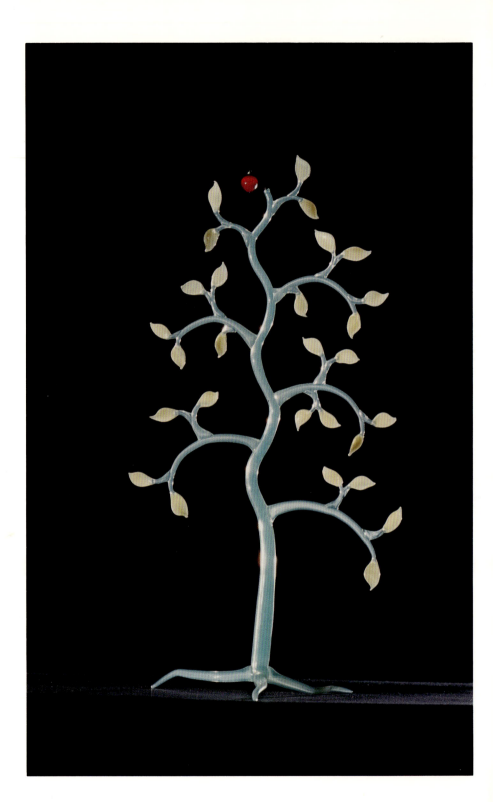

Plate 2.
an idealized tree
of knowledge,
with Eve's apple
on top

Plate 3.
costume jewelry

Plate 4.
fish swimming past
a coral formation

Plate 5.
miniature blown
objects that amateurs
can make

Plate 6.
a collection of
glass dishes

Plate 7.
a set of swans

Plate 8.
a glass deer

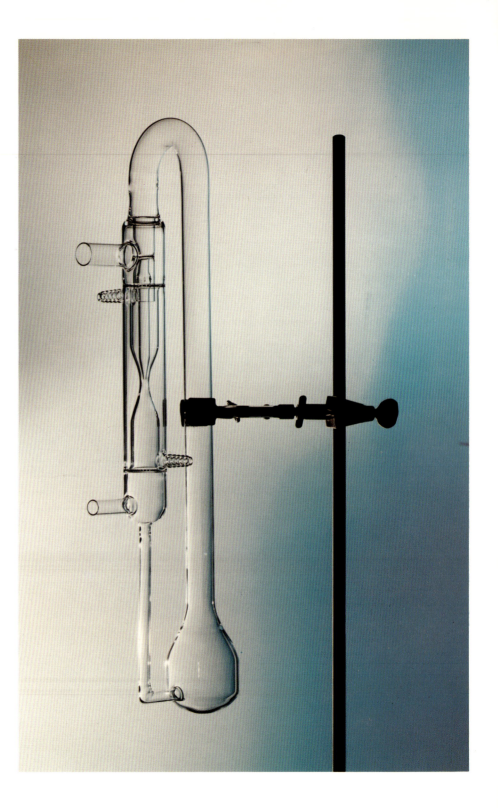

Plate 9.
a two-stage
diffusion pump
of the
Kurth-Ruggles type

Glass tubing: Basic operations

The seemingly infinite variety of shapes into which the artisan converts glass tubing consist, essentially, of variations and selected combinations of only a few basic forms. Each form is the consequence of an equally basic manipulation or operation. Four of these have been discussed in Section III: *cold cutting, fire-polishing, fire-cutting,* and *pressing.*

Additional operations that are employed, in particular, to alter the form of the tubing include *pulling a point,* stretching the ends of a tube into relatively narrow tapers that are closed at the tips; *the maria,* a ring-like bulge encircling a tube that is made by pushing the ends inward while heating a cylindrical zone at some intermediate location; *shrinking,* permitting surface tension to constrict the plastic zone of a heated tube; *the dimple,* a depression made by creating a partial vacuum inside a vessel while softening a selected area by means of a pointed flame; *flaring,* expanding the end of a tube, or other object such as an opened bulb, into a conical shape; *bending,* altering the curvature of glass tubing while preserving its circular cross section and wall thickness; *bulb blowing,* expanding molten glass into spherical, ellipsoidal or spheroidal form; *sealing,* joining two or more pieces of glass, or glass to another substance, such as metal, by fusing the surfaces; *annealing,* reheating and cooling glass slowly to relieve internal stresses; *sagging,* transforming glass of sheet or lump form into desired shapes by letting the softened material flow into the contours of an appropriate mold.

Each of the basic operations is easy to master, particularly if practiced in the above sequence. You may consider an operation "mastered" when you can perform it confidently whenever you wish. The time required for attaining proficiency depends somewhat on the

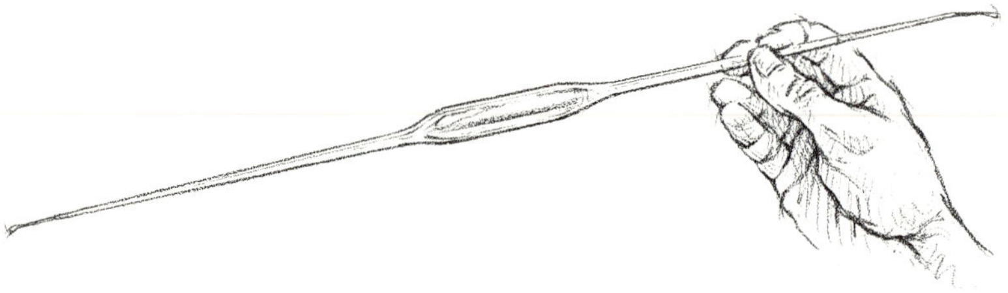

Figure 4-1.

aptitude of the individual. As in learning to drive an automobile, however, anyone can do it. The practice period is measured in weeks, not years. As with most minor arts, an hour of daily practice will count much more than a seven-hour session once each week. Keep at it regularly and the knack will soon be yours.

Pulling a point

Substantially every novelty in blown glass—miniature vases, urns, birds, animals, Christmas tree ornaments—begins as a point. This basic form variously modified is also found in most scientific glassware. Its fabrication is by far the most useful practice exercise for the beginner. A typical point consists of a section of glass tubing about 12 millimeters in diameter and 3 inches long with tapered ends averaging $\frac{1}{8}$ inch in diameter and about 7 inches in length (Fig. 4-1).

The tapered ends serve a variety of functions. For example, they are used as handles for manipulating the tubing that makes up the central section.

The tapered ends of well-made points are circular in cross section, are in perfect axial alignment with the center tubing, and have relatively thick, strong walls. When a good point is grasped by the tapered ends and spun between the thumbs and forefingers the center section runs true—as a cylinder of metal does when rotated by an engine lathe.

Snapping off the tip of one taper converts that stem to an open tube through which the worker can blow into the point for making a bulb. Similarly, the opened end permits air to escape. When the glass center is heated, the force of surface tension will constrict the central portion, shrinking it. The details of manipulating points in these and related ways are endless and occupy a substantial part of this book.

Incidentally, glass tubing is made in various wall thicknesses. In general, the heavier the wall, the more easily one can control the plastic glass. Doubling the wall thickness more than doubles the period that the hot material remains plastic and, hence, workable. Heat that is carried

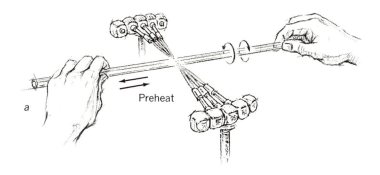

a
Preheat

Figure 4-2, a.

away from the surface by air currents is, in effect, replaced by that transferred from the interior. Moreover, the walls of heavy tubing tend to be more uniform in thickness than those of lightweight tubing. When purchasing glass tubing, request heavyweight material if you are a beginner.

As an initial exercise in point-pulling, select a length of tubing approximately 12 millimeters in diameter and about 2 feet long. Grasp the glass near either end by one hand, at a point of comfortable balance, and about 16 inches from the other hand. Adjust the crossfires as explained in Section II. While rotating the tubing by the technique explained in Section III, heat a zone of glass equal in length to about three tube diameters (Fig. 4-2, *a*). The heat may be applied at any convenient place along the tube.

Preheat the selected zone slowly by passing the horizontal tube up and down through the flame at the rate of about one pass per second. Simultaneously, shift the tube back and forth longitudinally to heat about an inch and a half of glass (in the case of 12 millimeter tubing). After approxi-

mately 30 seconds rotate the zone directly in the fire. The heated portion will soon begin to color the flame a bright yellow. This effect is known as *flare-off.* The yellow color becomes more intense as the glass heats, and it is a useful guide to the uniformity of the temperature of the glass. Within seconds of the onset of flare-off the heated zone will become perceptibly plastic; the tube will tend to bend out of axial alignment, and will feel wobbly.

Alter the motion of your hands to oppose the bend, to maintain true alignment. Do not pull the ends apart or push them together. Continue to rotate the tubing. Soon the heated zone will become quite flexible, as though the rigid portions of the tubing were connected by thick molasses. You are familiar with this "feel," of course, because it closely resembles that of a similarly heated rod. The glass should now stain the blue flame a dazzling yellow (but the glass itself should show no color).

Lift the heated zone out of the fire and, while continuing the rotation, begin pulling the ends apart and simul-

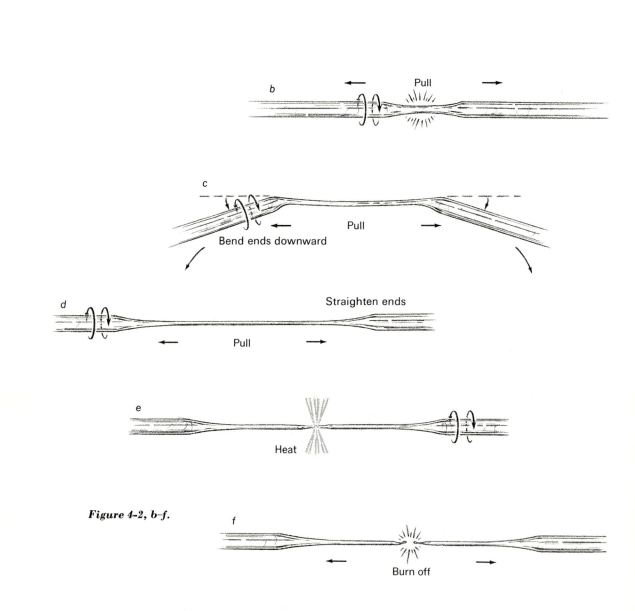

Figure 4-2, b–f.

taneously bend them downward at an angle of about 30 degrees (4-2, *b, c*). If you find that continued rotation in one direction is too difficult, rotate the glass alternately clockwise and counterclockwise—making approximately a full turn in each direction while simultaneously stretching the material. As the glass reaches a length of about 12 inches turn the end sections back up into axial alignment without interrupting the stretching motion (4-2, *d*). Stretch the piece to a total length of about 14 or 15 inches. The stretching operation should be completed in about 3 seconds.

At the end of the pull maintain just enough tension to prevent the material from sagging but not enough to stretch it beyond the specified length. In about 3 more seconds the pulled zone should have cooled enough to become rigid. Then heat the center of the pulled section. This portion of the tubing should now be about ⅛ inch in diameter, its wall much thinner than that of the original tubing. It will therefore heat to the plastic state in about a second.

When a zone ½ inch long has softened, promptly lift the glass about 3 inches above the fire and simultaneously stretch the heated portion to a length of about 1½ inches (4-2, *e*). The center of this stretched zone will be thinner than a pencil lead. Return the middle of this doubly stretched portion to the fire. It will immediately become red hot. Pull the ends apart *without lifting the glass from the fire.* This is another example of fire-cutting or "burning off" (4-2, *f*).

To pull a point, then, the glass must be heated three times; first to form the major constriction, second

to pull the small center constriction, and third to cut or to burn off.

At this stage only half of the point has been made. The short end of the tubing, together with its attached taper, is laid aside temporarily. The remaining taper serves as a handle for use in making a duplicate taper a short distance beyond. This one is formed by heating to softness a section of the tubing some 3 inches beyond the first taper and making the second pull. The result is a portion of tubing about 3 inches long terminated by 7-inch tapers on each end.

One difficulty in pulling points that often besets the beginner is the refusal of the glass to retain its smooth tubular form when heated to softness. As the material becomes plastic, the glass tends to twist out of shape. This is caused most often by rotating one end of the tubing at a different rate than the other, or by permitting the end sections to bend out of axial alignment, or both. Practice soon minimizes this difficulty. On the other hand, glass blowers know a trick that can help to make your practice pay off.

Observe that the trouble does not appear when the glass first softens. At this stage the material is so stiff that the entire tube can be rotated by one hand, the other hand serving merely as a loose bearing on which the glass turns. The difficulty arises when the glass becomes quite soft. Here, then, is the secret! *Don't heat the glass more than absolutely necessary to stretch it as desired.* Beginners tend to overheat the material. Glass, when sufficiently plastic for proper manipulation, is still rigid enough to contribute substantial support to the end sections—and there-

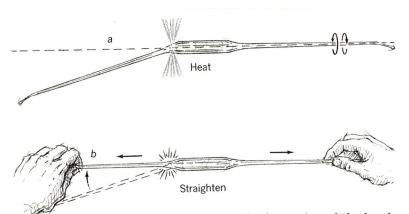

Figure 4-3.

Still another difficulty is the refusal of the tapers to assume the desired cross section; they come out oval-shaped or flattened, and do not roll smoothly between the thumbs and forefingers. This difficulty appears most frequently when the glass is worked in the crossfire, suggesting that the tubing has been most strongly heated on opposite sides as a consequence of nonuniform rotation. Flattened tapers can also result from uneven cooling. This occurs when rotation is discontinued as the piece is lifted from the fire.

In cases where the glass has been rotated first in one direction and then in the other—as when making the pull—the worker may hesitate longer than necessary before resuming rotation in the opposite direction, or he may fail to make a complete rotation in each direction. Uneven cooling results. The corrective measure is obvious. Maintain continuous uniform rotation. *Never hold hot glass still for examination whether the material is in or out of the fire.*

Occasionally, the tapered ends become laterally displaced at the point where they join the tubing. They should be nicely centered like the handles of a rolling pin. Centering is accomplished by another trick: bending the ends downward at the angle of 30 degrees while simultaneously making the first part of the pull, as mentioned.

The off-axis angle of the pull distributes the plastic glass uniformly around the center as the material is stretched. The evenly distributed mass is then brought into precise alignment as the ends are straightened just before the end of the pull.

The tapered ends may also become

fore to guide the motion of the hands. Each hand can "feel" the movement of the other through the plastic zone.

Do not be discouraged if the tapered ends of the first point are not in axial alignment. This difficulty may be experienced for some time. Such points are easily salvaged. Nick the tip of one taper with the file and snap it off. Grasp the point by its tapers and preheat the crooked taper at the point where it joins the center tubing (Fig. 4-3, *a*). When the first trace of flare-off appears hold the base of the taper close to, but not necessarily inside, the hottest part of the fire. The thin glass will quickly reach the plastic state.

While continuing to rotate the piece, drop the point out of the fire (1 or 2 inches below the flame), and exert a gentle pull, perhaps 8 ounces, on the tips of the tapers. This will straighten the bent taper and bring it into axial alignment (4-3, *b*). If the remaining taper is also bent, correct it similarly.

too thin to support the weight of the central tube or, conversely, they may be much thicker and shorter than they need be. Thin, spindly tapers result from overheating part or all of the zone, or from heating a zone less than three diameters in length, or both. Heat the specified length of glass just enough to make the pull—and no more. This assumes that the pull is commenced *immediately* after the piece is removed from the fire.

In regard to the size of the heated zone, err if you must by heating too much glass. Short zones result in thin tapers. Thick, stubby tapers are the result of zones that are too long. Glass that is too cool stiffens before the pull can be completed. The same difficulty occurs when the worker hesitates before starting the pull. The delay of a second or two permits the glass to cool and stiffen. Short, stubby tapers result. *Cultivate the habit of working promptly, continuously, and at a moderate pace.* Avoid jerky, abrupt movements.

The short end of the tubing with its single taper that was initially laid aside can now be salvaged and converted into a complete point. First, fuse the open end of the tube to a rod of convenient diameter and length, as discussed in Section III. Then, as the glass stiffens, stretch the seal just enough to bring the rod into axial alignment with the taper. Using the rod as one handle and the taper as the other, heat a zone near the seal and draw out the tubing into a twin of the previously formed taper. An identical taper will be attached to the rod, of course. Part the pair. Cut (and discard) the taper that is attached to the rod.

The maria

As discussed briefly in Section III, the maria consists of a bulge in an otherwise straight rod or tube. It can be made anywhere along the piece, at the ends or in between. The maria has numerous applications, both practical and aesthetic. For example, it often appears as a finger support on stemware such as a wine glass, as a wax catcher on a candelabrum, and as ornamentation on vases. In laboratory glassware the maria serves as the foot on muddlers, a support for metal parts, ridges on hose connections, stops on tubing inserted in perforated corks, spacers in coaxial tubing, and so on. For acquiring the knack of keeping a glass tube in axial alignment when the middle has softened, no exercise is more effective than making marias.

Although the maria can be formed in any convenient length of rod or tubing, the beginner is urged to make an initial series in glass points. The tapers of the point serve as convenient handles of relatively small diameter and, therefore, minimize the finger movement required for rotating the glass. In addition, the beginner simultaneously acquires the "feel" of working with points.

First, select a point. With the file first nick and then snap off one tip. The opening will permit air to enter the point through the taper and prevent the formation of a dimple when the glass is subsequently softened. (The dimple will form because the point was sealed off when hot, when the air was expanding; the lowered pressure of air trapped in the cooled glass permits the pressure of the atmosphere to deform the glass inward and any area that is subsequently softened, unless the inner and outer pressures are equalized by first opening the point to the atmosphere.)

Grasp the tapers between thumbs and index fingers and test for trueness of spin. Do not discard the piece if it fails to run true. You can correct the defect, as previously explained (page 90).

You are now ready to make the maria. While rotating the point, preheat the tubular body. Then concentrate the fire on a narrow central zone. Continue to rotate; push the ends gently toward each other. An ounce or so of pressure does the trick. Keep the ends in axial alignment. Watch the heated zone closely. A low encircling bulge will appear that grows larger as the glass softens, assuming the form of a thin wedding ring (Fig. 4-4). Continued heating (and pushing) will transform the ring into an expanding disk that will grow to substantial proportions—as large as two or three tube diameters. All disks should run true, like well made wheels.

A wobbly maria, one that is eccentric, indicates failure either (1) to keep the tapers aligned, (2) to prevent them from becoming laterally displaced, (3) to heat the glass uniformly, or all three. Misalignment and lateral displacement usually encourage wobbling, uneven heating, eccentricity. Study the effect by deliberately making each of the three errors, one at a time. Watch the incipient bulge closely during its early stage of growth. It is important that the glass of the maria fuse to a solid state—the condition illustrated in-

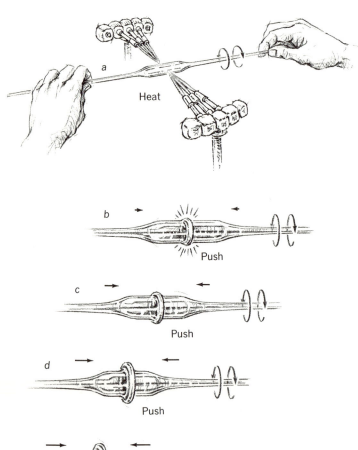

Heat

b Push

c Push

d Push

e Push

Figure 4-4.

vites cracking (Fig. 4-5). On large bulb-like marias the hollow construction is quite safe (Fig. 4-6).

If the glass softens too quickly for comfort, drop the tubing partly out of the fire. Don't rush. You have lots of time. Rest your elbows on the bench. This helps to steady your hands. The glass configuration is unstable, of course, because the solid ends of the point are flexibly connected by soft glass in the middle. They tend to buckle when compressed, or to skid sideways, bending the softened portion into an **S** shape. Heat the narrowest possible zone *just soft enough to bulge*. When buckling is observed drop the work out of the fire and straighten the piece by exerting a gentle pull and, perhaps, bending it a trifle.

If the tapers become laterally displaced, again drop the piece out of the fire and apply the indicated corrective force. You are already familiar with the cure for eccentricity occasioned by uneven heating. Apply it. Do not attempt to make a large, disk-shaped maria on your first try.

Begin by pushing the tapers inward just enough to make a barely perceptible bulge. Lift the work partly out of the fire to inspect the bulge— but keep the glass hot. Then return the piece to the fire. By such easy stages, let the maria grow into circular form, the wedding ring. Having succeeded, stop work for 24 hours and think about what you have done. During the next practice session duplicate the wedding ring. Make a half dozen. Then, let a wedding ring grow into a disk.

You can conserve glass by making four or five small marias on each

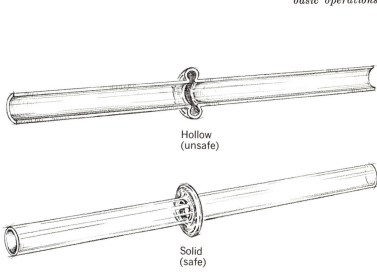

Hollow
(unsafe)

Solid
(safe)

Figure 4-5.

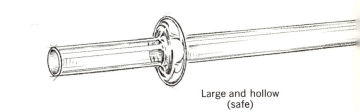

Large and hollow
(safe)

Figure 4-6.

point. A single point should also accommodate two small disks or a single large one. Practice no other operation until you can make a maria of any size you wish whenever you wish. Then try your hand at making several in tubes that range in diameter from 6 to 20 millimeters. Even a rank beginner should find it possible to complete the project in less than a week.

Shrinking or constricting

Frequently, tubing must be reduced in diameter—even to the point of conversion into glass rod. Wall thickness must also be altered—made thicker or thinner. Occasionally the artisan wishes to reduce the end of a large tube to the diameter of a smaller one, simultaneously mating the wall diameters. The technique of making all such alterations is called "shrinking," whether the wall is made thicker or thinner. The operation exploits surface tension, the natural tendency of fluids to behave as though covered by a thin, stretched membrane under tension that tends to contract. The property explains why raindrops and soap bubbles assume a spherical shape when they fall through the air. Molten glass behaves the same way for the same reason.

The technique of shrinking varies according to the desired result. You will find it not difficult *if you have mastered the two preceding operations of pulling points and making marias.* You must now, at last, learn to manipulate glass in semifluid form. Heated glass never becomes water thin. On the other hand, it is not as viscous, nor as easily handled as soft tar. In general, hot glass shrinks at a reasonable rate when its viscosity approaches that of heavy molasses. You will acquire the knack of manipulating it in easy stages.

Select a point and proceed as though you were going to make a maria. As the central zone softens, however, neither push the ends together nor pull them apart. A depressed ring will form all around the heated zone. Let the zone deepen until the center has narrowed a few wall thicknesses. Drop the piece out of the fire and stretch the softened zone to approximately twice its original length. Maintain just tension enough thereafter to keep the work straight until the glass stiffens.

As an expert point-puller you doubtless found this exercise easy. Now cut the constriction at the middle and inspect the wall thickness. It will be thinner than that of the tubing (Fig. 4-7). Select another point and repeat the exercise, but this time heat a zone equal in length to that of the constricted part of the piece just made— and keep on heating the zone without pulling or pushing on the ends until it shrinks to the outer dimensions of the constriction previously made by pulling. Don't panic if the middle twists and closes the bore.

Heat the next piece that you attempt to shrink to a slightly lower temperature. (The art of rotating the ends in synchronism becomes more difficult as the viscosity of the glass decreases, of course. In addition, the force transmitted by each hand to the other through the softened zone diminishes, but it never disappears. Concentrate on sensing this force. Remember, too, that the fingers must

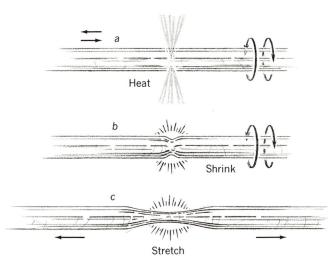

move sequentially when rotating the glass—like the feet of a crawling caterpillar. This motion must become second nature. Practice it with a lead pencil now and then when you are away from the bench. Don't skimp either hand during this practice. Both must be equally trained.) The cooler glass may require as much as a minute to shrink to the desired dimension. The present objective is not speed, however, but a constricted piece of circular cross section and of normal wall thickness.

If you still have difficulty at the lowered temperature, decrease the width of the softened zone on the succeeding attempt. By trial and error you will soon discover the minimum temperature at which the glass will shrink at a reasonable rate and the maximum zone-width that you can manipulate without twisting and closing the tube. Thereafter, increase both the temperature and the zone-

width little by little until you can shrink a 1-inch zone in 15-millimeter tubing within 30 seconds.

Select three pieces so made and, with the aid of the file, cut one at the middle of the shrunken zone, another about a third of the distance to the edge of the zone and the third close to the edge of the zone. Examine the wall thickness of each. It should not differ substantially from that of the unconstricted tubing (Fig. 4-8, *a*). If it is thicker, make another constriction, slightly narrower, and stretch the glass to the full width just before it stiffens. The exact amount that is meant by "slightly narrower" must be learned by trial and error.

Next assume that you wish to reduce the outer diameter of a tube and, simultaneously, to increase the wall thickness of the constriction. Just heat the zone as before but this time as the work is rotated, let the ends move toward each other slowly as the

Figure 4-7.

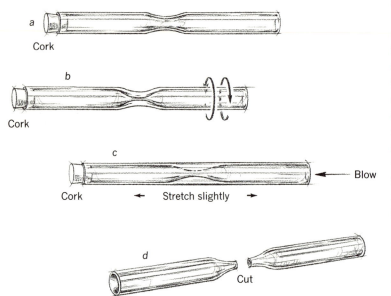

a

Cork

b

Cork

c

Cork   ← Stretch slightly →   Blow ←

d

Cut

Figure 4-8.

in from the adjacent tubing and, finally, blow the constriction to the desired outside diameter, stretching the softened portion just enough to straighten the tube (4-8, *b*, *c*).

A tube can be partially or fully closed simply by rotating the end in the fire, as you have already discovered for yourself. You have observed the excessive thickening of the edges as the bore narrows and the end becomes rounded. Little practical use is found for this form. It is not an example of end shrinking in the sense that we have been considering. Strictly speaking, ends as such are rarely shrunk. A tube with a constricted end is made by shrinking an intermediate portion of tubing (that may be near an end). This constriction is then cut either by nicking the glass transversely and pulling the piece apart (4-8, *d*), or by fire-cutting (the fire cut would be made by shrinking the middle of the constriction completely shut, pulling the closed portion into a thread, burning off the thread, and, finally, heating the tip, blowing a small bulb and cracking it off).

The dimple

In laboratory glassware dimples can be used as pivots to limit the motion of other parts including pointed rods or spheres, as finger grips, as a means to increase surface areas for the radiation of heat, and so on. The reverse side of the dimple, the inward bulge, also serves a variety of functions. The convex surfaces can act as stops to restrict the motion of internal components and to separate surfaces such

glass becomes fluid. If the bore threatens to close in the middle of the constriction, blow into the point enough to keep it open. In effect, you are feeding additional glass from the tubing into the constriction (4-8, *b*).

If the wall in the center becomes disproportionately thicker than at the edges of the constriction, alternately blow the material to a diameter slightly larger than the tubing and shrink it back again. This kneading action will tend to distribute the glass uniformly.

Occasionally the need arises to constrict the bore of a tube without altering the outside diameter. Having mastered the above operations you will find this an easy exercise. Simply shrink the tubing to make a wall of maximum thickness by feeding glass

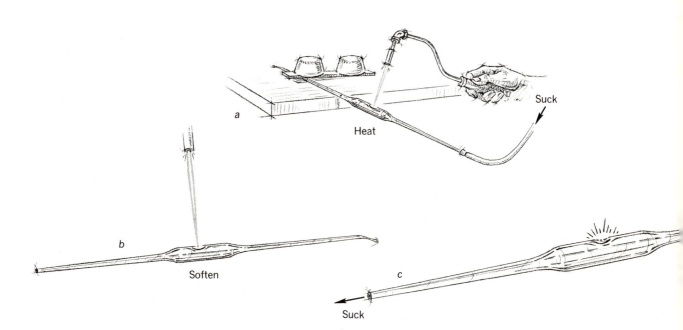

as coaxial tubing, and as barriers that retard the flow of gases and liquids. As a decorative device, the dimple is popular as a design element in vases, tumblers, costume jewelry, and, particularly, in the baubles used as ornaments on Christmas trees.

The dimple is so easy to make that you will turn out a good one on your very first try. Select a point, open one of the tapers at the tip, warm the central portion of tubing carefully, and lift it up under the fire so the flames play on a selected area near the center at the top. When the glass softens, a shallow depression will form. Heat the center of the deformed area to yellowish orange (Fig. 4-9, *a*). Remove from the fire and suck gently on the open tip. Atmospheric pressure will force the soft glass inward (4-9, *b*).

The size of the resulting dimple will depend on the diameter of the heated area. Its depth will vary in proportion to the force and duration of the suction. Make several dimples of various sizes. Then make a number of the same size—preferably in one piece of tubing.

Flaring

Expanding the end of a tube (or the opened end of a glass bulb) into a conical or funnel shape is termed "flaring." This form appears as an element of design in objects as diverse as vacuum pumps, ornamental urns, wine glasses, and medicine droppers. The end of the tube (or the opened end of the bulb) is softened in the fire

Figure 4-9.

diameters and, in shape, from a gentle taper to a fully developed, right-angular flange.

As an initial exercise you may manufacture a useful tool: the mouthpiece of a blowing hose. Select a convenient length of 6-millimeter tubing. Preheat one end and while rotating the glass in the fire watch for the onset of flare-off, then continue heating until the edge is nicely fire-polished. Remove the work from the fire (Fig. 4-11, *a*). While continuing to rotate the piece, promptly insert the warmed tine of a file (or similar flaring tool) to a distance of about ⅜ inch into the bore of the tubing.

The tool must not touch the glass; particularly, do not let the metal tip touch the inner wall. Now *lift* the *side* of the tool *lightly* into contact with the *inner edge* of the glass. A perceptible bead will form that encircles the edge (4-11, *b*).

If the work has stiffened, remove the tool and return the piece to the fire. When it has reheated to its former working temperature remove the glass from the fire, replace the flaring tool, and again *lift* the soft edge. In effect you are stretching the material a bit at a time *at its point of contact* with the metal.

Once the small portion in contact with the tool has been thus stretched it tends to retain its new shape until the next revolution carries it into contact with the metal where it is stretched a little more. Expand the end into a cone about ¼ inch long and approximately ⅜ inch across at the base, or open end. All of this should require only a matter of seconds; the glass should still be at working temperature. If it has cooled, however, re-

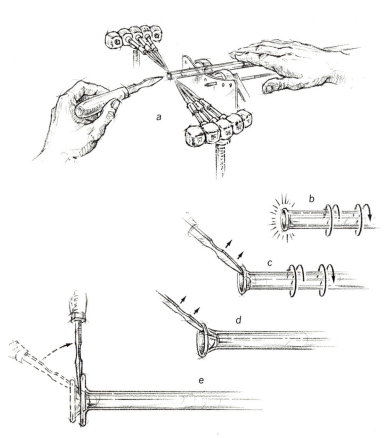

Figure 4-10.

and rotated at a constant rate. A smooth metal rod, called the flaring tool, is placed in the opening and gently pulled against the plastic edge of the glass.

The resulting force stretches the glass and therefore expands the end of the tube into a cone (Fig. 4-10). Flares can range in size from a barely perceptible ring of thickened glass to a taper equal in length to many tube

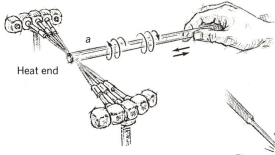

Heat end

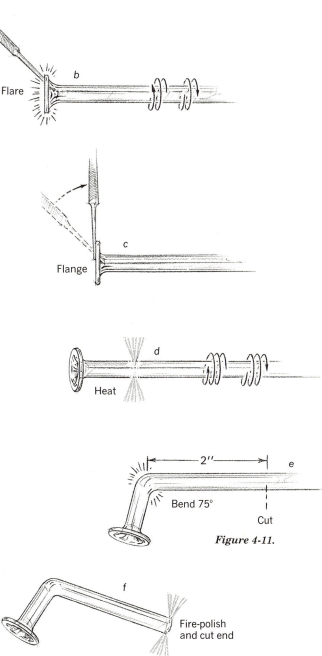

Flare

b

Flange

c

Heat

d

2″

Bend 75°

Cut

e

Figure 4-11.

Fire-polish
and cut end

f

move the flaring tool and return the work to the fire. Then remove the re-heated piece from the fire, reinsert the flaring tool, and lift the outer edge by increasing the angle between the axis of the tool and that of the tube—in effect, sweep the tool around like the hand of a clock. This motion expands the base of the cone without increasing its altitude or height.

Your object is to transform the cone almost but not quite into a right-angular flange: a cone that slopes upward, say, about 80 degrees. The base of the completed flare should measure about ½ inch in diameter (4-11, *c*). After the piece cools, return the tubing to the fire and heat a zone about an inch long at a point about an inch away from the flare.

When the glass softens remove it from the fire, support the tubing horizontally, and let the flared end droop to an angle of about 70 degrees. You have now made a "bend" (4-11, *d*). Then cut the tube about 2 inches from the bend and fire-polish the cut end (4-11, *e*, *f*). Insert the polished end into the blowing hose. You have a glass mouth piece, a very good one. In use, let it dangle from the mouth with the flare just behind the teeth. (It will not fall out even when you talk while working.)

made by *lifting* the hot glass, not by prying or pushing it. Do not attempt to flare the work in the fire.

There are exceptions to this rule, but not for the beginner. When making a small flare the application of heat can be general. The portion of the glass to be expanded may be heated uniformly. Larger pieces—those of 10-millimeter diameter and greater—require more heat at the outer edge of the flare to compensate for the greater stretching in this region of the glass. In addition, the softened outer edges must be supported by glass that is increasingly rigid toward the apex of the cone; this means that the center portion must be cooler than the edge. Should the inner portion of the flare be heated more than the outer edge, the flare will tend to buckle. Graded heating is achieved by the lateral motion of the glass in the fire; the flame is permitted to play on the outer portion of the flare for longer intervals than on the inner portion.

Never let the flame play on the tool. Glass "wets" hot metal and sticks to it like chewing gum. Keep the tool warm but not hot. Sometimes you must cool the tool. (It picks up heat from contact with the hot glass.) Many professional glass blowers simply plunge the working blade into a block of beeswax. This not only cools the metal but deposits a film of wax on the metal that discourages the glass from sticking to the tool.

Do not attempt to expand tubing into a right-angled flange by a single operation on your first try. Make the flare in at least two steps, first a cone and then the flange.

Make a half dozen mouthpieces.

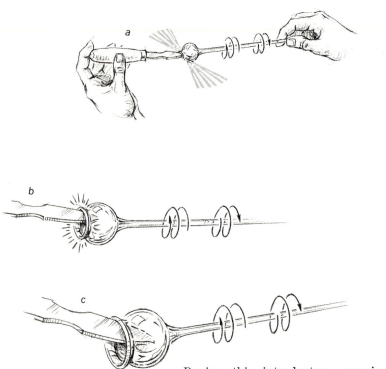

Figure 4-12.

During this introductory exercise in flaring, several things can go wrong. First, you may jab the flaring tool into the softened glass instead of inserting it into the space of the bore. This is simply a case of poor marksmanship. Aim for the bore.

Cultivate the habit of resting your elbows on the bench, a position that takes a lot of jitter out of your hands. Secondly, resist the temptation to place the tip of the flaring tool against the inner bore of the tubing beyond the softened zone where it can find solid support acting as the fulcrum of a lever. You will merely gouge the glass and encourage the softened part to wind onto the tool. A flare must be

You will need them later because, unfortunately, they appear to be magically attracted by floors, particularly those made of concrete, and are accordingly expendable. Tubing larger than 8-millimeters is flared more easily with the aid of a set of hand rollers. Cork or stopper the far end to avoid the rush of heat through tube. Rest the glass on the rollers and rotate it by stroking the palm of one hand back and forth *across* the tubing. Shift the piece longitudinally by pushing the palm sideways.

Place the roller so the tubing is level with the focal point of the flames. The end of the tubing should point toward the focal point of the flames and be located at a distance such that the work can be slid into and out of the fire as desired. Manipulate the flaring tool by the free hand. The size of the flaring tool should be proportionate to the diameter of the tubing—narrow enough to enter the bore and wide enough to make contact with at least 10 angular degrees of the inner edge.

At first you may have difficulty in making flares that run true. They may wobble or show eccentricity or both. The wobble develops most frequently from attempts to expand the glass too quickly. The cure: slow down. Eccentricity can arise from failure to cut the tubing square (so the cut end is perpendicular to the axis), or it can arise from failure to heat the end uniformly, or both. The cure is obvious (see pages 98 and 100). Now make about 100 flares of various sizes in tubing ranging from 10 to 25 millimeters in diameter. Few techniques in the glass blower's bag of tricks are more useful. Bulbs are flared by the identical procedure. (Fig. 4-12).

a

Stretched
excessively

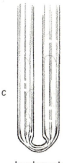

b

Inadequate
stretching
or heating

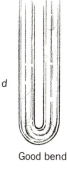

c

Inadequate
blowing

d

Good bend

Figure 4-13.

Bending

Anyone can easily make a good bend of 90 degrees in glass tubing of 6 millimeters or less in diameter, as you discovered when you made your mouthpiece. Simply rotate the tube in the fire while simultaneously shifting it back and forth longitudinally to soften a zone about an inch long, remove the glass from the heat and lift the ends to the desired angle. Difficulty appears when relatively sharp bends must be made in 10-millimeter tubing, and it increases in proportion to the diameter thereafter.

When tubing is bent, whether made of glass or metal, the material on the outer radius of the bend must be stretched and that on the inner radius must be compressed—the outer wall of the bend must become thinner; the inner wall, thicker. Moreover, the forces of tension and compression tend to shorten the radius of the outer wall, to pull the material inward, and to buckle the inner wall (Fig. 4-13). The glass blower sets up counteracting forces by a combination of stretching the soft glass longitudinally and expanding it by blowing.

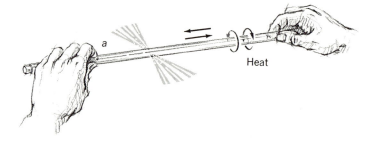

One end of the tubing is corked and the blowing hose is attached to the other. A zone of the glass where the bend is to be made is preheated slowly and then softened, usually to a deep red color. The piece is then removed from the fire and simultaneously bent, stretched, and blown—all in a fraction of a second (Fig. 4-14). The stretch should be as little as possible to produce symmetry, and should not exceed one tube diameter. The stretching maneuver prevents the inner wall of the bend from buckling. A 90-degree bend of a 1-inch radius in 10-millimeter tubing would tend to compress the inner wall of the bend about $\frac{1}{10}$ inch. The outer wall, having greater radius, would tend to be stretched about 50% more than the inner wall was compressed. (To this must be added the stretch that is applied by the glass blower.)

The outer wall of the bend tends to expand readily, in contrast to the inner wall, because of the diminishing wall thickness. Now, try it. The secret here is speed. At first you may stretch the glass too much. This is the common error of beginners. Excessive stretching results in a piece that, in effect, contains a pair of 45-degree bends connected by a short, relatively straight run of tubing. Insufficient stretching results in buckling the inner wall of the bend.

It is possible for even a rank beginner to bend tubing successfully on the very first try if time is no object and the worker is willing to settle for a bend that is functional but not necessarily of professional appearance. Clamp the tubing in the horizontal position at one end. Let one end project over the edge of the workbench and place a weight on the other end. With a hand torch equipped with fishtail burners to produce a crossfire, preheat a zone of the tubing at a point at least 15 tube diameters from the projecting end. The preheated zone need be only a couple of tube diameters in length. Support the projecting end by one hand, just enough to limit its motion when the tubing softens. Now heat the zone until you

Figure 4-14.

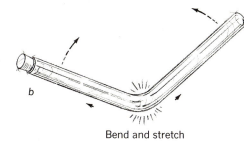

Bend and stretch

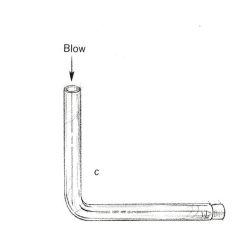

feel the glass sag about ¼ inch. Remove the heat. When the glass stiffens, apply the torch again, this time a small fraction of an inch closer to the projecting end. In effect, you will be making a series of small bends. Neither the inner nor outer wall can misbehave seriously because the softened zone is supported in cylindrical form by the stiff adjacent glass. The radius of the bend must be controlled by eye, of course. Even helical coils can be made by this technique.

The formation of long, sweeping curves and circles that appear in some scientific apparatus and in the gas discharge tubes of advertising signs requires the use of the ribbon burner, as described in Section II. Making bends with the use of this burner in tubing up to 16 millimeters in diameter is almost child's play. Proceed by stoppering one end of the tube with a cork, then mark the glass by means of ordinary blackboard chalk at two points that designate the location and length of the proposed bend. For an introductory practice exercise with

15-millimeter tubing these marks might be placed 6 to 8 inches apart at the approximate center of a tube 30 inches long.

Adjust the burner to develop a ribbon of fire about 10 to 15% longer than the bend to be made. (Modern ribbon burners are equipped with an adjustable slide that can be set for masking any desired portion of the burner surface.) The same result can be achieved in the case of old-fashioned burners by covering part of the surface by a wet strip of asbestos paper, as illustrated in Figure 4-15, *f*.

Grasp the tube by the ends with the palms of the hands up and support the marked portion of the glass in the flame about ½ inch below the flame tip. Rotate the tube continuously and simultaneously shift it from side to side about 1 inch. When the glass starts to soften, change from rotation in one direction to alternate clockwise and counterclockwise rotation but continue the alternate side to side movement (Fig. 4-15, *a*).

When the glass becomes wobbly and

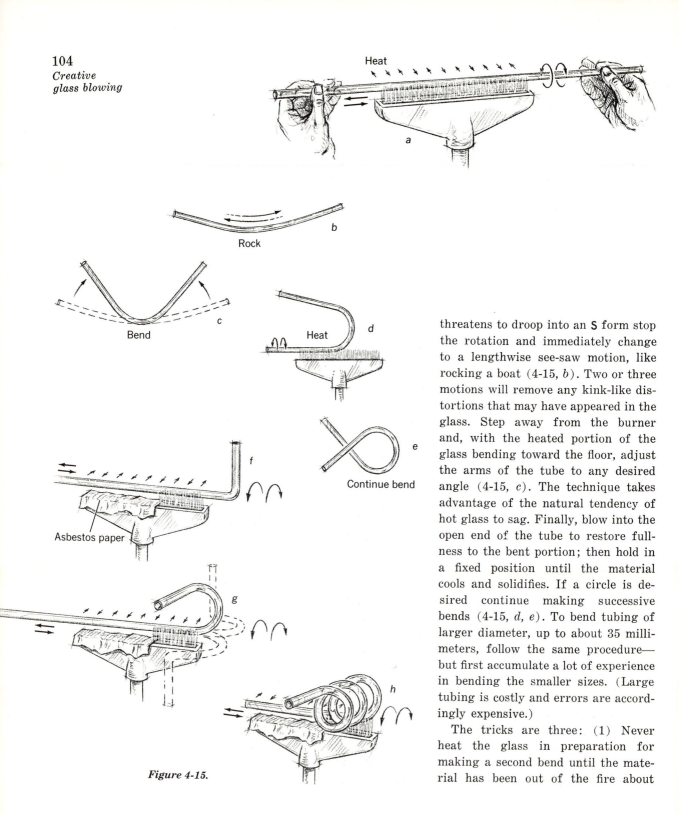

Rock

Bend

Heat

Continue bend

Asbestos paper

Figure 4-15.

threatens to droop into an **S** form stop the rotation and immediately change to a lengthwise see-saw motion, like rocking a boat (4-15, *b*). Two or three motions will remove any kink-like distortions that may have appeared in the glass. Step away from the burner and, with the heated portion of the glass bending toward the floor, adjust the arms of the tube to any desired angle (4-15, *c*). The technique takes advantage of the natural tendency of hot glass to sag. Finally, blow into the open end of the tube to restore fullness to the bent portion; then hold in a fixed position until the material cools and solidifies. If a circle is desired continue making successive bends (4-15, *d*, *e*). To bend tubing of larger diameter, up to about 35 millimeters, follow the same procedure— but first accumulate a lot of experience in bending the smaller sizes. (Large tubing is costly and errors are accordingly expensive.)

The tricks are three: (1) Never heat the glass in preparation for making a second bend until the material has been out of the fire about three times longer than the interval required for heating it to softness. In other words, permit the material to solidify completely after each bend but do not let it cool to room temperature. Failure to observe this precaution will tend to produce kinks at the end of the first bend. (2) When reheating the glass for the second bend always heat at least an inch of the preceding bend. This encourages bends of smooth continuity. (3) Having made one bend, you can no longer rotate the glass continuously in one direction when heating for subsequent bends. You must therefore rotate the work in alternate directions through half turns, 180-degree arcs, grasping the previous bend by one hand and the straight portion of the tubing by the other. Always pause between bends for the work to solidify before proceeding with the next bend.

Helical coils may also be made by means of the ribbon burner. First make a right-angled bend at the end of the tubing, a short length, say, 6 inches long. This will subsequently serve as a handle for manipulating the piece (4-15, *f*). On the assumption that the diameter of the completed helix will be, say, 1½ inches and will be made of 8-millimeter tubing, next soften a zone approximately 3 inches long. Rotate the work alternately (half turns), shifting it lengthwise and from side to side. (Ribbon burners tend to develop "hot spots" along their length. The compound motion tends to even out these inequalities.) When the glass softens, step back from the fire and, by the technique previously described, make the bend (a third- to a half-circle, depending on your proficiency) at right an-

gles to the 90-degree handle, as illustrated in Figure 4-15, *g*. Now, *let the work solidify*—as when making a simple bend. Finally, return the piece to the fire and reheat another portion of the tubing—remembering to soften approximately 20% of the bend just made. Thereafter continue to bend, portion-by-portion, until you complete a helix of the desired number of turns (4-15, *h*).

Bulbs

If you can make a soap bubble don't hesitate to blow one in glass. It will be just as much fun, your product will be just as pretty—and the bubble will last longer. Try it. Select a length of tubing of, say, 10 millimeters in diameter and 2 feet in length. Draw off one end with a piece of rod, as in making a point. Burn off close to the tube. Rotate the end in the fire until it melts. Then, remove the piece from the fire, rotate it in the air about 4 seconds, and then puff gently into the open end. Examine the result. The end should have expanded into a hemisphere. The thickness of the wall in the blown portion should approximate that of the tubing.

If the end has not fully rounded, reheat the glass and blow either more forcefully or longer on the second try. Conversely, the glass may have expanded into a small bulb of greater diameter than the tubing. If so, reheat the work and shrink it. Try again, using less pressure. Within three or four attempts you will doubtless have achieved the desired hemispherical shape. If so, you have now made the bottom of a conventional test tube.

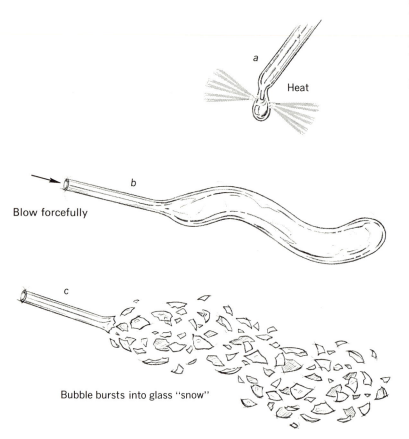

Heat

Blow forcefully

Bubble bursts into glass "snow"

Figure 4-16.

the open end. A huge bubble will form, one of irregular shape perhaps 3 feet long (4-16, *b*). If you keep blowing hard enough it will explode into a cloud of iridescent flakes. If the bubble fails to break, maintain pressure and strike the glass with your knuckle. The accompanying "bang" may shatter your nerves but will do no harm (4-16, *c*). The colorful flakes (synthetic "snow") have numerous applications as decorative material. On examination the flakes are found to be as flexible as plastic film and will not cut the skin, even if you crush them in your hand. The first portions of the bubble formed will be relatively heavy, and *can cut you,* however. The flakes can be collected in quantity by exploding bubbles in a large container, such as a box.

Next, blow a spherical bulb—one with a wall of substantial thickness. To make this shape, select a point, open one tip for use as a blowpipe, and while rotating the glass heat a narrow zone uniformly at a point in the tubing about two and a half diameters from the junction of the opened taper (Fig. 4-17, *a*). A constriction will form in this zone.

When the zone reaches an orange color slowly stretch the glass. After the material has been stretched 4 or 5 inches concentrate the fire on the hot glass adjacent to the tubing attached to the blowpipe. Continue pulling. The glass will quickly narrow to thread-like dimensions and part at the junction, leaving a thickened drop at the center of the tubing to which the blowpipe is attached. This thick drop is called a "bleb." It must be made smaller by removing some of the molten glass (4-17, *b*).

Reheat the hemisphere, remembering to rotate the glass uniformly. By the time the material reaches yellow heat, the bottom will have shrunk and thickened substantially. Heat at least ½ inch of tubing, elevating the cool end about 45 degrees to form a teardrop shape (Fig. 4-16, *a*). Remove the piece from the fire and point the heated end directly at the floor. Blow gently until a "sausage" starts to form, 1 to 2 inches long, then blow forcefully for as long as you can into

To do so, retrieve the discarded taper with your free hand, snap off the thread of glass now attached to it, and, after warming the large end, remove both pieces from the fire and promptly touch the large end of the taper to the tip of the bleb (4-17, *c*). The molten bleb will adhere to the taper. Simultaneously rotate the taper (to wind a thread of hot glass from the bleb onto the large end of the taper) and pull the two apart. This should remove most of the glass that makes up the bleb. If it does not, repeat the operation.

When the size of the bleb has been reduced substantially, reheat the end of the tubing and blow it into a hemisphere (4-17, *d, e*). Next, heat the remainder of the tubing uniformly from the hemispherical end to the junction of the blowpipe. Rotate the piece so the tubing does not sag. The technique is much the same as that of gathering a spherical ball of glass on the end of a rod, as described in Section III.

When the glass has heated to a deep red, remove it from the fire, hold the piece vertically with the heated part down, and, after about 2 seconds, blow into the end of the taper to form a bulb about an inch in diameter, assuming that you start with a 15-millimeter point (4-17, *f, g*). Always rotate the tubing as you blow. Next, make an identical bulb, but incline the piece about 10 degrees from the vertical. Then proceed with still other bulbs of the same size and made in precisely the same way, except that each in succession is inclined farther and farther from the vertical. The final bulb should be blown in the horizontal position.

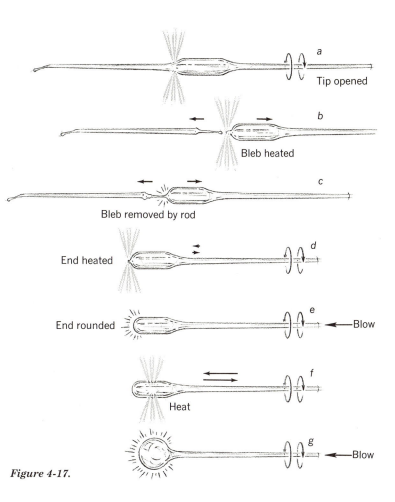

Figure 4-17.

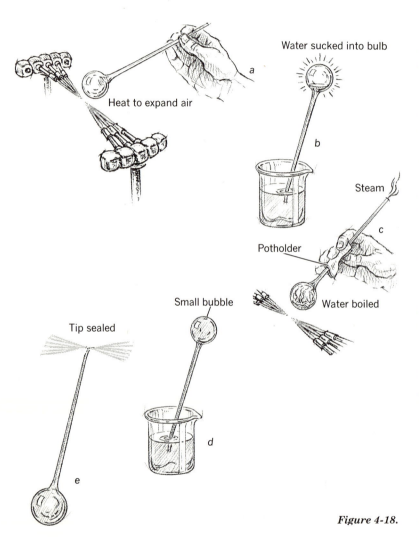

Heat to expand air

Water sucked into bulb

Steam

Potholder

Water boiled

Small bubble

Tip sealed

Figure 4-18.

By this practice you will master the art of rotating the soft glass so that it does not sag and also so that it cools uniformly while being blown. Air currents are set up by convection around all hot objects, including hot glass. Cold air rises from beneath the object, is heated by the glass, and carries off the heat above. For this reason the bottom of hot glass tends to cool more quickly than the top. Constant rotation assures uniform cooling and therefore symmetrical bulbs.

Before proceeding to the next practice exercise, you can now make an interesting magnifying glass. First, provide a glass of water and a few square inches of any cloth that can be folded to serve as a potholder. Next, rotate one of the glass bulbs (that you have just made) close to the fire but not in contact with the flame. Your objective is to heat the air inside the bulb and thereby expand it. The expanded air escapes through the blowpipe (Fig. 4-18, *a*).

Now quickly invert the piece and thrust the open end of the blowpipe into the glass of water. After a few seconds the trapped air will contract and a small amount of water will be sucked up into the bulb (4-18, *b*). Next, grasp the blowpipe by means of the folded cloth potholder, and hold the bulb close to the fire until the water comes to a boil. Because a few drops of scalding water may be shot out of the blowpipe, do not point the opening at anyone. The object of using the potholder now becomes apparent. The glass taper becomes scalding hot (4-18, *c*). When steam has been issuing from the blowpipe for, say, 5 seconds, quickly reinvert the tip of the blowpipe in the glass of water. Soon water will rush up into the bulb. Indeed, it may rush in and out several times when repeatedly turned to steam by the hot but cooling glass. After a short while, things will settle down and the bulb will fill completely except, perhaps, for a small bubble (4-18, *d*). The initial heating expands the air, which, when contracted, draws only a limited amount of water up into the bulb. Converting the water to steam expels all the air, and causes the bulb to fill completely with water when the steam condenses.

Remove the blowpipe from the glass of water and invert the piece so the remaining bubble enters the blowpipe. If you now tap the bulb against the palm of your hand the bubble will rise to the open tip of the blowpipe. Then, holding the water-filled bulb with the blowpipe uppermost, expose the tip of the blowpipe to the hottest region of the fire. It will promptly seal shut (4-18, *e*).

You now have rather an excellent magnifying glass of high power. The blowpipe serves as the handle. Hold the bulb about ¼ inch away from your

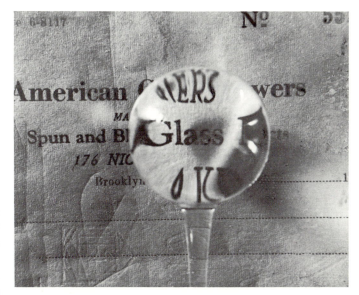

eye and bring any object close to the other side of the bulb. The object will appear grossly distorted near the edges, but a clear, greatly enlarged image will occupy the center field (Fig. 4-19).

Having mastered the trick of blowing spherical bulbs on the end of a glass tube, you are prepared to tackle egg shaped, round, and doorknob-shaped bulbs made in the middle of tubing. Begin practice by making an elliptical bulb. This is easy. Select a point, open one end, and straighten the tapers if necessary. Then soften a central zone equal in length to about two and a half tube diameters. Remove the piece from the fire.

Figure 4-19.

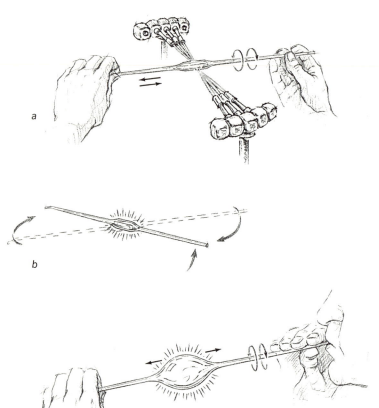

a

b

c

Figure 4-20.

fingers. It should run true, just as the point did. If it wobbles you will immediately recognize the cause: nonuniform heating or cooling (Fig. 4-20).

Make three or four elliptical bulbs in various proportions (Fig. 4-21, *a*). Then heat the glass at the junction where the closed taper joins the bulb and remove the taper by pulling it to a thread and melting the thread so it separates. Having burned off the taper, remove the bleb from the bulb by the same procedure that was used when making the magnifying glass.

Next, heat a zone of the taper that is still attached to the bulb—about an inch long—and close to the bulb. When the thin tubing softens bend it into a U shape and burn off the end to form a small hook. Now you have the beginning of a handsome Christmas tree ornament, as you will see if you next dip it in colored enamel and dust generously with glass snow.

Although elliptical bulbs are easy to make, doubtless you will find that some practice is needed for turning out a series identical in size and proportion. Learning to judge size and proportion by eye comes with experience.

Next tackle bulbs of the doorknob shape (4-21, *b*). They require more hand control than elliptical bulbs because you must simultaneously rotate the hot glass and blow it while pushing the tapers toward each other, rather than stretching as when forming elliptical bulbs. You can think of the doorknob bulb as rather a large maria. Similar skills are required for making both.

The tubing that supports each end of the softened glass must be kept in axial alignment despite the natural

Promptly blow and simultaneously pull, while rotating the piece, to form a bulb about an inch in diameter. By the way, when blowing bulbs, apply gentle air pressure at first, then gradually but promptly increase the force. Otherwise you may accidentally blow an oversized bulb, one that may even explode. Blow from the cheeks rather than the lungs. The length of the elliptical bulb will depend on how much you stretch the glass. Elliptical bulbs can be made in any desired proportions, short and stubby like fat eggs, or long and thin. Spin the completed piece between the thumbs and fore-

tendency of the hot portion to buckle or bend sideways into an **S** form when pressure is applied to the ends. Moreover, a new "feel" will appear when the bulb is blown; the expanding glass exerts a perceptible pressure against the ends of the attached tubing in opposition to the force applied by the hands. This "new" pressure increases in proportion to the size of the bulb. If the applied force is relaxed the tapered ends tend to move apart. In other words, the bulb behaves somewhat as a rubber balloon that is squeezed.

To make a bulb shaped like a doorknob (an oblate spheroid), open the tip of a point and heat the center tubing just as when preparing to make an elliptical bulb. Then, instead of pulling on the tapered handles, simultaneously blow, and as the bulb expands push the handles toward each other about a quarter of an inch.

The completed piece should run true when spun between the thumbs and forefingers. Doubtless the first one you make will wobble. If the glass has been heated uniformly (which ought to be a safe assumption at this advanced stage of practice) the wobble must be the consequence of failure to maintain the handles in axial alignment. Either the hot glass was permitted to bend or the handles, although parallel, became displaced laterally.

Blowing an oblate spheroid is *not* one of the easier operations. On the other hand, corrections can be made while the bulb is expanding. Watch the work carefully, particularly when the bulb is in the early stage of expansion. If the hot glass bends so the tapered handles form an angle, stop blowing momentarily and stretch the

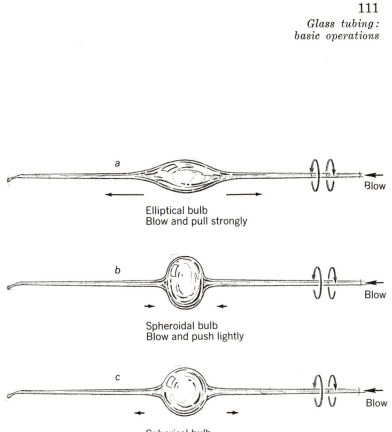

Elliptical bulb
Blow and pull strongly

Spheroidal bulb
Blow and push lightly

Spherical bulb
Blow and pull lightly

work just enough to straighten the piece. Then promptly complete the bulb.

You must work quickly because the glass soon cools. The hand motions should be smooth and deliberate. Lateral displacement of the handles becomes immediately apparent; instead of remaining centered, the junction between the bulb and handle that serves as the blowpipe moves in a circular path that increases in radius in proportion to the lateral displacement.

The correction is obvious; when evidence of the circular motion appears, promptly exert just enough lat-

Figure 4-21.

eral pressure to center the blowpipe. The earlier the correction is applied, the easier it is to make.

Do not discard wobbly bulbs. Line them up on the bench in the order they were made and examine them sequentially from time to time. They are a record of your progress. Suppose, however, that after collecting an array of twenty or thirty bulbs you can detect no progress?

In this unlikely event you may wish to backtrack a little. Return to the exercise of making elliptical bulbs. This time you should vary the technique slightly. Instead of stretching the glass as you blow the bulb, hold the handles in their original position; neither push them together nor pull them apart. Also, blow the bulb to a diameter only half again as large as the tubing.

This small bulb will be elliptical and you will have no difficulty in making a symmetrical one that runs true. Having made one or two of these, blow another small one but, this time, push the handles together slightly. Thereafter blow a succession of bulbs each a trifle larger than the last and simultaneously push the handles together more and more until at last you are moving them a full quarter of an inch.

Doubtless this sounds like work. It is. But it does not require nearly as much effort as most enthusiasts spend in perfecting a new dance step and it is just as interesting. Naturally, one consumes a lot of glass tubing. Fortunately, glass is cheap. So, as convenience permits, keep at it. Finally, having overcome the wobble, make a dozen or so spheroids of identical size and proportion. It is one of the most useful shapes found in glassware, both scientific and ornamental.

The blowing of spherical bulbs comes next (Fig. 4-21, *c*). The sphere is the unique form that lies midway between the ellipsoid and spheroid. To make it, blow without stretching the glass until the initial elliptical bulb becomes spherical. In this case it is easier to tell you *what* to do than *how* to do it. Success in blowing spherical bulbs in the center of a glass tube comes largely with the development of a good eye and a sensitive touch.

A soap bubble assumes the spherical shape automatically because the internal air pressure exerts a symmetrical outward force against the soap film; only gravity acts as a distorting force. The same forces operate in a glass bulb that is blown at the end of a single tube. In the case of a bulb blown between a pair of glass handles, as when a point is converted into a spherical bulb, additional nonsymmetrical forces can be introduced by the handles. This is where the difficulty arises.

The weight of the closed taper (the one that has not been cut off at the tip) must be supported by the glass blower. No longitudinal force—neither push nor pull—may be exerted between the two handles. In essence, the bulb, supported by the handles, must float in air and must be rotated at a rate that precisely counteracts the force of gravity tending to make the bulb droop. In other words, strive for a light touch.

Bulbs that are slightly elliptical can be corrected during the last split second by puffing just a trifle harder and pushing the handles together lightly. Conversely, spheroidal bulbs can often be made spherical by pulling slightly on the handles while maintaining the internal air pressure.

Spherical bulbs can also be made by at least two other techniques. One requires the use of the time-honored blowpipe of rigid metal.

Procure a 12-inch length of iron tubing of ⅛-inch inside diameter. Square off one end on a grinding wheel and smooth the other end to serve as a mouthpiece. Stainless steel makes a nicer blowpipe but is scarcely worth the extra cost. Next, warm and then heat to softness the end of an 8-millimeter rod of soft glass. Simultaneously heat the squared end of the blowpipe, but not to redness (Fig. 4-22, *a*). Wind a small amount of molten glass onto the *end surface* of the heated blowpipe and manipulate the blowpipe so the glass closes the opening of the pipe (4-22, *b*).

Remove the pipe from the fire and promptly blow a small bubble in the molten glass (4-22, *c*). More glass will be added subsequently, but unless the small bubble is blown at this stage the pipe will become plugged. Do not permit glass to flow up over the outer surface of the pipe. It must "wet" only the end *edge,* the face that you ground on the wheel. Now, while keeping the bubble hot with one hand, heat ½ inch or more of the glass rod until it becomes runny. Then wind this softened glass onto the hot bubble —as though you were making a glass bead on a wire (4-22, *d*).

Continue to heat the accumulated blob. Blow from time to time as necessary to maintain the size of the bubble. (It will shrink as the glass heats.) The blowpipe must be rotated contin-

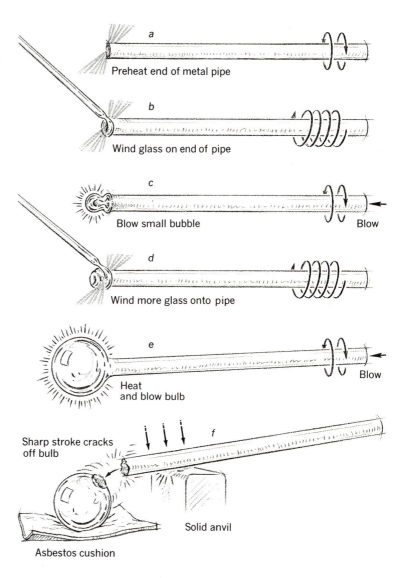

a

Preheat end of metal pipe

b

Wind glass on end of pipe

c

Blow small bubble   Blow

d

Wind more glass onto pipe

e

Heat and blow bulb   Blow

f

Sharp stroke cracks off bulb

Solid anvil

Asbestos cushion

Figure 4-22.

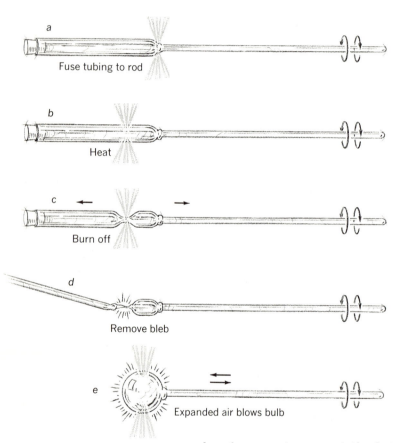

Figure 4-23.

a — Fuse tubing to rod

b — Heat

c — Burn off

d — Remove bleb

e — Expanded air blows bulb

an angle that encourages the glass *to creep up the outer surface of the pipe.* When the accumulated glass reaches yellow heat, and is about the consistency of thick molasses, remove the blowpipe from the fire and, while maintaining uniform rotation, blow the bubble into a bulb by a series of short puffs from the cheeks (4-22, *e*).

To detach the completed bulb, strike the outer end of the blowpipe smartly, downward, against a solid object such as a heavy iron rod or pipe. The shock of impact will crack off the bulb at the point where it joins the metal (4-22, *f*). The completed bulb may be caught on a sheet of asbestos paper cushioned by a pad of folded cloth beneath. Bulbs up to 2 or 3 inches in diameter that have reasonably substantial walls can be made by a blowpipe of this size.

Spherical bulbs can also be formed without an external source of air pressure. To make one, preheat the end of a convenient length of 4-millimeter rod, and simultaneously preheat the closed end of a similar length of 15-millimeter tubing (Fig. 4-17).

Now rotate the hot ends of each piece just inside the flame of the crossfire. The ends should face each other on opposite sides of the fire and be in axial alignment. When the tips of each end have become molten, bring the two into contact. They will promptly fuse (Fig. 4-23, *a*). Do not press the pieces together with enough force to form a maria. Simply let them join.

Now drop the work out of the fire. Continue the rotation. As the glass begins to solidify, exert just enough pull on the pieces to straighten the joint. When the glass has stiffened, return it to the fire. Heat a narrow

uously, of course, to prevent the hot glass from sagging. During most of the operation the blowpipe should be angled downward about 30 degrees (glass at the lower end) but may be occasionally held horizontally to maintain the spherical shape of the blob.

Never point the blowpipe upward at

zone that girdles the tubing about ½ inch away from the fused joint (4-23, *b*). When the glass softens, pull the piece apart (4-23, *c*) and burn off to leave a closed half inch of tubing attached to the rod (4-23, *d*).

Using the rod as a handle, return the tubular portion to the fire. Rotate the piece to prevent sagging. As the tubing softens, the cylindrical shape will slowly expand into a perfect sphere that gradually increases in size. A bulb is being "blown" by trapped and expanding air.

When the sphere has developed fully, lift the glass slowly upward and finally out of the fire—taking at least 30 seconds. This procedure permits the bulb to cool and yet keeps the trapped air sufficiently expanded to support the spherical shape until the glass solidifies (4-23, *e*). Tipless bulbs so made have applications in the poppet valves of scientific apparatus and clappers in all-glass hand bells.

Bulbs of irregular shape are easiest to make by the technique of mold-blowing, expanding the hot glass in a cavity of refractory material that limits the distribution of the material to a predetermined form. Anyone who can blow a spherical bulb in air can do mold-blowing as a matter of routine. The making of molds, however, is an independent field of craftsmanship that will be discussed only briefly. The interested reader should consult one or more of the excellent references on molding techniques that are listed in the bibliography (see page 191). Neither will we discuss in detail the art of making models, the objects to be duplicated in glass. In general, the model should be reasonably smooth, and free of extended projections, deep indentations, or undercuts. Cubes and other polyhedrals present no problems, and neither do small bottles or similar shapes. Figures such as miniature Santa Clauses used as ornaments on Christmas trees require, in general, molds made in a number of independently removable sections so that indented or projecting parts of the figure do not bind in the cavity during disassembly.

Sealing

Joining glass parts by the technique of placing molten surfaces lightly in contact until they solidify is perhaps the most basic and useful stratagem of the glassworker. It is known as "sealing." The procedure has been fully discussed with respect to solid objects in Section III. Frequent need arises for butt seals, straight tubing of various sizes and all proportions, joined end-to-end as well as to rod, bulbs, and so on. The applications of this sealing technique are myriad.

As an introductory exercise, cut two pieces of 8-millimeter tubing about a foot long. Stopper the end of one length. Fit one end of the second length with a blowing hose equipped with an L-shaped swivel, as described in Section II. The hose connection of the swivel may be joined to the glass by an inch or so of rubber tubing that makes a snug fit with each.

Grasp a length of glass in each hand and bring the pair roughly into axial alignment, with the facing ends separated about ½ inch. Now, rotate the tubes alternately clockwise and counterclockwise, about one-fourth of a turn in each direction at the rate of about one turn per second. Strive to keep the pieces moving in synchronism. Don't be discouraged if you fail to do it perfectly. No one, not even the most skilled artisan, can. It is also impossible to support unattached tubes in perfect axial alignment by hand. Just do the best that you can.

Now, while maintaining the best possible synchronism and alignment, transfer the tubes to the crossfires and preheat the ends. Take it easy. You have lots of time. Just move the glass up and down through the fire at the rate of about one pass per second—as you have been doing in other practice exercises (Fig. 4-24, *a*). After 15 or 20 seconds support the edges of the cut ends just barely inside the flames while continuing the quarter-turn rotations at the same unhurried pace. Soon the yellow flare-off will appear and the sharp edges will soften. When the edges become red hot to a depth of perhaps $\frac{1}{32}$ inch, and fully rounded, bring them lightly into contact.

Observe how easily the tubing can now be rotated in synchronism. The force exerted by each hand is plainly felt by the other.

When the surfaces have made contact, drop the joint out of the fire immediately and, after about 2 seconds, puff lightly into the blowhose to expand the glass about one wall thickness. Then, while continuing the alternate rotation, stretch the piece a little, just enough to straighten the seal.

The appearance of this first seal may not please you (4-24, *b*). Doubt-

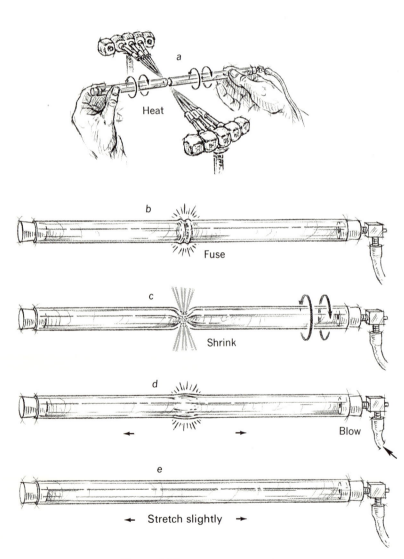

Figure 4-24.

less, an irregular ridge of thickened glass will extend completely around the joint. Perhaps you did not succeed in bringing the molten edges together in perfect register; they may be slightly offset. Even so, this seal would be functional for many purposes. The ridge and partial offset, if they exist, can be eliminated.

Simply return the seal to the fire and, while maintaining alternate rotation, let the glass shrink to about half the diameter of the tubing (4-24, *c*), then blow it out to full diameter or even a little more, drop it out of the fire, and straighten the work (4-24, *d*). You may have to repeat the blowing and shrinking several times in the case of gross ridges. The finished seal, if well made, should closely resemble straight tubing (4-24, *e*).

Having made this first seal, nick the tubing (when cool) about an inch away from the seal with the file, pull the glass apart, and repeat the procedure.

You can make at least a dozen practice seals in each pair of tubes. Within an hour you will be highly pleased with your work. Then shift to tubing of 15 millimeters in diameter. Traces of the old defects may now reappear, but you know the cure. Apply it.

Next, cut a point in half and seal the center tubing. The tapered handles of the point do not provide the rigid support of full-sized tubing. Being thinner, they tend to bend under load. This is counterbalanced by supporting the work at a slight upward angle. Seal the cut ends.

Sealing tubes of unequal diameter must be accomplished either by shrinking one end of the larger tubing to the diameter of the smaller, or by flaring the end of the smaller tube so that it matches the diameter of the larger. The technique of shrinking has been discussed on page 94 and flaring on page 97.

After the diameters of the ends have been matched by either technique, make the seal just as though the tubes were of equal size. The subsequent manipulation involved in completing the seal differs somewhat from that of sealing uniform tubes, of course, because of the unequal diameters of the tubes. One set of fingers must travel farther than the other to rotate the pieces synchronously. Practice the manipulation briefly with cold glass prior to attempting the first seal.

Tubes of differing wall thickness as well as unequal diameter must be joined on occasion, particularly in fabricating scientific glassware. When the larger tube has the thicker wall, the job is easy. Simply heat a zone of the larger tube and draw it out to matching size.

Usually the smaller tube has the thicker wall; capillary tubing of the type used in thermometers and barometers is an example. If the bore of the capillary exceeds 2 millimeters in diameter, the end can be opened conveniently by the flaring technique. If not, it must be expanded by blowing an end bulb and opening it.

To "expand" a small capillary by this technique, first blow a bulb of approximately the same diameter and wall thickness as that of the tubing to which the piece is to be sealed. When the bulb solidifies, heat the outer hemisphere strongly and blow a second bulb about twice the diameter of the first. The wall of the second bulb will be paper thin. Strike it off with the edge of the file (Fig. 4-25). Return the jagged edge to the fire and heat until the glass gathers into a smooth rim. Seal the rim to the larger tubing. If the flare, or rim of the blown-out capillary, is too thin, you have not heated a sufficient area of glass to form the bulb that was blown first.

Capillary tubes of equal size are sealed by much the same stratagem. The bore is so small (frequently only a fraction of a millimeter) that, unless enlarged, it will promptly close when the glass softens. For this reason the ends must be expanded and then sealed. In consequence, a cavity is formed in the otherwise smooth bore but this can be taken into account when the piece is designed, or, if absolutely necessary, it can be shrunk to any desired diameter.

Frequent occasion arises for making T seals, that is, joining one tube to another at a right angle. The procedure entails making a hole in the crossarm of the T at the desired point of attachment and then sealing the leg of the T to the opening. Seals of this type can be made in the crossfire.

In fact, skilled glass blowers make T's by means of the crossfire as a matter of casual routine and think little of manipulating what amounts, in effect, to three lengths of tubing joined

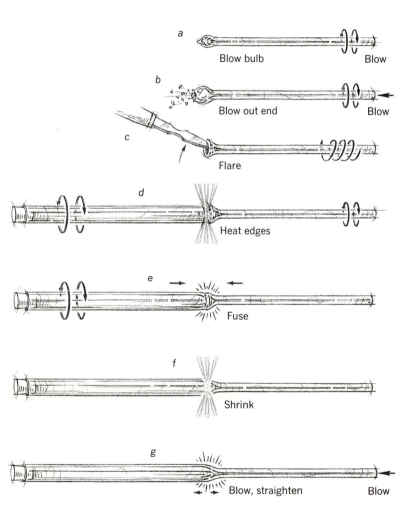

a   Blow bulb   Blow

b   Blow out end   Blow

c   Flare

d   Heat edges

e   Fuse

f   Shrink

g   Blow, straighten   Blow

Figure 4-25.

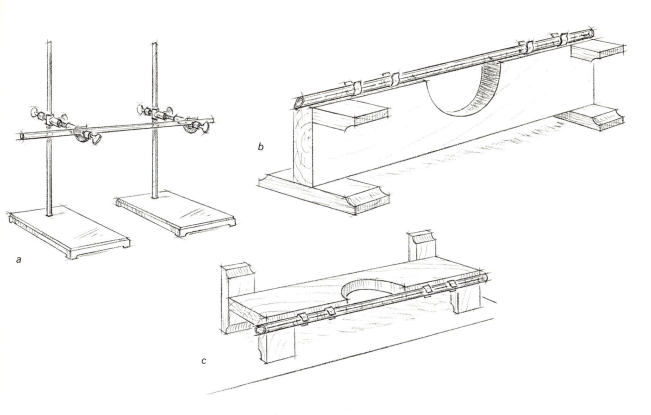

by a mass of soft glass. Beginners do not find this procedure so easy.

For this reason, the novice is urged to acquire two hand torches: one of the crossfire type equipped with a pair of fishtail burners and the other with a simple burner that develops a needle-point flame. Both torches can be made at home for an outlay of about $15.00, as explained in Section II, or they may be purchased ready-made for about $30.00.

Hand torches are rarely used in novelty glasswork—such as miniature utensils, animals, costume jewelry, and so on—but they are indispensable for assembling scientific apparatus such as rigid systems of tubing. Moreover, they are worth many times their cost to the beginner when he is learning how to make small pieces, such as T seals.

The following discussion assumes that you have acquired a pair of hand torches. In addition, you should improvise an armrest, one located a few inches higher than the work. It may be placed on either side of the work, depending on whether you are right-handed or left-handed.

Thus equipped, clamp a 12-inch length of 12-millimeter tubing near its ends to prevent the tube from buckling downward when the middle of the glass has been softened. Two of the many possible clamping schemes are depicted in Figure 4-26. Stopper one end, and fit the blowhose to the other. Then, using the fishtail torch, preheat about an inch of glass in the middle of the tubing. The procedure differs from preheating in the fixed crossfire only in that the torch is moved instead of the glass.

Figure 4-26.

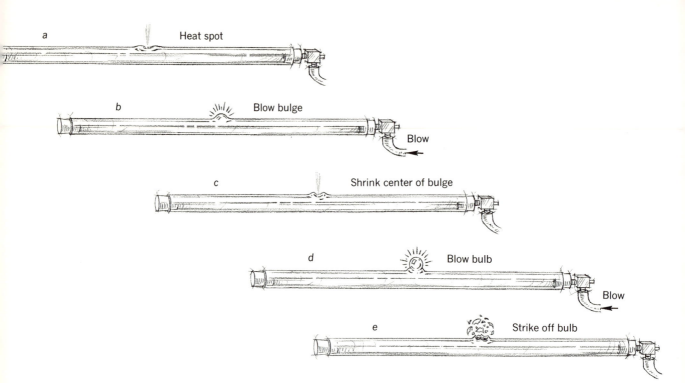

a — Heat spot

b — Blow bulge / Blow

c — Shrink center of bulge

d — Blow bulb / Blow

e — Strike off bulb

Figure 4-27.

When the first trace of flare-off appears, substitute the needle-flame torch for the fishtail burners. Direct the flame squarely downward so the bright, inner cone of the fire is almost but not quite in contact with the center of the tubing. Yellow flare-off will promptly appear. Within seconds a small area of glass will redden and sag slightly to form a shallow dimple (Fig. 4-27, a).

Let the dimple expand to a width of about ¼ inch. Remove the fire and blow the dimple into a bulge about as high as it is wide (4-27 b). Then heat the top of the bulge with the needle-flame until half of the area sags (4-27, c). Remove the fire and blow a bulb about ⅜ inch in diameter (4-27, d). Break off the bulb with the edge of the file and brush the fragments away (4-27, e).

Now, stopper one end of the tubing that will become the leg of the T and hold it vertically over the hole just made in the crossarm. The openings should be spaced about ⅛ inch apart. Utilize the armrest for holding the tube steady.

Preheat both the end of the tubing and the edge of the hole with the fishtail torch and then concentrate the flame simultaneously on edges of the two openings (4-27, f). (If updraft from the fire becomes uncomfortable to the hand that supports the leg of the T, stop work and fit the tubing, near the top, with a heat shield in the form of a 4-inch square of asbestos paper perforated in the middle to make a snug fit with the glass.)

Rotate the torch alternately clockwise and counterclockwise to heat the glass all around until the end of the

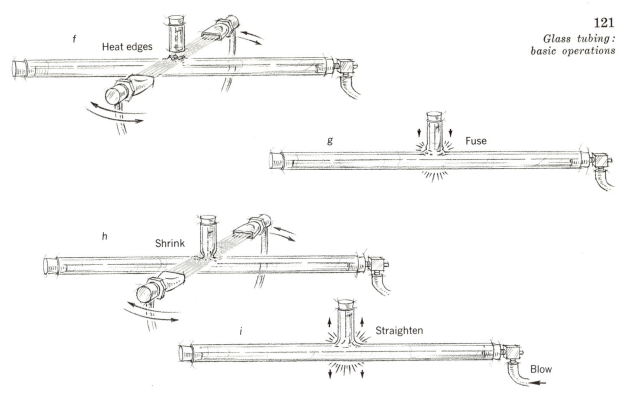

tubing shrinks to the diameter of the hole. If necessary to this end, concentrate more flame on the tubing than on the edges of the hole. When the edges become molten, and match in size, lower the tubing until the surfaces make light contact and fuse (4-27, *g*). Remove the fire and inspect the joint.

If a small hole is found, reheat, and then incline the tube in the direction of the leak, wobbling it a bit if necessary to close the hole. Then return the tube to the vertical position and lift it a fraction of an inch to stretch the glass slightly. Remove the fire and immediately suck on the blowhose just enough to constrict the joint perceptibly. Failure of the joint to constrict under the partial vacuum may indicate the presence of a second, previously undetected leak.

Close the leak by the technique just described. Apply suction again. When the joint constricts, indicating a good seal, blow the glass out to its former dimension and, while holding the tube motionless, continue to heat the work until the junction shrinks about 20%. Remove the fire (4-27, *h*).

Let the material cool about 3 seconds. Then simultaneously stretch the glass and expand it by blowing until the bore and wall thickness of the seal match that of the tubing (4-27, *i*). Cool gradually by passing the flame up and down over the glass—to anneal the joint partially.

You have now made a T seal. The procedure may seem somewhat difficult in prospect, but experience will demonstrate that it is easier than making a simple butt seal in the crossfire.

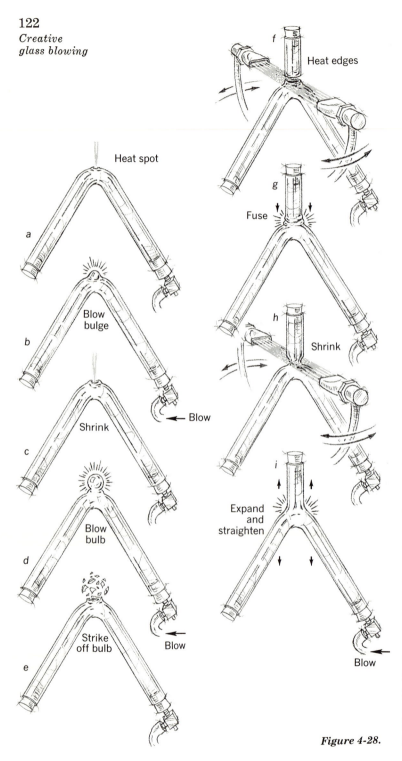

Figure labels (left column):
a — Heat spot
b — Blow bulge
c — Shrink · Blow
d — Blow bulb
e — Strike off bulb · Blow

Figure labels (center column):
f — Heat edges
g — Fuse
h — Shrink
i — Expand and straighten · Blow

Figure 4-28.

Occasionally it becomes necessary, when making special T seals, to join a leg of narrow tubing to a crossarm of greater diameter, or vice versa. If you are making a T seal with a narrow leg, the job is easy. Simply blow a small hole of matching size in the crossarm and proceed as though the tubes were of equal size. On the other hand, if the leg is the thicker member of the pair, shrink one end to the diameter and wall thickness of the crossarm, and then proceed.

The technique of executing a Y seal differs from that of the T only to the extent that the diverging arms of the Y are prepared first by making a V bend in the tube that would otherwise form the cross of the T. The bent piece is supported by the clamps as an inverted V and the hole blown in the apex.

Complete the seal by alternately blowing and shrinking to form smooth contours (Fig. 4-28). Crosses, or X seals, may be assembled by installing a second, opposing leg on the T or, alternatively, by sealing the apexes of a pair of V's that have first been opened as though a Y seal were to be made.

Sometimes a seal must be made without the use of air pressure. In making these, proceed just as though you were making a T seal except that, at the point where you would normally blow the dimple into a bulge, you touch the center of the heated area

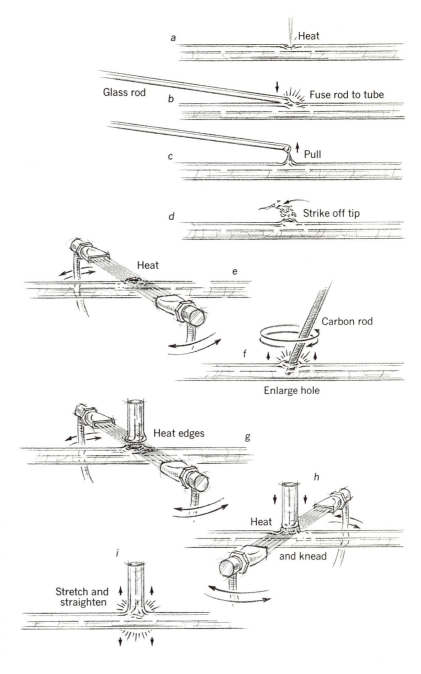

with the preheated end of a thin glass rod (Fig. 4-29, *a*). When the end of the rod fuses to the heated area (4-29, *b*), pull the glass out to a sharp point (4-29, *c*). Break off the point with a stroke of the flat file (4-29, *d*). Then heat the opening that has been made so that it runs down forming a hole about ⅛ inch in diameter (4-29, *e*).

While the glass is still soft, insert a thin, round rod of either carbon or steel into the opening and quickly rotate it, at a slight angle (4-29, *f*). This operation will result in a raised, thickened ring around the hole. Repeat the operation until the ring that borders the hole is equal in thickness to that of the wall of the tubing.

The end of the tubing that is to be sealed to this opening should be flared slightly to compensate for any subsequent shrinkage. Next, proceed as for a normal seal; heat the edge of the flared tubing and the ring until soft, and place them in contact so they fuse (4-29, *g*). In this operation there is no room for error. The facing edges must be evenly and well heated to assure an air tight joint at the first touch. Permit the seal to cool for a few seconds. Then reheat the work and knead the glass by pulling the leg member up and down slightly for distributing the glass (4-29, *h*) and, after about 3 seconds, pull just enough to align the work (4-29, *i*). The seal is then ready for annealing.

Figure 4-29.

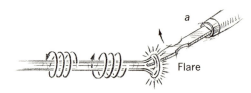

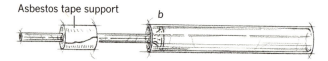

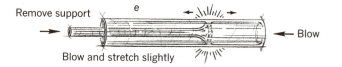

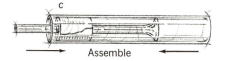

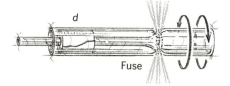

Figure 4-30.

Frequent occasion arises for sealing a small tube inside a larger one, in coaxial arrangement. Several procedures have been devised for making such pieces. In one, for example, the end of the smaller tube is flared so that it fits snugly within the bore of the larger. The flared end of the smaller tube is then slid into the larger, so it rests at the desired position (Fig. 4-30, *a, b*). A means must be devised for independently supporting the inner tube. One way is to wind just enough asbestos tape around a part of the smaller tube so that it fits snugly within the bore of the larger tube (4-30, *c*).

For the roll of asbestos tape, you can substitute a rubber stopper, one that has an accurately centered perforation, which fits snugly around the small tubing, plus another off-centered perforation to which a blowing hose can be connected. If the small tube is to extend beyond the larger, simply push it through the center perforation of the rubber stopper and insert the stopper into the larger tube.

On the other hand, if the smaller tube must be completely contained by the larger, push an appropriate length of glass rod through the center perforation of the rubber stopper and couple its inner end to the unflared end of the smaller tube by a short length of thick-walled rubber hose. The stopper now supports the rod which, in turn, both closes and supports the smaller tube. Connect blowing hoses both to the open end of the large tube and to the off-centered perforation of the rubber stopper.

To fuse the flare to the inner wall of the larger tube, first preheat the larger tube in the vicinity of the flare and then concentrate the fire in a narrow zone completely around the flare (4-30, *d*). The wall of the larger tube will shrink into contact with the edge of the flare and fuse. Lift the work out of the fire. Incidentally, the roller becomes a most useful tool for making seals of this type.

Promptly puff into first one and then the other of the blowing hoses (these may be connected with a T to a single blow hose for ease of operation) to expand the larger tube to its former dimension and simultaneously stretch the hot glass just enough to straighten the work. You have now made a "ring seal" (Fig. 4-30, *e*).

Immediately rotate the completed seal in the hot region of the fire just above the flames (but not so close that flare-off occurs) and lift it out of the heat at a rate of about an inch per minute for a period of 3 minutes. Wrap the completed piece in several folds of preheated asbestos paper and reheat in direct flame for 3 seconds with rapid compound motion before cooling to room temperature.

Many versions of the ring seal appear in scientific glassware, including the insertion of two or more flares in an envelope of larger tubing. All must be fully annealed before use because damaging strain develops when the fused region shrinks around the relatively cold flare. (See "Annealing," page 134.)

Another common seal involves what, in effect, amounts to inserting a tube through the wall of a larger piece—perhaps inserting the smaller tube through the bottom of a test tube or the side of a flask, or extending a centered coaxial tube out through the side of its envelope. Joints of this type are known as "triple seals" because they are frequently made of three pieces of glass.

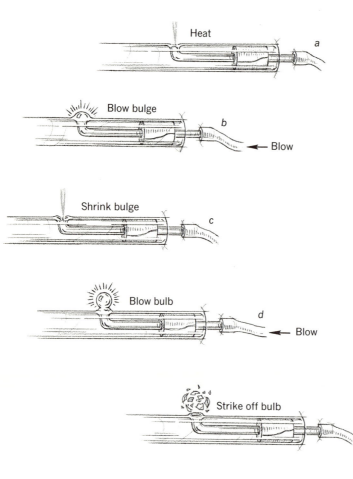

Figure 4-31.

The end of the small inner tube is first placed against the inner wall of the larger tube at the point where the seal is to be made and, if necessary, it is clamped or otherwise supported in this position by an improvised fixture. A blowing hose is attached to the other end of the small tube. The general area of the seal is then preheated.

Finally, the flame is concentrated on the outer wall of the larger tube, as though a dimple were being made over the end of the inner tube (Fig. 4-31, *a*). The glass softens, sinks slightly, and fuses to the inner tube, closing the end. The soft glass is then blown out, by pressure applied to the inner tube, and the bulb cracked off (4-31, *b*, *c*, *d*, *e*). A second length of small tubing is then sealed to the opening, by the same technique that is used for making a T seal (4-31, *f*, *g*, *h*). The joint is then kneaded by alternate shrinking and blowing, to eliminate any irregular contours (4-31, *i*).

In some applications, a variation of the triple seal is made with only two lengths of tubing. An example is a small tube that runs coaxially through the bottom of an otherwise conventional test tube. This arrangement is a nice practice exercise in making triple seals.

Begin the project by making a test tube about 8 inches long from 25-millimeter tubing. First, shrink and burn off a convenient length of tubing and then blow the hemispherical bottom. Be sure to remove the bleb. Next, blow a hole in the bottom that matches the outside diameter of 8-millimeter tubing.

In a convenient length of 8-millimeter tubing make a small maria and

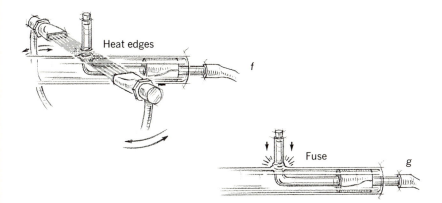

Heat edges

f

Fuse

g

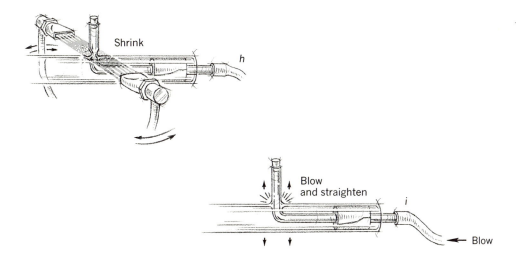

Shrink

h

Blow
and straighten

i

← Blow

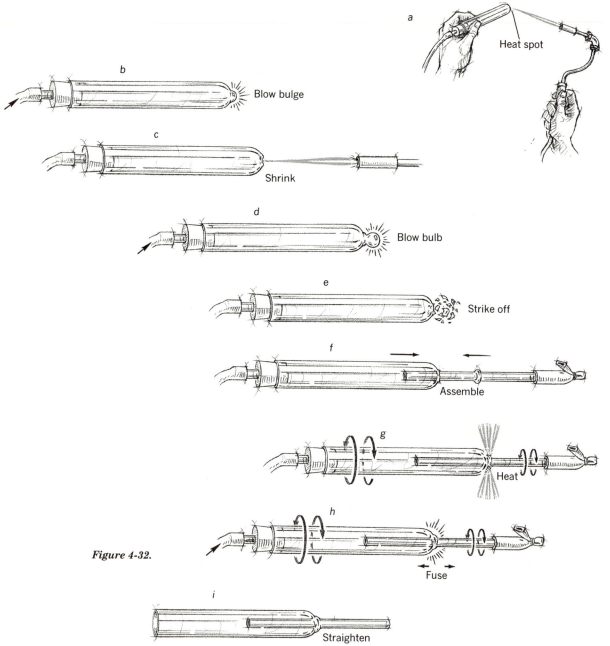

Figure 4-32.

cut the tubing at a point about 2 inches distant. When the test tube has cooled, stopper the large end. Push the 2-inch length of the small tubing through the hole until the maria rests snugly against the bottom on the outside (Fig. 4-32, *a-f*). Fit the blowing hose to small tube, preheat the junction, fuse the maria to the rim of the hole, and by alternate blowing and shrinking convert the surfaces into smooth contours (4-32, *g, h, i*). Rotate to prevent the softened inner tube from sagging; it must be kept centered by eye. Anneal the triple seal (partially) by the procedure used for the ring seal.

Having made a few triple seals by this simplified procedure, prepare an identical test tube. Into this tube insert, coaxially, a smaller glass tube of about twice the length of the test tube so that the end of the smaller tube rests firmly against the hemispherical bottom. It can be rigidly supported in this position by a centrally perforated rubber stopper that fits snugly in the opening of the test tube. Fit the blowing hose to the smaller tube.

With the glass assembly in the vertical position and the hemispherical end uppermost, heat the center of the bottom by means of the needle-flame hand torch until a circular area of glass shrinks into contact with the smaller tube and seals to the end of it. Let the glass stiffen (just until it shows no red color), and then reheat, in the center, a spot that is about two-thirds of the diameter of the smaller tube. Blow a bulge of approximately equal width and height. Reheat the top of the bulge, blow a thin-walled bulb, and crack it off. (This operation

is similar to that shown in Figure 4-31, *a-e*.)

Now transfer the operation to the crossfire or the fishtail torch. Keep the seal hot but not soft. Stopper one end of a similar length of small tubing, preheat the other end, and butt-seal it to the opening in the bottom of the test tube. (This procedure is similar to that shown in Figure 4-31, *f-i*.) Preanneal in the crossfire.

To make a seal of this type in the wall of an envelope such as a flask or other bulb, bend the inner small tube at a right angle so that the end butts against the wall at the point where the seal is desired. Support the tube in this position by a perforated rubber stopper or equivalent device and proceed as discussed above.

Incidentally, it is almost impossible to reheat an annealed triple seal of soft glass without breaking the work. The coeffecient of expansion is so great that rupturing stresses develop when heat is applied to the accessible surfaces. Both triple and ring seals must be annealed in an oven that heats all parts uniformly at a rate not exceeding 10 degrees Centigrade per minute (21 degrees Fahrenheit).

Occasionally the need arises for sealing a U-shaped tube into the side of a vessel, which may be a tube of larger diameter, a flask, or a bulb. Usually the width of the U greatly exceeds its height, and its arms bend at 90 degrees.

Whatever the proportions, start by making two bends to produce a U of the desired width; one of the bends should be 90 degrees and the other about 45 degrees. Cut the arms of the U to the desired length. Then at one of the points in the vessel to

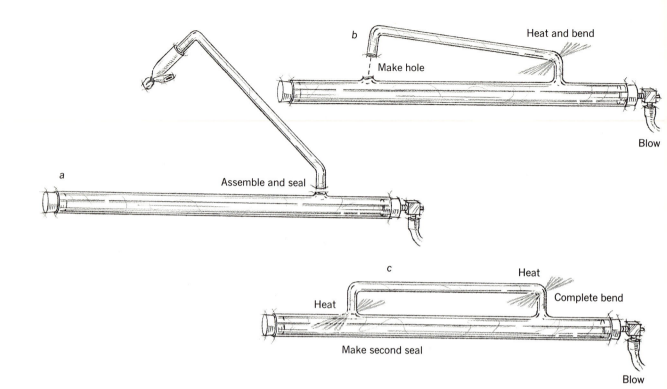

b

Make hole

Heat and bend

Blow

a

Assemble and seal

c

Heat

Heat

Complete bend

Make second seal

Blow

Figure 4-33.

which the U will be attached blow a hole that matches the diameter of the U tubing. (Make a bulge. Then blow and crack a small, thin-walled bulb, as shown in Figure 4-33.) Seal the arm with the 45-degree bend to this opening by means of the now familiar technique of the T seal. Apply the heat by the hand torches.

Next, locate the point in the vessel at which the other end of the U is to be sealed and mark it with a china-marking pencil. Blow the second hole. Preheat and then soften the 45-degree bend. Now bend the softened glass so the open end of the U is located squarely over the hole but not quite in contact with the edge of the opening; it should be within $\frac{1}{16}$ inch of contact (4-33, *b*).

Preheat the surfaces and complete the second T seal (4-33, *c*). If the U is fairly wide and consists of slender tubing you will find that the glass is sufficiently flexible that it can be bent enough to bring the molten surfaces into contact. If it is not wide, the bend in the opposite leg of the U must be softened simultaneously so that the molten ends can be placed in contact. The services of a helper can be enlisted to wield a second torch to this end, or you may accomplish the same result by rapidly transferring one torch back and forth between the bend and the T seal. The strain that is caused by the surfaces being forced into contact will be relieved by subsequent annealing. An alternative method of attaching the U tube, where space permits, is to prepare the larger vessel by setting on it two 1-inch stubs of tubing to receive the U ends, and butt-sealing the U ends to the stubs, using the fishtail hand torch.

Among the more difficult seals for the beginner to make is the so-called Dewar seal: joining at one end two coaxial tubes of substantially the same diameter to form a re-entrant edge. This seal is found at the mouth of the Dewar flask, or "Thermos" bottle. To tackle this ambitious project, first make a conventional test tube of, say, 25 millimeters in diameter. Flare the opening so that it fits snugly within a larger tube of, say, 35 millimeters in diameter. At about an inch from the end of the 35-millimeter tubing, seal a short length of 6-millimeter tubing, a typical T seal (Fig. 4-34, *a*). Such so-called "side arms" of small tubing are known as "tubulations" and are used both for blowing and, in some scientific apparatus, for exhausting the air from vessels. Attach the blowing hose to the tubulation.

Next, insert the test tube into the 35-millimeter tubing and, by means of an improvised support, fix its position so the flare is in contact with the end of the 35-millimeter tubing. Stopper the other end of the 35-millimeter tubing, and then fuse the flare to the end of the 35-millimeter tubing. By alternate shrinking and blowing, knead the seal to remove irregular contours. Remove the improvised support (4-34, *b*). Finally, shrink the 35-millimeter tubing at a point just beyond the bottom of the test tube, burn off, remove the bleb, and blow the closure into a smooth hemisphere, as illustrated (4-34, *c*). Anneal the finished piece in the oven (4-34, *d*).

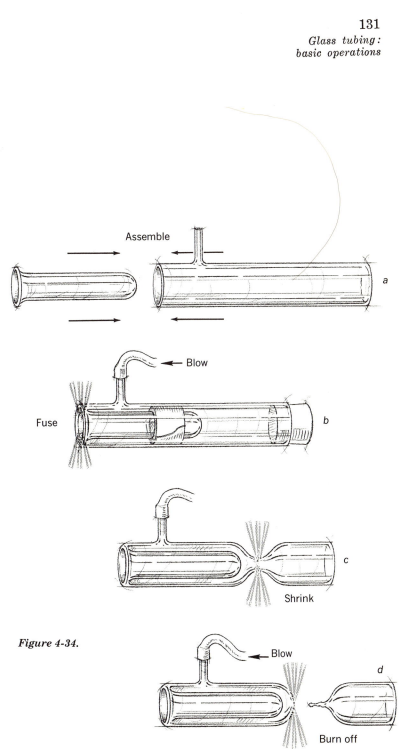

Figure 4-34.

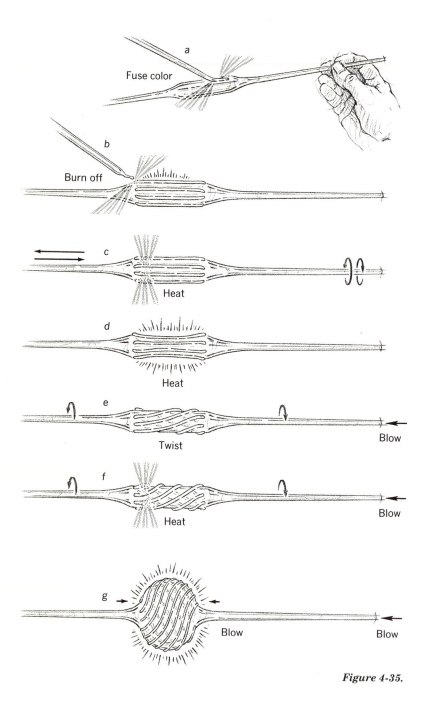

Figure 4-35.

Sealing rod to hollow forms

Certain ornamentation can be applied to blown work, either by sealing glass rod to tubing and then blowing the combination, or by applying the softened end of a rod to the surface of a bulb and blowing the rod into a hollow configuration as the heated mass softens the wall of the bulb. In addition, the end of a glass rod can be sealed to hollow ware and subsequently bent as desired to form the handle of a pitcher or comparable vessel, or to be a brace in scientific apparatus.

To make an ornamented bulb, first preheat the body of a point and then support it close to the flame, but not immersed in it. Simultaneously preheat and then soften the tip of a rod of colored glass. When the tip becomes molten touch the soft glass to a spot near one end of the body of the point and draw it lengthwise along the body, much as you would make a stroke with a crayon (Fig. 4-35, *a*). Having completed the stroke, burn off the rod. You have now sealed a line of colored glass to the body, the color being parallel to the axis of the tubing. Now rotate the point slightly and similarly seal another line of color to the body. Continue until six or more equally spaced stripes of color have been applied around the body (4-35, *b*, *c*).

Next, heat the region you have just striped until the glass softens enough so that you can twist the material (4-35, *d*). Make a twist of about *one-third of a revolution*, 120 degrees of arc (4-35, *e*). The body may shrink somewhat. Having made the twist, return the work to the fire and heat it just enough for blowing the body out to its *original* size, not more. Then, if desired, make another twist, but *not more than one-third of a revolution.* Again, restore the body to its original size by blowing (4-35, *f*).

Continue this sequence until the stripes acquire the desired amount of twist. Finally, restore the point to its original size and, while soft, blow it into a bulb of the desired size and shape (4-35, *g*). A polka-dot effect can be achieved by applying spots of color instead of stripes.

To blow a rod into hollow form, heat the end and apply it to the pre-heated wall of a bulb (Fig. 4-36, *a*). The molten tip of the rod will instantly fuse to the thinner wall of the bulb and soften it (4-36, *b*). Blow into the bulb. A bubble will form in the end of the rod that will become tubular in form if the rod is simultaneously pulled away from the bulb (4-36, *c*). The shape and proportions of the bubble can be controlled as desired by the same techniques that have been described for altering the form of the tubing. Indeed, having made a hollow projection with blown rod, you can make a second projection of like form on the wall of the first, and so on. Just burn off the rod from the bubble, reheat its end, and repeat the procedure by applying the heated rod to the hollow projection instead of to the bulb (4-36, *d*).

When handles of rod are applied to hollow ware such as miniature vases, it is customary to blow the work slightly immediately after the rod has been fused to the vessel. The result is a seal in which the thickness of the rod diminishes gradually (because of the incipient bubble) to the thick-

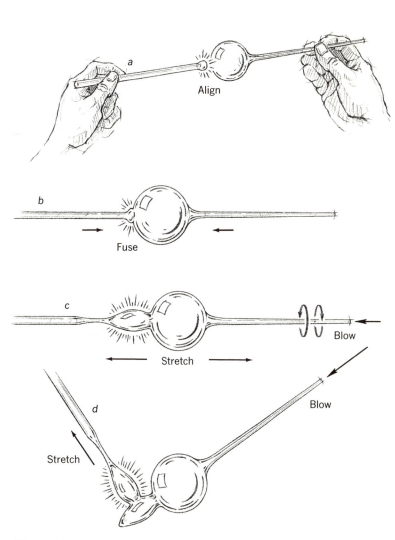

Figure 4-36.

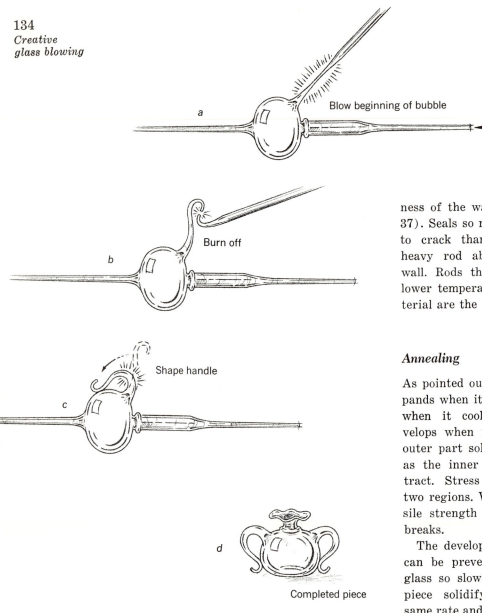

a   Blow beginning of bubble

b   Burn off

c   Shape handle

d   Completed piece

Figure 4-37.

ness of the wall of the bulb (Fig. 4-37). Seals so made have less tendency to crack than those in which the heavy rod abruptly joins the thin wall. Rods that soften at somewhat lower temperature than the bulb material are the easiest to blow.

Annealing

As pointed out in Section I, glass expands when it is heated and contracts when it cools. Internal stress develops when molten glass cools; the outer part solidifies and cannot yield as the inner part continues to contract. Stress develops between the two regions. When it exceeds the tensile strength of the glass, the piece breaks.

The development of internal stress can be prevented by cooling molten glass so slowly that all parts of the piece solidify at substantially the same rate and at the same time. Small, relatively simple pieces can be fully annealed in the crossfire by slowly removing them from the heat—at a rate of about 10 minutes per inch of movement. This assumes that the work is continuously rotated. The rotation distributes the stresses uniformly; it prevents the growth of local stresses in any region of the surface from exceeding the tensile strength of the glass.

A partial anneal, one that reduces the stress enough so that work will not break during ordinary changes in room temperature, can be made by completing the removal from the flame in 3 or 4 minutes and then protecting the work from drafts until it cools to room temperature. Even more effective partial anneals are made by shutting off the air supply and rotating the work in the smoky flame until it acquires an opaque coating of soot.

Better still is a container of asbestos wool maintained at a temperature of 600 to 750 degrees Fahrenheit. Work is simply buried in the hot asbestos until the end of the session. The heat is turned off and the asbestos permitted to cool slowly. This is an ideal method of annealing small novelties, miniature vases, urns, parts for costume jewelry, and so on.

Models of sailing ships in glass, which include fine rods (forming the rigging) and similar pieces, cannot be successfully annealed. The finer lines sag out of shape long before the heavier parts anneal. Larger pieces such as ash trays and scientific glassware that contain other than simple butt seals must be annealed in a tem-

perature-controlled oven that need be large enough only to accommodate the work.

Glass is said to have a "strain point," an "annealing point," and a "melting or working point"; this implies that at one temperature the material can be stretched, at another internal strain is relieved, and at a still higher temperature the glass becomes semifluid. As mentioned in Section I, glass by its nature is in the fluid state even at room temperature, but with a viscosity so high that it is for all practical purposes a rigid solid.

In other words, glass behaves like very stiff tar or pine pitch. Its tendency to flow varies continuously with its temperature. For this reason internal stress should automatically disappear in time from a glass piece at room temperature—perhaps in a few million centuries! Heating the object merely accelerates the process.

The heating must not be carried too far, however, because the object is continuously subjected to another force, gravity. Fortunately the gravitational force is much weaker than the forces of internal stress. An object that weighs an ounce, for example, may contain an internal stress of 20,000 pounds per square inch or more. The annealing procedure takes advantage of this differential. The piece is heated just enough to permit the glass to yield under the great internal forces without sagging appreciably under the force of gravity.

Ordinarily internal stresses in soda lime glass (that is 1 millimeter thick) are relieved in 4 minutes at a temperature of 510 degrees Centigrade (950°F). The annealing time, which varies with the square of the thickness, is determined by multiplying the square of the thickness by the 4. Hence, a piece 2 millimeters thick would require an annealing interval of 16 minutes, a piece 3 millimeters thick would require 36 minutes, and so on. Huge pieces, such as glass blanks for telescope mirrors, remain in the annealing oven for many months. As a general rule, small, compact objects are placed in the oven, heated gradually during an interval of 15 to 20 minutes, and then maintained for 5 minutes at the annealing temperature. The heat is then shut off. A well-made oven requires about 3 hours for cooling to room temperature. No sagging due to gravity should be evident in annealed work.

On the other hand, you must take into account the gravitational force when you are annealing other than compact pieces. For example, a 10-inch tube of thick-walled capillary 8 millimeters in diameter will develop pronounced sag during the anneal if supported only at the ends. When possible, rest such pieces on a flat surface, such as a heavy plate of metal, or in the V of a straight length of angle iron.

Projections, such as slender tubes sealed to the sides of flasks or cylinders, should be supported by braces made from Transite or similar heat-resistant material. When it is impractical to brace the work, or to rest it on a flat base as in the case of the inner tube of a coaxial pair, suspend the piece vertically. It may elongate slightly. This should be anticipated during design.

Attempts to prevent distortion by annealing at low temperature for a long period invariably fail. Glass responds without favor to all mechanical forces, including gravity. Time and temperature merely determine the rate of its response.

Sagging

Sagging, the bane of the annealer, becomes a prized technique to the craftsman intent on making glass objects of irregular shape. A sheet of glass of appropriate shape is placed on a mold of fireclay, dental stone, plaster of paris, or equivalent refractory substance, and it is softened in the annealing oven. The glass sags into contact with the mold, conforming roughly to the contours. The shape of the mold is limited to open contours. The glass cannot sag to fill undercuts. Scientific glassware, such as watch glasses that take the form of uniform spherical sections, petri dishes, and similar shapes are easy to make. Comparable novelty forms include ash trays, candy dishes, and so on. The novelty forms may be ornamented by placing bits of colored glass in the forms of thin rod, or frit (glass in granular form) on the object prior to firing.

Novelty glass work

This section introduces the art of combining the basic operations of glass blowing to form novelties and trinkets. By duplicating the pieces to be described, the beginner will acquire the knack of selecting sequences of operations that minimize the expenditure of time and materials when making pieces of other design. The urge to improvise may then be given free play. No attempt will be made to explain how novel designs are created. This is largely a matter of natural endowment. However, the pages that follow will explain the general rules of procedure and the techniques through which creative talent can find expression.

The exercises have been arranged so that skills acquired when making the first pieces are subsequently applied. The beginner is urged to do the exercises in the order of their presentation. A few rules should be observed. First, place all required ma-terials within easy reach of the work position before lighting the fires. A hot piece laid aside, while the worker hunts for a special kind or size of glass, will cool and is likely to break when reheated. It is possible, of course, to provide a furnace in which to store hot work. If one is acquired, it too should be located within easy reach of the work position.

In general, too, the sequence of operations should be planned so that all details within a given region of a piece are completed before work is undertaken at a remote region. For example, in making a vase, complete the top and attach the handle before starting work on the bottom—or vice versa. Thin parts, such as bulbs, can usually be reheated locally without risk of breakage. Even so, beginners are urged to cultivate the habit of keeping each region hot until it is finished.

Avoid abrupt transitions in thick-

A glass candlestick

A relatively simple exercise that illustrates the order in which glasses are heated when making a piece involves the fabrication of a miniature candlestick. The materials may consist of a 20-inch length of 12-millimeter ruby tubing, a 10-inch length of 8-millimeter opaque white tubing and two 10-inch lengths of 6-millimeter rod, one of crystal and the other of opaque orange. The sizes and colors are not critical nor are the dimensions of the completed piece. In novelty glass work proportions are determined not by the yardstick but by the aesthetic tastes of the artisan.

Begin the construction by pulling a point from the ruby tube. Shrink the center to the diameter of the opaque white tubing and make a maria as illustrated (Fig. 5-1, *a*). The point should have been straightened and opened at one end, of course. Next, heat the constricted tubing close to the maria on the opened side of the point (5-1, *b*). Blow off and discard the opened taper (5-1, *c*). Next, flare the maria slightly so that its inner diameter matches that of the opaque white tubing (5-1, *d*). Seal the opaque white tubing to the maria (5-1, *e*). Then heat and blow off the remaining taper (5-1, *f*). The base of the candlestick is now made with the flaring tool. Open the ruby bulb into a funnel shape and continue by sweeping the soft glass up and over in the form of a re-entrant edge as illustrated (5-1, *g*). When forming a reverse curve of this type, keep the outer edge of the flare substantially hotter, and hence softer, than the in-

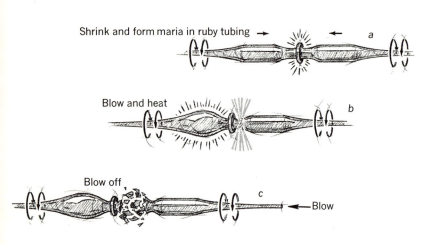

Shrink and form maria in ruby tubing →   *a*

Blow and heat   *b*

Blow off   *c*   ← Blow

Figure 5-1.

ness when making seals. Such discontinuities encourage the development of internal stresses and lead to spontaneous breaks. When attaching a handle of rod to a thin bulb, for example, always blow into the bulb lightly when the molten end of the rod is placed in contact with the thin wall. The molten end of the rod will immediately soften the wall and a bubble will start to form in the end of the rod in which the thickness gradually increases. This tapered form minimizes internal stress. Watch the growing bubble carefully and stop blowing when it becomes a perceptible depression. (Continued blowing will cause the seal between the wall and rod to expand into a conventional bulb and spoil the piece). Finally, always let the completed piece cool slowly, preferably in an annealing oven.

ner zone. If the inner zone becomes softer than the edge, the glass will buckle.

Next, attach the handle (5-1, *h*). If desired, the rod may be first heated, partly flattened, and twisted to simulate the strands of a rope, or a plain handle may be made according to the tastes of the worker. Having added the handle, rotate the piece at a distance of about 2 inches above the fire and, during an interval of a minute or so, lift the work gradually to a height of about 4 inches. This slowly lowers the temperature of the base. Next, warm a holder, grasp the base in the jaws, and burn off the opaque white tubing at a point approximately 2 inches from the base (5-1, *i*). Finally, apply "wax drippings" of crystal glass to the top of the candle (5-1, *j*) and add a "flame" of orange rod. A realistic flame can be simulated by heating the tip of the orange rod and flattening the soft glass between the serrated jaws of a tweezers. The outer tip of the flattened portion is then pulled into a stubby point by the tweezers. Seal this tip to the tip of the candle, soften the orange glass at a point just beyond the seal, stretch the mass into the shape of a flame, and burn off (5-1, *k*). Anneal the completed piece (5-1, *l*).

A toy top

Many novelties involve the fabrication of distorted bulbs. One such novelty is the glass top, in which a flattened bulb serves as the spinning mass. To make the top, pull a point in 15-millimeter tubing of any desired color. Shrink

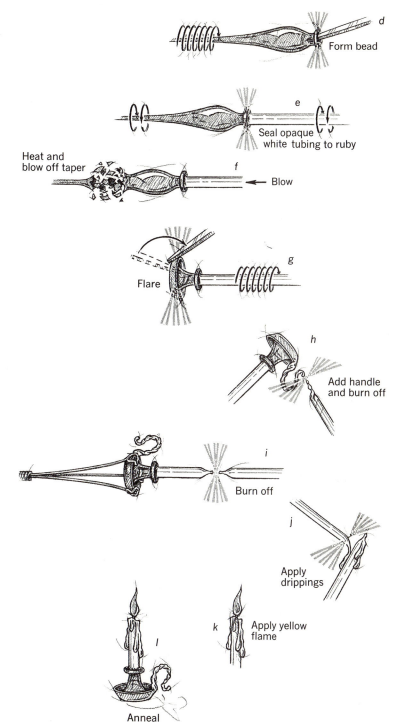

d Form bead

e Seal opaque white tubing to ruby

Heat and blow off taper

f ← Blow

Flare

g

h Add handle and burn off

i Burn off

j Apply drippings

k Apply yellow flame

l Anneal

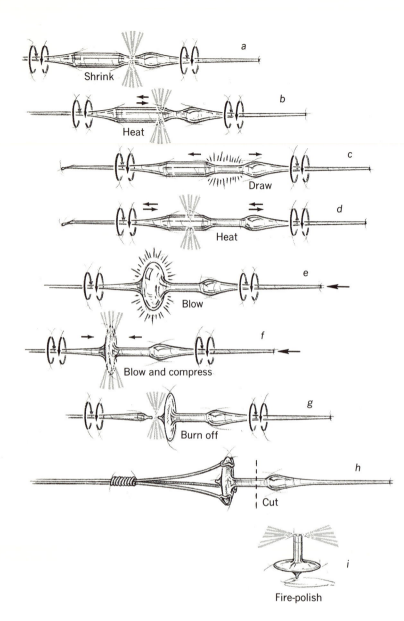

Figure 5-2.

heats will be required until the draw can be completed in one heat. Next, heat and blow a doorknob-shaped bulb in the remaining portion of the body (5-2, *d*, *e*). Soften the outer rim of the bulb, then blow and simultaneously compress the glass to form a shape resembling a large, hollow maria (5-2, *f*). The glass must be heated to the plastic state but it must not be allowed to become so soft that the walls of the bulb twist out of control. Do not let the flame play directly on the thin wall of the bulb. Sufficient heat is provided by the edge of the fire. Burn off the closed taper (5-2, *g*). During this operation, keep the glass well centered so that the top will spin true on the tip that remains fixed to the body. Finally, nick the straight tubing with the file an inch or so from the body, break off the taper (5-2, *h*), and fire-polish the cut end.

A tea set

One of the more popular products of itinerant glass blowers who give demonstrations at amusement centers, schools, and so on, is the miniature tea set, consisting of a tea pot, sugar bowl, and creamer. The pieces may be made in any convenient sizes and colors. Fifteen-millimeter tubing is frequently used. To make the tea pot, pull a point with a body about ¾ inch in length and form a maria close to one shoulder, as illustrated (Fig. 5-3, *a*). Heat the remainder of the body and blow a doorknob-shaped bulb (5-3, *b*). Burn off the closed taper (5-3, *c*). Apply a handle of rod stock and blow a slight depression

the body of the point near one end, as illustrated (Fig. 5-2, *a*). Next, soften one shoulder of the body (5-2, *b*) and stretch the material to form a tube of uniform diameter about 2 inches in length (5-2, *c*). Beginners may find the operation easier if the tube is formed by making a succession of heats and draws. With practice, fewer

into molten seal (5-3, *d*). Soften the handle and bend it into final form, using the warmed tip of the rod as a tool (5-3, *e*). Similarly, apply the spout (5-3, *f*). Next, soften the bottom of the bulb and press it against a flat surface, such as a block of Transite that has been covered with a sheet of asbestos paper (5-3, *h*). *Do not use a block of uncovered carbon.* Carbon chills the glass so quickly that severe internal stress develops. Grasp the bulb in a holder and burn off the taper (5-3, *i*).

This is a tricky operation, but relatively easy to master. The difficulty arises from air that is trapped inside the bulb when the taper is burned off. The trapped air is at atmospheric pressure. Upon cooling, it creates a partial vacuum in the bulb. If the glass is now softened, the higher external pressure may cause the material to collapse. On the other hand, when the trapped air is strongly heated, the softened wall may bulge outward. The solution consists in burning off the taper and immediately moving the bulb just above the fire. Watch the softened glass closely. If the glass starts to collapse, lower the bulb; if a bulge appears, raise the bulb. In a few seconds the glass will solidify—and the trick is turned.

Finally, seal the end of a colored rod to the tip of the lid that was formed when the taper was burned off. Burn off the rod (5-3, *j*) and rotate the adhering mass horizontally in the fire until the knob of the pot becomes pear-shaped (5-3, *k*). Watch for distortion that may be caused by trapped air and heat or cool the bulb to counteract the effect, as discussed. Anneal the completed pot (5-3, *l*).

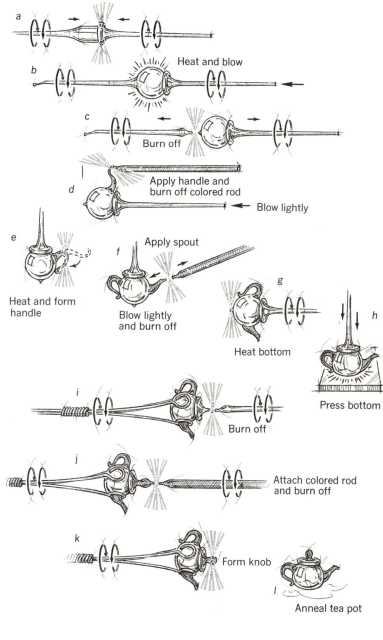

Figure 5-3.

Figure 5-4.

Add second handle
and anneal sugar bowl

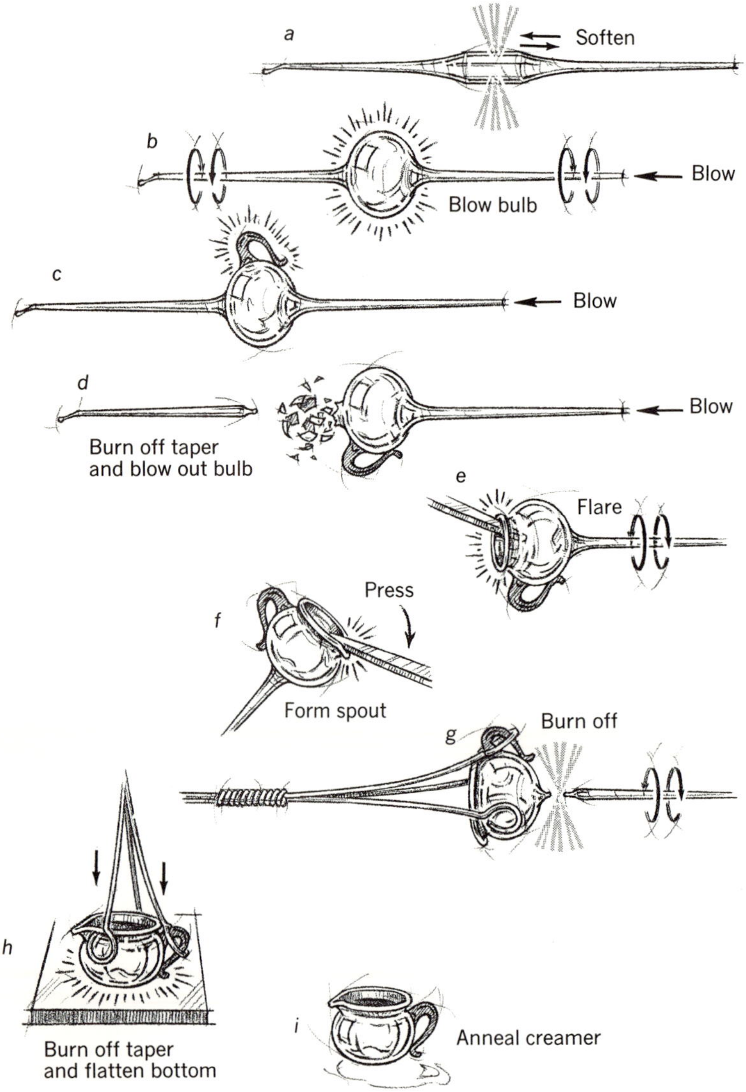

The sugar bowl of the set is made by an identical sequence of operations except that twin handles, instead of one handle and the spout, are applied (Fig. 5-4). Making twin handles is one of the more difficult operations encountered in novelty work. No one can make two things exactly alike by hand. Just do your best.

The operating sequence involved in making the creamer of the tea set introduces a flaring operation. The conventional point is pulled and the bulb blown. The handle is then added and blown because the bulb must be opened for the flaring operation. (The handle cannot be blown after the bulb is opened but may be applied to the rim of the flares.) Soften the point (Fig. 5-5, *a*). Blow the bulb (5-5, *b*). Apply and blow the handle (5-5, *c*). Burn off the closed taper and open the bulb (5-5, *d*). The opening should be kept small, not exceeding one quarter of the diameter of the bulb. Otherwise, sufficient glass will not accumulate at the edge of the flare to form a substantial bead around the rim of the vessel (5-5, *e*). Heat a portion of the beaded rim diametrically opposite to the handle and, by means of the flaring tool, form the spout (5-5, *f*). Next, grasp the rim in the jaws of the holder, burn off the remaining taper (5-5, *g*), flatten the softened bottom (5-5, *h*), and anneal the completed creamer (5-5, *i*).

a ← Soften

b ← Blow
Blow bulb

c ← Blow

d ← Blow
Burn off taper
and blow out bulb

e Flare

f Press
Form spout

g Burn off

h
Burn off taper
and flatten bottom

i Anneal creamer

Figure 5-5.

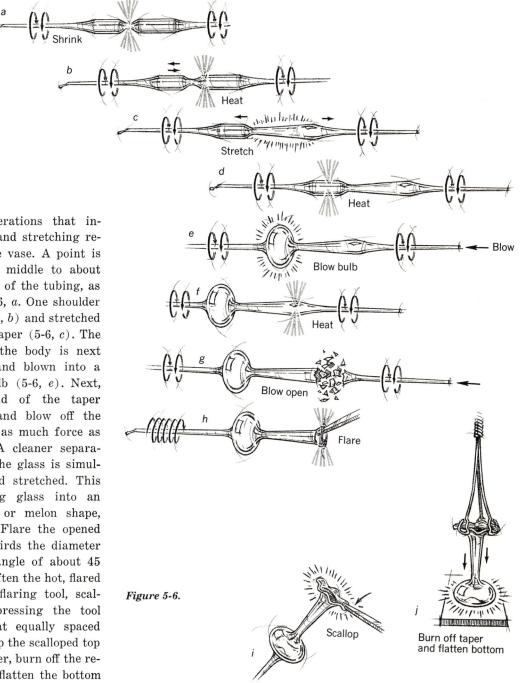

A miniature vase

A sequence of operations that involves both flaring and stretching results in a miniature vase. A point is first shrunk in the middle to about half of the diameter of the tubing, as shown by Figure 5-6, *a*. One shoulder is then softened (5-6, *b*) and stretched to form a straight taper (5-6, *c*). The remaining half of the body is next softened (5-6, *d*) and blown into a doorknob-shaped bulb (5-6, *e*). Next, heat the large end of the taper strongly (5-6, *f*) and blow off the softened glass with as much force as possible (5-6, *g*). A cleaner separation may result if the glass is simultaneously blown and stretched. This pulls the expanding glass into an elongated ellipsoid, or melon shape, that breaks easily. Flare the opened end to about two-thirds the diameter of the bulb at an angle of about 45 degrees (5-6, *h*). Soften the hot, flared end and, with the flaring tool, scallop the edge by pressing the tool against the glass at equally spaced points (5-6, *i*). Grasp the scalloped top in the jaws of a holder, burn off the remaining taper, and flatten the bottom (5-6, *j*).

Figure 5-6.

Shrink

Heat

Stretch

Heat

Blow bulb — Blow

Heat

Blow open

Flare

Scallop

Burn off taper
and flatten bottom

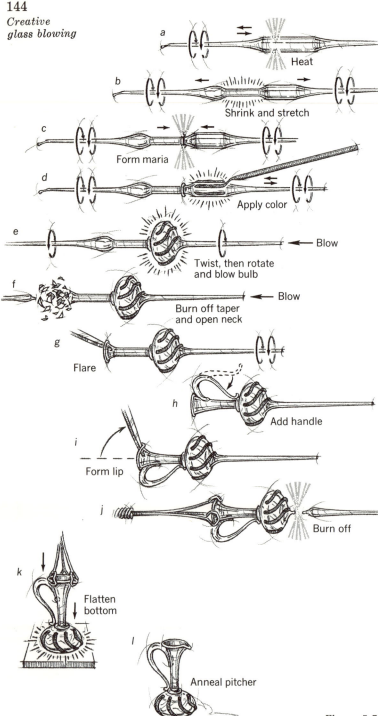

Heat

Shrink and stretch

Form maria

Apply color

Blow

Twist, then rotate
and blow bulb

Blow

Burn off taper
and open neck

Flare

Add handle

Form lip

Burn off

Flatten
bottom

Anneal pitcher

Figure 5-7.

An ornamental pitcher

By introducing a few variations, you can convert a simple vase into an ornamental pitcher. First, heat a relatively broad zone in the body of a point near one end (Fig. 5-7, *a*) and stretch the softened portion into an elongated section that tapers outward from the middle (5-7, *b*). Form a maria in the tapered portion close to the larger portion of the body of the point (5-7, *c*). Next, apply narrow strips of colored rod to the body (5-7, *d*). Heat the body to softness and, while applying just enough air pressure to maintain the normal diameter of the body, twist the taper handles gently in opposite directions. The twist converts the colored lines into spirals. Reheat the body and blow a conventional doorknob-shaped bulb (5-7, *e*). Strongly heat the closed taper at the point where it joins the body of the point and blow it off (5-7, *f*). Flare the open end slightly (5-7, *g*), and seal a handle to the flared edge. In this case the seal between the handle and the vessel cannot be blown. If the seal is made close to the thickened edge, however, internal stress will not usually exceed the breaking strength of the glass and the piece will remain intact for annealing. While the top of the pitcher is still hot, soften the rim at the point directly opposite the handle and, with the flaring tool, form a spout (5-7, *i*). Grasp the top of the pitcher in the holder and burn off the remaining taper (5-7, *j*), flatten the bottom (5-7, *k*), and anneal the completed pitcher (5-7, *l*).

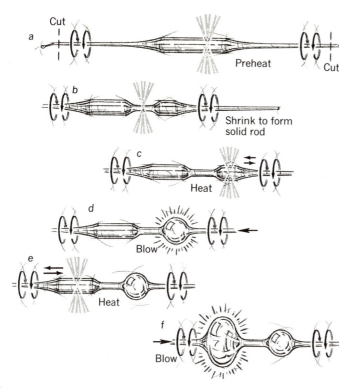

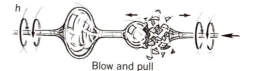

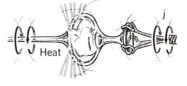
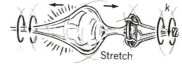
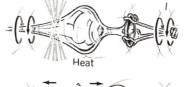

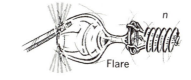

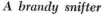

A brandy snifter

Stemware is made by shrinking a zone in tubing until the glass collapses to form a solid rod. Both ends of a point are opened, the shrinking operation is performed, and then bulbs of appropriate size are blown, opened, and flared to form the bowl and base of the vessel. A relatively simple example is the brandy snifter. The body of the prepared point is heated at a point about one quarter of the length from one end (Fig. 5-8, a), it is shrunk until the glass collapses (5-8, b), and a spherical bulb is blown in the smaller portion of the body (5-8, c, d). The remaining portion of the body is then softened (5-8, e) and blown into a doorknob shape (5-8, f). The smaller bulb is softened (5-8, g), blown open

Figure 5-8.

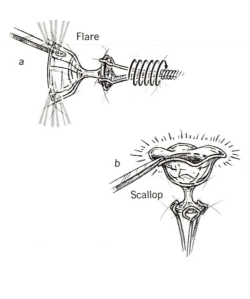

Flare

Scallop

Figure 5-9.

A fruit bowl

With additional flaring, the brandy snifter would become a dessert dish, a wine glass, or a fruit bowl. A fruit bowl, for example, requires for the step shown in Figure 5-8, *n*, a broad flare instead of a bead (Fig. 5-9, *a*). To complete the fruit bowl, make a series of shallow scallops around the edge (5-9, *b*).

The epergne

If you make the fruit bowl with a hollow stem, it can be used as the lower member of an epergne. To make the hollow stem, the point is collapsed abruptly at one end and tapered gradually at the other. Otherwise, the procedure is identical with that used for making the fruit bowl (Fig. 5-10, *a*). The centerpiece of the epergne is made by a technique similar to that used for forming the neck of the simple vase (Fig. 5-6, *a, b, c*). One end of the body of a point is collapsed to form a solid tapered rod and the remainder is stretched to form a straight taper (Fig. 5-10, *b, c, d*). The piece is then blown open at the wide end (5-10, *e, f*), flared (5-10, *g*), and scalloped (5-10, *h*). The scalloped end is then grasped by the holder and the taper burned off (5-10, *i*). The small end of the piece must be adjusted so that it fits snugly into the hollow stem of the bulb (5-10, *j*), an operation that calls for some judgment. If the fit is too loose, heat the tip and thicken. Conversely, if the tip is too large, heat and stretch the glass.

(5-8, *h*), and flared to form the base of the vessel (5-8, *i*). The base is grasped in a holder and the opposite side of the large bulb is softened in the edge of the fire (5-8, *j*). As in the case of the glass top (Fig. 5-2, *f*), the material must not be heated directly in the fire. The thin wall of the bulb softens quickly. If overheated, it can flow out of control. Stretch the softened zone until the bulb assumes a pear shape (5-8, *k*). Heat the narrow end of the resulting bulb (5-8, *l*), and open it by simultaneously stretching the glass and blowing (5-8, *m*). Heat the ragged edge of the opening and form it into a smooth bead by means of the flaring tool (5-8, *n*). Anneal the completed vessel (5-8, *o*).

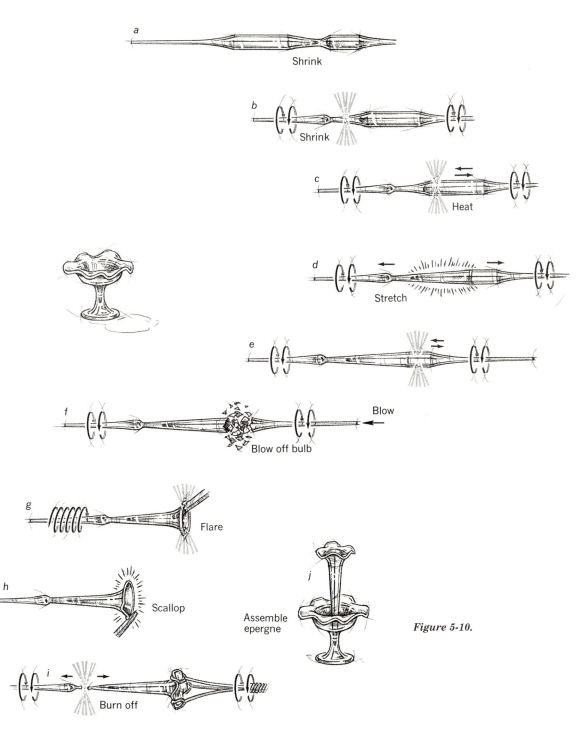

a Shrink

b Shrink

c Heat

d Stretch

e

f Blow off bulb — Blow

g Flare

h Scallop

i Burn off

j Assemble epergne

Figure 5-10.

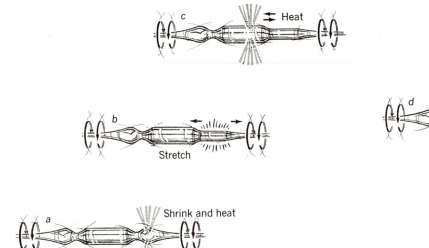

Figure 5-11.

An urn

An urn can be made of a single length of tubing and a rod. The construction begins with a point.

The body of the point is first shrunk at two zones about a tube diameter from each end; this step violates the general rule of completing all details in a heated zone before transferring operations to a remote zone. The small bulb at the open end of the point is then softened (Fig. 5-11, *a*) and blown slightly until it is about five-eighths of the diameter of the body (5-11, *b*). Approximately three-fourths of the glass remaining in the central portion of the body is then softened adjacent to the portion just heated and is blown into a doorknob-shaped bulb (5-11, *c*, *d*). The wall of this bulb, which faces the closed end of the point, is next softened and stretched to form a straight taper by means of

a very gentle blow (5-11, *e*, *f*). Then strongly heat the junction of the remaining taper and blow it off (5-11, *g*, *h*). This opens the small bulb. Flare the opening to form the base of the urn (5-11, *i*). When the work has cooled, close the bottom of the urn with a cork and grasp the base by a holder (5-11, *j*). Strongly heat the remaining taper at the point where it joins the straight tube and blow off (5-11, *k*). Bead the ragged edge by means of the flaring tool (5-11, *l*) and complete the urn by adding a pair of symmetrical handles (5-11, *m*).

The swan set

Few trinkets of glass have more charm than sets of miniature swans. Their fabrication involves the bending of tubing and making small tapered bulbs of solid rod. Realism may

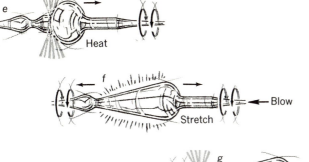

e Heat

f Stretch — Blow

g Heat

h Blow open — Blow

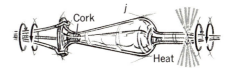

i Flare

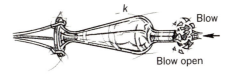

j Cork — Heat

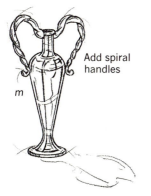

m Add spiral handles

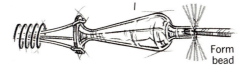

k Blow — Blow open

l Form bead

be accentuated by the use of opaque white tubing. If 15-millimeter tubing is used, a point should be pulled with a body about 2 inches in length. Soften half of the body as shown in Figure 5-12, *a*, and blow an elliptical bulb approximately 1¼ inches in diameter and 2 inches long. Promptly flatten a portion of the bulb by pressing the softened glass against a block of Transite at an angle of approximately 20 degrees (5-12, *b*). The flattened portion should be about 1 inch long. Next, heat the opened taper at a point where it joins the bulb and bend it upward at an angle of about 5 degrees (5-12, *c*). The angle enables you to judge the relative position of the flattened zone during subsequent operations. It complicates the manipulation of the piece slightly because the tapered points are now out of alignment, so the body of the point no longer runs true. This will cause no great inconvenience, because extended rotation will not be required. Next, soften the remaining portion of the body of the point. Uniform heating can be achieved by rotating the work first one way and then the other. Ignore the wobble. The softened zone should extend from the large bulb almost to the point where the closed taper joins the body of the point (5-12, *d*). The head of the bird and its S-shaped neck are now formed by simultaneously blowing, stretching, and quickly bending the S curve. The stretched glass is forced upward and backward in a continuous sweep that must be completed in not more than a second. The whole success of the operation depends upon the speed with which the bend is made (5-12, *e, f, g*). Do not become discouraged if you fail on your first attempt. Two of the most common failures are illustrated by Figures 5-12, *h* and *i*. The form shown in *h* results from applying too much air pressure to stiff glass, or, alternatively, from working so slowly that the glass has cooled, stiffened, and kinked. Much the same result is observed when the neck is first pulled, then blown, and finally bent. All three operations must occur at the same time. The bend is started before the pull is completed. At the opposite extreme is the example in 5-12, *i*, in which the glass has been overheated, stretched, and bent—but with insufficient air pressure.

When the neck has been formed, strongly heat the taper attached to the head of the bird and separate it from the head by lifting the taper upward, a motion that forms the bony structure above the base of the bird's beak (5-12, *j*). Next, seal a yellow rod to the beak position (5-12, *k*). By simultaneously blowing and stretching the molten tip, blow the rod into a tapered bulb that forms the beak (5-12, *l*). After the rod has been burned off (5-12, *m*), fuse to each side of the head the eyes, which must be blown slightly to distribute the added glass so they introduce no abrupt change in thickness (5-12, *n*). Then apply pupils to the eyes (5-12, *o*). Complete the swan by heating the remaining taper strongly at the point where it joins the bulb. Then lift the taper off (don't pull off) to form the bird's tail (5-12, *p*). (Eyes may be put on before the beak if desired.) You can make swans assume a variety of poses by bending the neck in the form of other characteristic attitudes, as illustrated by Plate 7.

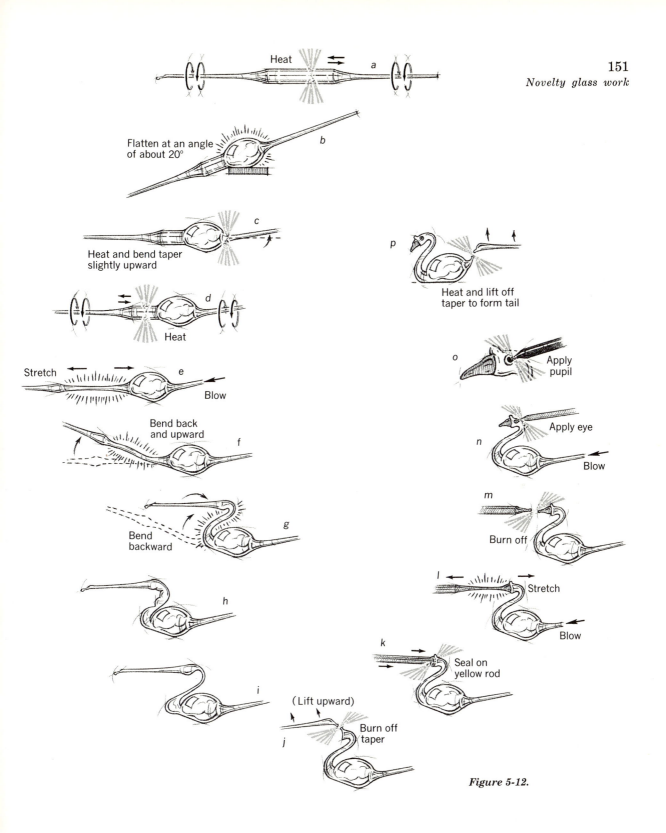

Figure 5-12.

The hurricane lamp

The miniature hurricane lamp illustrates an application of the triple seal. The required materials include a 10-inch length of opaque white tubing of 5 millimeters in diameter, and two 20-inch lengths of 12-millimeter tubing, one of ruby and the other of crystal.

Begin the construction by burning the opaque white tubing in two (Fig. 5-13, *a*). With the file, make a square cut at a distance of about 1 inch from the point where the tube was burned off. The resulting piece will become the candle of the hurricane lamp. Next, use the file to cut off the tip of the candle, but retain as much of the pointed end as possible (5-13, *b*). This step opens the tube so that air can pass through the candle. From the crystal tubing next pull one taper of a point and insert the candle in the body of the point so that its squared end rests against the taper (5-13, *c*). Then pull the second taper and, with a file, cut off the first taper close to the body, but not so close that the resulting opening is larger than the diameter of the candle (5-13, *d*). Next, make a similar point of ruby glass and in the same manner remove one taper (5-13, *e*).

The two points just made will constitute the base and chimney of the lamp. Now join them by a triple seal that includes the candle. Soften the ends of the two major pieces in the edge of the fire, and then, with the crystal piece uppermost, bring the points into contact. The axis of the assembly must make an angle of approximately 45 degrees with respect to the vertical so that the candle will slide into contact with the molten seal. When the pieces fuse, remove the assembly from the fire, blow to preserve the diameter of the seal, and simultaneously rotate the piece so that the candle becomes accurately centered in the crystal tubing (5-13, *f*).

Now form the base of the lamp by blowing a doorknob-shaped bulb in the body of the ruby tubing (5-13, *g, h*). The triple seal must not be permitted to cool during this and subsequent operations. Next, soften a zone in the body of the crystal point adjacent to the triple seal. The zone should be about a tube diameter in length (5-13, *i*). Blow a spherical bulb about 50% larger in diameter than the crystal tubing (5-13, *j*). Next, soften a zone of the crystal tubing about 1¼ inches long that includes the upper hemisphere of the spherical bulb just blown (5-13, *k*) and stretch the softened glass to form a straight taper (5-13, *l*). Seal the handle of the lamp to the base (5-13, *m*). The triple seal may now be cooled slowly. Next, heat and blow off the outer end of the crystal point (5-13, *n, o*), flare the ragged edge of the chimney (5-13, *p*), reheat the flared end, and form a pattern of scallops (5-13, *q*). Clamp the scalloped end of the chimney in a holder, burn off the taper of the ruby point (5-13, *r*), and flatten the base of the completed lamp (5-13, *s*).

153

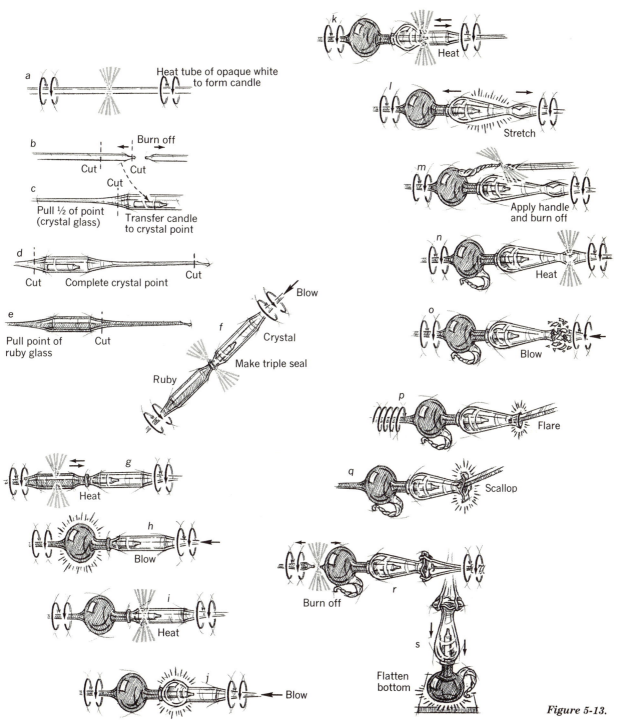

a Heat tube of opaque white to form candle

b Burn off
Cut | Cut

c Cut
Pull ½ of point (crystal glass)
Transfer candle to crystal point
Cut

d Cut Complete crystal point Cut

e Pull point of ruby glass Cut

f Blow
Crystal
Make triple seal
Ruby

g Heat

h Blow

i Heat

j Blow

k Heat

l Stretch

m Apply handle and burn off

n Heat

o Blow

p Flare

q Scallop

r Burn off

s Flatten bottom

Figure 5-13.

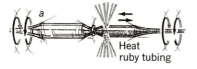

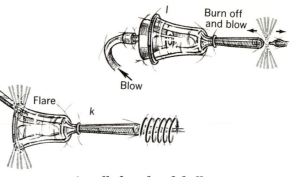

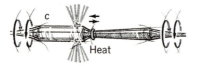

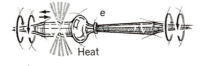

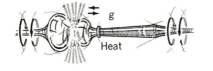

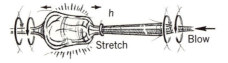

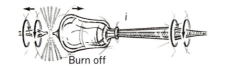

Figure 5-14.

An all-glass hand bell

The final exercise is the fabrication of an all-glass bell and clapper assembly. It incorporates a shape formed by superimposing portions of two bulbs and stretching the junction into a tapering curve. Start by pulling points of 15-millimeter ruby and 20-millimeter crystal glass, cutting off one taper of each and sealing the squarely cut ends as illustrated (Fig. 5-14, *a*.) Heat and stretch the ruby tubing into a straight taper that increases in diameter uniformly toward the outer end (5-14, *b*). The tapered section will become the handle of the bell. Next, soften approximately ¾ inch of the crystal tubing adjacent to the seal and blow a doorknob-shaped bulb about 1 inch in diameter (5-14, *c, d*). Then heat the remaining portion of the crystal tubing and, adjacent to the first bulb, blow a second doorknob-shaped bulb about 1½ inches in diameter (5-14, *e, f*). Heat the zone between the two bulbs. Blowing as necessary, stretch the softened glass into a bell-shaped curve (5-14, *g, h*). Burn off the closed taper close to the bulb and blow the bulb open (5-14, *i, j*). The diameter of the opening should be about ⅜ inch. Soften the opened end and flare the material into the classical bell shape (5-14, *k*). Two or more heats may be required for

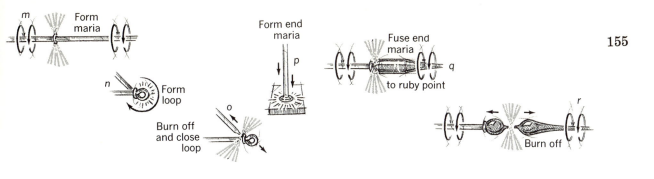

completing the flare. When it is cool, close the open end of the bell by a large cork which has been fitted with a glass tube and a blow hose. Preheat with care and burn off the ruby taper and blow the closed end of the handle into a hemisphere (5-14, *l*). Anneal the completed bell.

The clapper assembly is made in two parts: the clapper rod and hammer, and a linkage for supporting the clapper in the bell. Make the linkage first. Use 2- or 3-millimeter crystal rod. Form a maria in the middle of a convenient length of the rod (5-14, *m*) and, without permitting the glass to cool, heat a ¾-inch length of rod adjacent to either side of the maria and make a loop. The internal diameter of the loop should be about 7 millimeters, or slightly larger (5-14, *n*). Burn off the excess rod, heat the end of the loop strongly, and, with tweezers, bend the helical shape into a true loop. Seal the free end to the maria (5-14, *o*). Let the completed piece cool slowly.

Next, from rod of the same size, form an end maria (5-14, *p*) and seal the maria to the squarely burned off end of a ruby point (5-14, *q*). Burn off the body of the point about one tube diameter distant from the maria (5-14, *r*) and rotate the small resulting bulb in the fire until trapped air expands the glass into a true sphere

(5-14, *s*). When the bulb has cooled, cut the rod and form an open hook in the end (5-14, *t*). The distance between the hook and bulb should be made slightly less than the depth of the bell. The assembled clapper will then swing free when the completed bell rests on a flat surface. The correct length of the clapper assembly, which includes the linkage piece first made (see 5-14, *o*), must be estimated by eye. Next slip the hook through the loop of the linkage piece, heat the outer portion of the hook, and bend it into a closed loop (5-14, *u*). When performing this operation, remember to warm the linkage piece slowly to avoid cracking the maria. Complete the bell by cutting the rod of the linkage piece about ¼ inch from the maria. Coat the resulting stub with epoxy cement and slip it into the opening of the inverted bell handle (5-14, *v*).

With the completion of the bell, you graduate from the status of beginner. You are equipped with all of the essential skills of the novelty glass blower and need not hesitate to tackle more complicated projects. Some of these are suggested by the examples in Plates 1 through 8. Numerous others will be suggested by the objects and living forms that surround you. Remember, if you can mold it in clay, you can blow it in glass.

Scientific glassware

Although the fabrication of scientific glassware entails essentially the same skills as novelty work, it differs somewhat in concept and general approach. For example, the use to which an apparatus will be put, rather than aesthetic considerations, largely dictates its size and shape. This is not to suggest that a well-made piece need be unattractive. On the contrary, leading art museums have on more than one occasion exhibited chemical apparatus in support of the thesis that pleasing forms can arise from purely functional design. The same approach guides the selection of raw materials. Glasses used in apparatus are chosen for such physical properties as mechanical strength, chemical inertness, and resistance to thermal shock. In addition, designs frequently specify materials other than glass: ceramics; enamels; and natural substances, such as mica and a variety of metals in forms that include electrodes, contacts, springs, reeds, supports, and torsion fibers. Finally, in devices that measure some quantity, such as a simple graduate, or in those that alter a velocity, such as a vacuum pump, the precise control of dimensions becomes a critical factor.

These requirements can be met by careful planning. Before undertaking the construction of an apparatus, the experienced craftsman learns how the device is supposed to work and identifies its critical parts and dimensions. A working plan is developed and the operations to be performed are listed in sequence. In general, inner parts are assembled first and progressively enclosed by outer parts. Full-scale outline drawings of the more complex parts, as well as of the complete assembly, are made on asbestos paper. Hot parts may be placed directly on the drawings for checking dimensions. Alternative working procedures may be possible. Select the procedure that seems best and try it. Experience thus gained may suggest modifications. If so, rewrite the plan and try again. This approach will conserve not only glass but your temper and, if you are a beginner, your confidence in your growing skill.

The exercises in this section have been arranged roughly in order of increasing complexity. Having constructed the series of pieces, you should have no difficulty in improvising a working plan for other designs. Unless specified to the contrary, all parts are to be made of Corning 7740 Pyrex or equivalent glass and are to be worked in oxygen-enriched fires. Didymium goggles should be worn when the glass is heated. They will protect your eyes from the blinding flare-off. Borosilicate glass may feel strange during your first hour of practice. It hardens in less time than soda-lime or lead glass and must therefore be worked promptly. Even so, don't hurry. You will have ample time to complete the basic operations. If the glass should become stiff before an operation is complete, simply return it to the fire. Nothing will be lost but time. Borosilicate glasses up to 3 millimeters in thickness require little if any preheating. If a piece should crack, preheat the work uniformly in the vicinity of the break, apply a needle flame to the inner end of the crack and sweep it slowly toward the outer end. Usually the crack will close beneath the flame as though the torch were the slide of a zipper.

A stirring rod

When commencing work with strange glass always try out a length of rod in the fire, preferably a piece 6 to 8 millimeters in diameter. Plunge an end of Pyrex rod directly into the flames. Observe the color as the glass heats, the time required for it to become fire-polished, and the length of time the softened portion remains plastic after the piece has been removed from the fire. Heat each end until surface tension pulls the glass into a hemisphere. The product is a stirring rod.

A glass propeller

Make a second stirring rod, but this time continue heating the second end until about a centimeter of the glass has become plastic. From it make an end maria. Return the completed maria to the fire. When the glass has become plastic, cut the maria in two at opposite points on the diameter by means of a pair of tin snips or a wire cutter as illustrated (Fig. 6-1, *a*). Reheat the glass. Then, by means of tweezers fitted with tips in the form of flat plates, grasp the halves of the maria and twist them to an angle of about 20 degrees to form a small propeller (6-1, *b*). Next, hold the completed propeller blades in the flame of a Bunsen burner until a pale violet flare-off is seen (6-1, *c*). (Do not wear didymium goggles during this exami-

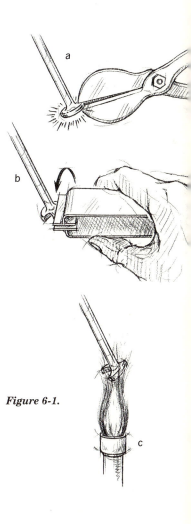

Figure 6-1.

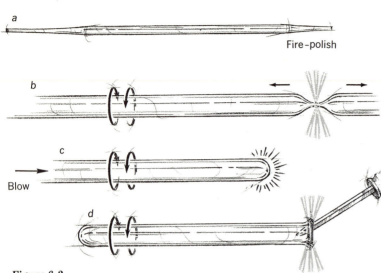

Figure 6-2.

from the bulb and the other about 3 centimeters distant. Fire-polish the cut ends (Fig. 6-2, *a*). Make the test tube of 20-millimeter stock. First burn off one end of a 30-centimeter length of tubing (6-2, *b*). Blow the end to hemispherical shape. Be sure to remove the bleb (6-2, *c*). When the work has cooled, cut the tubing at a point about 15 centimeters from the closed end. With the flaring tool, make a bead approximately 2 millimeters thick around the open end (6-2, *d*). Anneal both ends in the Bunsen flame.

Wash bottle

No chemical laboratory would be complete without a dispenser for distilled water. The device consists of a 1-liter flask, a two-hole rubber stopper, and a pair of specially shaped 6-millimeter glass tubes as illustrated (Fig. 6-3). Air blown into the flask by the mouth forces water from the nozzle of the longer tube. Make the longer tube first. In a piece of tubing approximately 40 centimeters long, pull a constriction with uniform walls about 27 centimeters from one end. Cut the constriction in the middle and lightly fire-polish the end. Then cut the tubing about 3 centimeters from the constricted end, and fire-polish both cut ends. This completes the nozzle. Next, at a point about 5 centimeters from the cut end of the tube, make an angle of approximately 30-degree bend. The radius of the bend as measured at the center of the tubing should be about 3 centimeters. Fire-polish the unconstricted end of the tube. Finally, connect the

Figure 6-3.

nation.) Place the hot end on asbestos paper to cool. (The Bunsen flame anneals the glass.) When the piece has cooled, wrap an inch or so of the rod near the rounded end with a single layer of adhesive tape. When the taped end is chucked in a vertical drill press, the piece becomes a motor-driven stirring rod, one that is relatively inert chemically.

A *pipette and test tube*

Articles such as pipettes and test tubes are so inexpensive that it does not pay to make them except as practice exercises. Making them can be an effective means for acquiring the "feel" of borosilicate glass, however, particularly during the first hour that you work with the material. To make the pipette, first pull a point in 8-millimeter tubing. With the file, cut one taper approximately 6 centimeters

nozzle to the short end of the bent tube with a short length of rubber tubing. (The flexible nozzle permits the stream of water to be directed as desired).

Next, cut a second tube to a length of 16 centimeters, bend a V of 135 degrees at a point about 7 centimeters from one end. Fire-polish both ends. Select a rubber stopper that has been perforated for 6-millimeter glass tubing, and wet the perforations and the glass. Assemble the dispenser as illustrated. (*Always wear a thick leather glove when pushing glass tubing through the perforations of rubber stoppers. The glass may shatter when forced into the rubber and cause a bad cut.* Grasp the tubing close to the stopper.)

Funnels

To acquire the "feel" of borosilicate glass during an extended flaring operation make up a pair of funnels, one conventional and the other of the thistle-tube type. Stopper one end of a piece of 12-millimeter heavy-walled tubing about 40 centimeters long. Near the center make a constriction 8 millimeters in diameter at the narrowest point. By stretching the glass and blowing as required, convert the larger portion of the constriction into a straight taper, as illustrated (Fig. 6-4, *a, b, c*). Cut the tubing at a point about 50 millimeters beyond the end of the straight taper (6-4, *d*). Flare the end just cut to a diameter of 50 millimeters to make a cone of approximately 45 angular degrees (6-4, *e*). Return the edge of the flare to the fire and form a 3-mil-

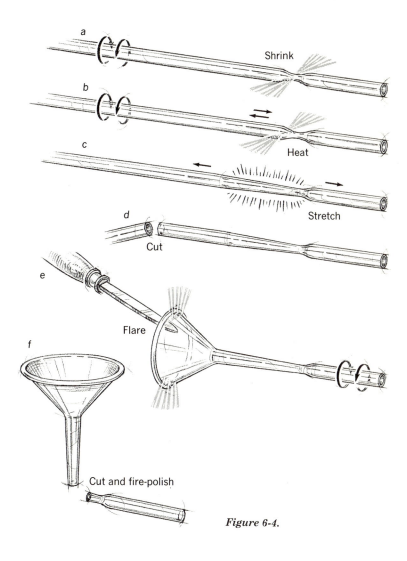

Figure 6-4.

A cylindrical graduate

Small graduates and similar vessels used for measuring the volume of fluids make little demand on the skill of the glass blower. Such vessels must be calibrated, however, an operation that requires the measurement of the volume in precise intervals as well as the placement of permanent markings on the glass, such as fiducial lines, numerals, and lettering. The fabrication of a cylindrical graduate demonstrates the art of marking glass.

Make the graduate 10 milliliters in capacity of 15-millimeter tubing. First, form a maria in the middle of a convenient length of the tubing (Fig. 6-6, *a*). Burn off the tubing close to the maria on one side and remove the bleb (6-6, *b*). Reheat the tip and work the glass to uniform wall thickness by alternately blowing and shrinking. Then press the end squarely against a sheet of asbestos paper that is supported on a flat surface of Transite (6-6, *c*). The tube is now closed by a flat flange that serves as the base of the graduate. Anneal the base. Cut the tubing at a point about 12 centimeters from the base, then grasp the maria in a wire holder, and flare the open end to a diameter of about 18 millimeters (6-6, *d*). Heat one edge of the flare and, with the flaring tool, pull the molten glass into a spout that protrudes about 6 millimeters (6-6, *e*). Stand the vessel upright on a smooth flat surface. If it tends to wobble, make a slurry of No. 120 carborundum grit mixed with water and grind the bottom of the vessel against a piece of ¼-inch plate glass. Simply grasp the tubing immediately above the maria, press it into

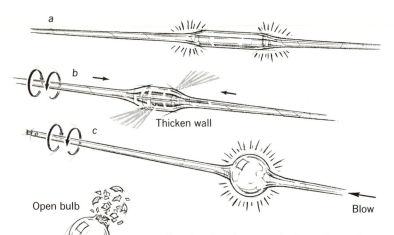

a

b — Thicken wall

c — Blow

Open bulb

d

e — Flare

f — Cut and fire-polish

Figure 6-5.

limeter bead around the edge. Complete the funnel by grasping the top in a wire holder and fire-polishing the end of the spout (6-4, *f*).

Make the thistle tube funnel by first pulling a point with thick, broad tapers. (To make the tapers thick and broad, heat about twice the normal length of glass until plastic but stiffer than normal, just hot enough that you can make a pull of about half the normal length.) Open the tip of one taper for blowing (Fig. 6-5, *a*). Heat the body of the taper, alternately blowing and returning the glass to the fire until the wall thickens to about three times its normal weight (6-5, *b*). Blow a spherical bulb approximately 35 millimeters in diameter (6-5, *c*). Burn off the closed taper, remove the bleb, and blow out the area formerly occupied by the taper (6-5, *d*). Flare the opening to a diameter of approximately 25 millimeters (6-5, *e*), and make a bead around the flared edge, as illustrated (6-5, *f*).

the slurry with a force of about 1 pound, and grind with an elliptical motion (6-6, *f*). From 20 to 30 strokes should suffice to remove all high spots.

To calibrate the graduate, stand the washed and dried vessel on an analytical balance that is capable of supporting a load of at least 500 grams and that is sensitive to a centigram. Add sufficient weight to the empty pan to balance the beam. Then add exactly 1 gram of distilled water to the graduate. (One gram of water is equal to one milliliter.) Then, with an artist's brush, from which all hairs but one have been removed, apply a thin line of india ink to the glass at the level of the *bottom* of the meniscus formed by the water. Similarly calibrate the vessel to 10 milliliters by adding the second gram of water, marking the meniscus, and so on. Finally, divide each milliliter into 10 equal intervals.

The markings may now be made permanent either by etching, enameling, or a combination of both. To etch the piece, first warm the glass to a temperature of about 180 degrees Fahrenheit (82°C) and coat the entire surface, both inside and outside, with a mixture composed of equal parts of beeswax and ceresin wax. Let the glass cool to room temperature. Then, with the ink marks as guides, cut fiducial lines through the wax with a steel needlepoint mounted in the handle of an artist's brush and similarly cut appropriate numerals as illustrated (6-6, *g*). If frosted markings are desired, invert the engraved markings over a shallow container of hydrofluoric acid for 2 hours. Fumes from the acid will attack the exposed glass. All spaces between the edge of

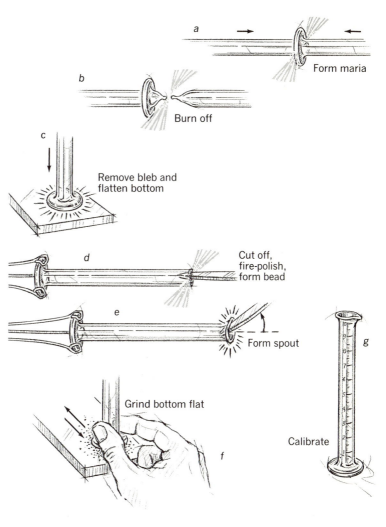

Figure 6-6.

the vessel containing the acid and the graduate should be closed with thin sheets of wax of the kind used by dentists for preparing models of dentures.

Alternatively, hydrofluoric etching ink of the kind described in Section I may be applied directly to the glass. This technique yields polished grooves that are difficult to see. They may be filled with an opaque enamel. If desired, enamel may be applied directly to the surface of unetched glass. This results in raised markings. Enamel is a form of glass that softens at relatively low temperature. It is made in a wide range of colors and consists of a flux containing lead oxide, boric oxide, silica (plus minor amounts of other oxides that increase the resistance of the material to the action of acids and alkalis), and selected metallic oxides that impart the color. Enamel is sold in the form of a finely milled powder. Like all glasses, it expands and contracts with changes in temperature. Unfortunately, no enamel has yet been compounded with a thermal coefficient of expansion which matches that of the borosilicate glasses. To minimize the strain that always develops when enamel is fired to borosilicate glass, the color is applied in the thinnest film that provides good visibility and it is fired only to a semigloss. If a thick coating is applied, or if the enamel is fired to a high gloss, the color will crack or craze upon cooling to room temperature. Because the surface of fired enamel is the surface of the glass, the surface of the piece is thus crazed and is weakened accordingly. The borosilicate glasses can nonetheless be enameled successfully by (1) applying the color as thinly as possible, (2) firing the enamel only to a semiluster, and (3) not refiring the ware. The coefficents of thermal expansion of most enamels approach those of the soft glasses.

For application to glass, the powdered enamels are mixed with an oily vehicle. The mixture may be a thin paste or a thick fluid, depending upon whether it is to be applied by printing, by stenciling, or with a pen. In quantity production the application is frequently made by the silk screen process, a form of stenciling. A relatively viscous mixture is best for filling in the depressions of an etched piece. The application is made by rubbing the color over the grooves and wiping off the excess. The piece is fired to a temperature of 530 to 645 degrees Centigrade (988° to 1193°F) until the enamel's surface becomes semiglossy. The authors prefer red enamel No. 2330 in squeegee oil as prepared by B. F. Drakenfeld and Company, New York, New York. For applying enamel to an unetched surface, we use the procedures recommended by Ray Andrews, director of research of the B. F. Drakenfeld Company. Lines are drawn on the clean glass by a pen equipped with a crow-quill nib. The "ink" consists of two parts of No. 2330 powdered enamel mixed with one part of ethylene glycol. The mixture is ground in a small ball mill to assure the dispersion of lumps.

For applying numerals and lettering, we use an alternate procedure, also recommended by Mr. Andrews, that involves a rubber stamp. A film of boiled linseed oil is first applied to a sheet of plate glass by means of a brayer. The oil film is then picked up from the plate glass by the rubber stamp and applied to the glass object. Powdered enamel is next picked up by a tuft of absorbent cotton and dusted on the oil impression. Particles of color adhere to the tacky oil and produce remarkably sharp lettering. Firing is done in two stages. The temperature is first raised to 400 degrees Centigrade (752°F) and maintained for 15 minutes. This evaporates the printing oil. The work is then heated to about 600 degrees Centigrade (1112°F) and maintained at this temperature until the enamel takes on the semigloss finish. Another satisfactory color for marking borosilicate glassware is Drakenfeld black, No. 2949. It is applied and fired by the same procedures.

The closed-end manometer

To the laboratory that operates a vacuum system the closed-end manometer is an indispensable instrument for measuring pressures between 1 and 10 torrs. (Standard atmospheric pressure at sea level is equal to 760 torrs.) The device consists of a capilary U tube closed at one end. The bore may be about 3 millimeters. The bend at the bottom of the U and the full length of the closed arm are filled with clean, triple-distilled mercury. When the system has been evacuated below 0.1. torr, the mercury seeks its own level, and stands midway in both arms of the U. When the vacuum is broken, air exerts pressure on the mercury in the open arm and drives the metal upward against the closed end. If the vacuum is broken abruptly, the metal may strike the closed end with sufficient force to break the glass. To prevent this it is customary to make a constriction about ¼ millimeter wide near the bottom of the closed arm. This narrowed portion of the bore limits the velocity of the rising column of metal and reduces the impact to a safe value.

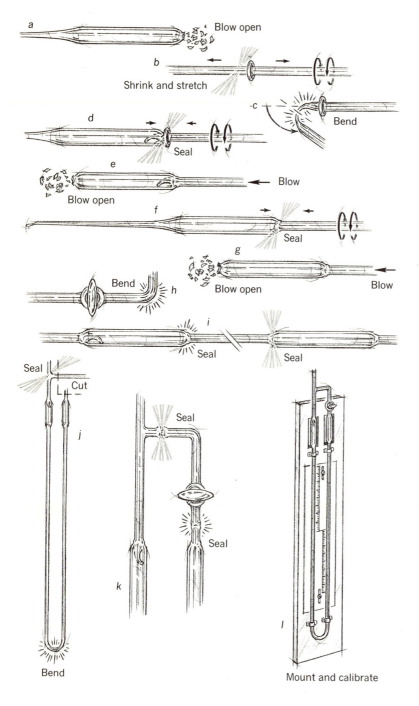

Figure 6-8.

to which the arms of the U are sealed may be made of 20-millimeter tubing approximately 15 centimeters long. The spacing between the arms is not critical, although it should be adequate for sealing the stopcock in place.

Make all of the parts before starting the assembly. Pull points for the two bulbs, burn off one taper, and open one end of each bulb as illustrated (Fig. 6-8, *a*). Next, make a maria in a convenient length of 8-millimeter tubing (6-8, *b*), draw the tubing to a point on one side of the maria, bend into a broad U, and cut in the narrowest zone (6-8, *c*). Attach the curved tube and maria to one of the bulbs and complete the triple seal (6-8, *d*). Blow an opening in the opposite end of the bulb in preparation for making a butt seal between the bulb and a length of 8-millimeter tubing (6-8, *e*). Seal a 20-centimeter length of 8-millimeter tubing to the opening of the second bulb (6-8, *f*) and blow out the opposite end in preparation for sealing to 8-millimeter tubing (6-8, *g*). Next, make a right-angled bend in one outlet tube of a stopcock (6-8, *h*). The outlet tubes of the stopcock should have a diameter of approximately 8 millimeters. When sealing stopcocks, remove the plug and clean the glass thoroughly. Close the openings of the shell with a pair of corks of the same size. The large end of the tapered shell opening should be closed by the large end of a cork. When heating the outlet tube, keep the flame at least 2 centimeters from the shell. When heat must be applied beneath a stopcock, always shield the shell with a sheet of asbestos paper.

Next, seal the two bulbs to a

straight length of tubing that will be bent into the arms of the U. Mark the center of the tubing with chalk, heat, and complete the bend. Seal a side arm to the inlet about 10 centimeters above the bulb and cut off the tubing about 2 centimeters from the seal, as illustrated (6-8, *j*). Finally, cut the outlet tubes of the stopcock to fit and seal into the system. The seal between the stopcock and bulb should be made first. The flexibility of the rigid tubing permits the bent portion of the stopcock tubing to be manipulated for completing the second seal (6-8, *k*).

The manometer may be mounted on a base of plywood by U clamps. Shims of sheet rubber should be placed between the glass and metal clamps. A scale of metric paper may be cemented to a sheet metal base containing slots for mounting screws. The slots permit the scale to be moved up and down for adjusting the zero point to the level of the fluid.

The McLeod gauge

An even more sensitive instrument for measuring low gas pressures is the McLeod gauge, essentially a U tube containing a reservoir of known volume from which gas is compressed by mercury into the closed end of the manometer. The pressure resulting causes a sensible difference in the level of mercury in the two arms of the U. Such gauges may be designed for measuring gas pressures from 10 torrs to a millionth of a torr. The McLeod gauge measures absolute pressure and therefore is used as the standard for calibrating gauges of other types, such as thermocouple and ionization gauges. It is a reliable instrument for measuring permanent gases, such as oxygen, nitrogen and the noble gases, but the presence of condensable gases, such as water vapor and the vapors of pump oils, degrades its performance.

A number of schemes have been devised for manipulating the mercury that is used to trap and compress the gas in the reservoir. One simple design that is convenient for measuring the pressure of helium and neon in a gas laser tube is illustrated in Figure 6-9. In this gauge, mercury is transferred between the two bulbs by rotating the instrument in the vertical plane. In the standby position, the gauge is horizontal with the larger bulb at the bottom. The center arm of the device is connected through flexible tubing to the vacuum system. Gas pressure in the gauge then equals that in the system. When the gauge is rotated to the vertical position, mercury flows under gravity from the large bulb into the smaller one (Fig. 6-9, *b*). All gas in the gauge beyond the seal of the center arm is trapped by the descending column of mercury. Accordingly, the gas is compressed into the closed-end capillary on top of the smaller bulb. The closed-end capillary and the center arm of the gauge constitute a manometer; the difference in the level at which mercury stands in the two arms is an absolute measure of the pressure in the system. The pressure range of the gauge is determined by the ratio of the volume of the smaller bulb to the volume of the closed-end capillary. A McLeod gauge made of standard wall tubing 13 millimeters

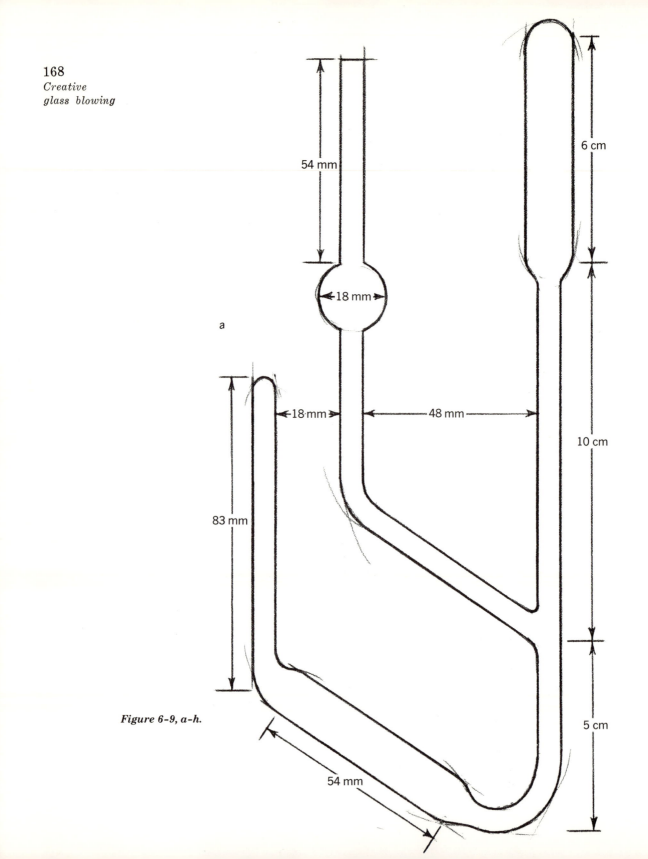

54 mm

18 mm

a

18 mm

48 mm

83 mm

6 cm

10 cm

5 cm

Figure 6-9, a–h.

54 mm

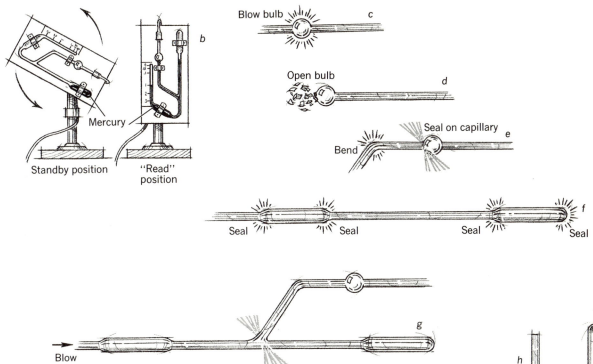

Blow bulb   c

Open bulb   d

Seal on capillary   e
Bend

Seal   Seal   Seal   Seal   f

Blow   g

Standby position   "Read" position
Mercury   b

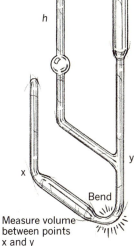

h

x   y

Bend

Measure volume
between points
x and y

in diameter and capillary tubing of 2-millimeter bore will have a useful range extending from 3 torrs to .01 torr, if made to the dimensions specified by Figure 6-9, *a*.

To make the gauge, first draw the layout (6-9, *a*) full scale on a sheet of asbestos paper. Pull two points in 13-millimeter standard wall tubing: one with a 54-millimeter bulb and the other with a 60-millimeter bulb. At the end of a convenient length of 8-millimeter standard wall tubing blow a spherical bulb of 18 millimeters in outside diameter (6-9, *c*).

Check the dimensions of each part, as made, against the layout. Open the spherical bulb and to it seal a 20-centimeter length of capillary (6-9,

d, e) and make the bend as indicated on the layout. Next, remove a taper and blow an opening in the 54-millimeter bulb. To this opening, seal a 20-centimeter length of capillary (6-9, *f*). Similarly, seal a 20-centimeter length of capillary to the 6-centimeter bulb. Remove the remaining taper of this bulb and blow the end into a hemisphere. Seal the central arm of the manometer to a 29-centimeter length of capillary at a point 10 centimeters from the 6-centimeter bulb as indicated in 6-9, *g* and on the layout. Finally heat and make the bend indicated (6-9, *h*).

Because the structure that has been made in this way is fragile, me-

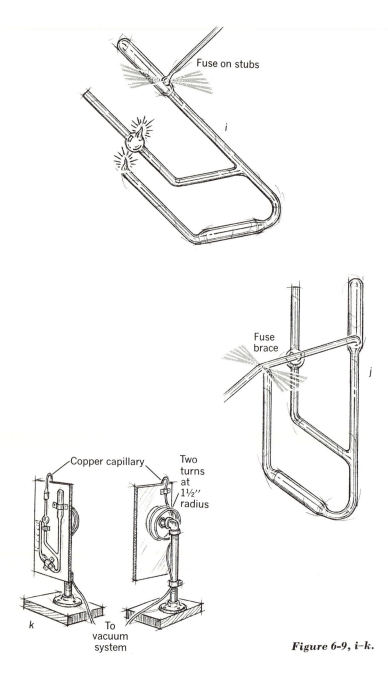

chanically, it should be braced. Braces may be added. First, heat and close the *end* of the capillary of the 54-millimeter bulb. In making the closure, pull a bleb from the capillary and bend it at a right angle with respect to the plane of the gauge so that it stands out about 8 millimeters. The brace will be fused to this stub (6-9, *i*). Fuse a similar stub to the 18-millimeter bulb. Finally, fuse the end of a 6-millimeter rod to the 6-centimeter bulb, and bend it into position for sealing first to the stub on the 18-millimeter bulb and next to the stub at the end of the 83-millimeter capillary, as illustrated (6-9, *j*). Anneal all seals and bends. (If the instrument is made of soft glass, the entire gauge must be annealed in an oven.)

The completed glasswork is mounted as illustrated (6-9, *k*). The mounting includes a scale plotted in torr that is placed adjacent to the closed capillary, the zero graduation coinciding with the closed end. Graduations representing higher pressures are plotted at appropriate distances below the zero graduation. Only two quantities must be determined to compute the locations of the graduations: (1) the volume of the closed capillary plus the volume of the bulb to which it is attached and the volume of the capillary that connects this bulb to the middle leg of the gauge; (2) the cross-sectional area of the closed capillary.

To measure the volume, first weigh the glassware (to a tenth of a gram), then fill the volume to be determined with mercury, and weigh it again. Subtract the weight of the glass from

Figure 6-9, i–k.

that of the glass and the mercury combined to determine the net weight of the mercury. Divide the net weight of the mercury by .0135 to determine the volume of the glassware in cubic millimeters. The cross-sectional area of a 2-millimeter capillary is approximately 3 square millimeters.

To determine the distance in millimeters at which mercury will stand below the zero graduation for any pressure, first multiply the volume just measured by the given pressure. Then divide this product by the cross-sectional area of the closed capillary. The square root of this quotient is equal to the distance in millimeters. For example, assume that the position of the graduation is desired for a pressure of 1.5 torr, that the volume of the closed capillary and its associated bulb and connecting tubing is 4500 cubic millimeters, and that the cross-sectional area of the closed capillary is 3 square millimeters. The distance between the zero graduation and the desired graduation is then equal to the square root of 1.5 x 4500/3, or 47.4 millimeters. To compute the entire scale, make a list of selected pressure intervals, such as .1, .5, 1, 1.5, and so on, and do the arithmetic. Plot the resulting distances in millimeters as graduations on a cardboard scale and cement it to the closed capillary with the zero indication adjacent to the closed end. If the volume of the closed capillary, its associated bulb, and connecting tubing is approximately 4500 cubic millimeters, a 75-millimeter scale will span the range of pressure from 0 to 3 torrs.

A gas-air mixer

Serviceable mixers for combining the gas and air supply for a glass fire can be made of glass. When provided with air compressed to approximately 1 pound per square inch (equivalent to the weight of a column of water 27.7 inches in height), the device will deliver fuel to the burners at a pressure of 6 ounces or more (equivalent to about 10.4 inches of water). The precise pressure at which fuel is delivered, as well as the ratio of gas to air, is controlled by needle valves or stopcocks inserted in the gas and air inlets to the device. The capacity of the mixer is fixed by the diameter of the air jet and the small end of the venturi tube. In an appropriate mixer for supplying fuel to a burner consisting of a single No. 3151 JC glass fire, which has a fuel capacity of 1825 Btu per hour, the air jet should have a diameter of about 1 millimeter and the diameter of the venturi inlet would be about 4 millimeters.

The diameter of the jet is made proportionately larger for supplying burners of greater capacity. In the case of a crossfire that uses a total of ten No. 3151 glass fires with a capacity of 18,250 Btu per hour, for example, the diameter of the jet would be increased to approximately 3 millimeters and the venturi inlet to about 9 millimeters. The dimensions are not particularly critical. Errors of as much as 50% can be tolerated.

To fabricate a mixer of this type, first make the usual full-scale outline drawing of the device, as depicted in Figure 6-10, *j*. Then pull a point of ap-

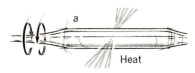

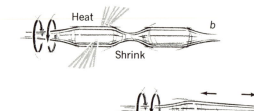

Heat

propriate size (6-10, *a*) and shrink the bulb in the middle (6-10, *b*). The inside diameter of the narrowest zone of the constriction should equal the size of the desired venturi opening. Soften the glass on one side of the constriction and pull it to form the conical portion of the venturi, which is equal in length to approximately five times the diameter of the narrow end (6-10, *c*). Next, reheat the glass beyond the end of the venturi and pull into a tube with straight walls equal in diameter to the large end of the venturi (6-10, *d, e*). Convert the end of the straight portion into a conventional hose connection, burn off, and open as illustrated (6-10, *f*). This completes the shell of the mixer.

The nozzle is made by first forming a maria in a convenient length of 8- or 10-millimeter tubing (depending upon the desired capacity of the unit). Make a constriction 2 centimeters beyond the maria (6-10, *g*). When the constriction is cut, the portion attached to the maria becomes the nozzle. The diameter of the nozzle must be judged by eye when the constriction is pulled. Do not fire-polish the tip of the nozzle; the softened

Figure 6-10.

glass may contract and reduce the diameter of the opening.

Now seal the maria to the shell of the mixer. If the layout was followed closely when the parts were made, the tip of the nozzle will extend just inside the inlet of the venturi and provide support for the nozzle when the triple seal is made. The softened glass will tend to sag under gravity but, by keeping an eye on the venturi and rotating the work, you can keep the nozzle centered in the opening of the venturi. If this operation proves to be too difficult, support the tip of the nozzle by means of a holder made of a wooden dowel with a stiff wire projecting into the nozzle (6-10, *h*). Complete the piece by sealing a side arm to the shell for admitting gas (6-10, *i*) and convert both this side arm and the air inlet into serrated hose connections (6-10, *j*).

A simple condenser

The separation of substances according to differences in vapor pressure by the process of distillation has been a favored procedure of the chemical

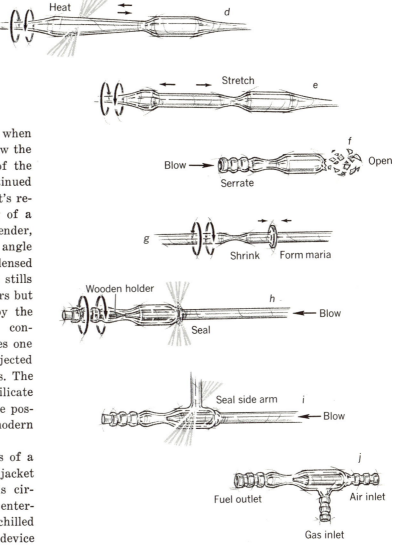

laboratory almost from the days when the first alchemist set out to brew the elixir of life. Up to the turn of the present century glass stills continued to take the form of the alchemist's retort—a simple boiler consisting of a glass bulb that opened into a slender, tapered spout bent at a right angle close to the bulb. Vapors condensed in the air-cooled spout. Modern stills still employ glass bulbs for boilers but the spout has been displaced by the more effective water-cooled condenser, a device that incorporates one or more triple seals that are subjected to widely differing temperatures. The high resistance of the borosilicate materials to thermal shock made possible the construction of the modern glass condensers.

The simple condenser consists of a straight tube surrounded by a jacket through which cooling water is circulated (Fig. 6-11, *d*). Vapors entering the tube condense on the chilled walls. The effectiveness of the device varies directly with the length of the cooled tube, a dimension that is fixed by the nature of the materials to be distilled. Normally, the cooled tube is attached at the ends to the sur-

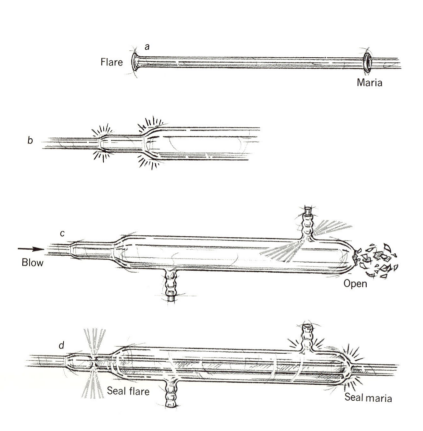

Figure 6-11.

(Fig. 6-11, *a*). Make the water jacket of 25-millimeter tubing and to one end seal a length of 13-millimeter tubing. Cut this tubing to a length of about 3 centimeters and to it seal a convenient length of 8-millimeter tubing (6-11 *b*). Complete the jacket by adding the hose connections, closing the large end, and blowing in it an opening about 11 millimeters in diameter (6-11, *c*). Assemble the inner tubing and the water jacket and make the triple seal. Blow the seal to a nicely rounded contour. The flare of the center tube will rest against and be supported by the inner wall of the 13-millimeter section of the jacket while the triple seal is made. Finally, make the ring seal. Both sides of this seal must be blown. You can accomplish this by fitting the blowing hose with a **Y** connection. Connect one arm of the **Y** to one of the hose connections and the other arm to the 8-millimeter tubing. Stopper the remaining hose connection and the other end of the 8-millimeter tubing. Anneal the completed piece.

The Graham condenser

The amount of heat liberated by a vapor when condensing to the liquid phase varies with the nature of the substance. Water vapor, for example, releases more heat than the vapor of alcohol. For this reason the cooling tube of a condenser designed for distilling water must be made longer than one designed for distilling alcohol, indeed, awkwardly long. There is no such size problem with the Graham

rounding jacket by means of triple seals. We have simplified the structure by substituting a ring seal for one of the triple seals.

Having made an outline drawing of the apparatus, form a maria about 12 millimeters in diameter in the middle of a 40-centimeter length of 8-millimeter tubing and flare one end to a diameter of about 10 millimeters

condenser, which contains a condensing tube in the form of a helix.

The sequence of operations for making a Graham condenser is begun by forming the coil, as described in Section IV. Add a maria and flare to the straight ends of the helix, as illustrated (Fig. 6-12, *a*). Then prepare the water jacket of appropriate tubing for housing the coil. Close one end and blow an opening through which the coil is threaded (6-12, *b*). The assembled coil is supported by a holder of asbestos tape and inserted in the open end of the water jacket. Then make the triple seal and add the adjacent hose connection *before* the seal cools (6-12 *c*). It is always desirable to install water connections close enough to the ends of the coil that as many turns as possible are exposed to running water. Triple seals are severely stressed when reheated because the fire acts only against the outer parts of the glass. For this reason water connections or other parts that must be installed close to a ring seal should be added before the triple seal cools. The hose connections may be prepared in advance and kept hot over a separate burner while the triple seal is being made. When the connection has been sealed, remove the asbestos holder, shrink the water jacket into contact with the flare at the end of the coil (as indicated by the dotted lines in 6-12, *c*), burn off the excess glass of the jacket, and blow the opening at the end of the coil. Add the second hose connection (6-12, *d*) and complete the remaining triple seal by adding a convenient length of tubing that matches the coil (6-12, *e*).

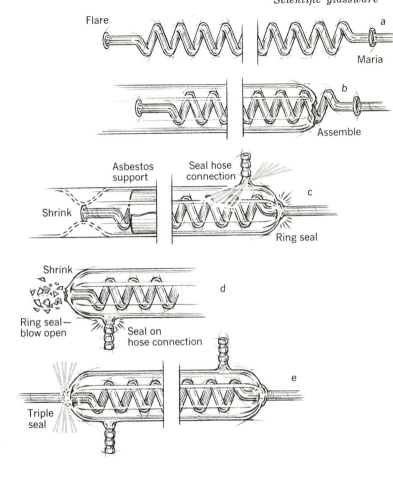

Figure 6-12.

Glass-to-metal seals

Frequent occasion arises for sealing glass to metal. For example, a handy dissection needle can be quickly improvised by pushing the eye-end of a heavy darning needle into the molten end of a glass rod. Holders of various kinds can be similarly made of glass rod and short lengths of wire or slivers of sheet metal. Almost any kind of glass and most of the base metals, if not more than a millimeter in diameter, can be so joined. The bonds have reasonable strength. In general, however, the thermal coefficient of expansion of metal greatly exceeds that of glass. Copper, for example, expands 167 parts in 10 million for each degree Centigrade of temperature rise, whereas soft glass, such as Corning code 0080, expands 92 parts in 10 million for each degree, and Pryex 7740 expands only 32.5 parts. As the joint cools, the metal contracts more than the glass and tends either to pull away from the bond or to set up a severe strain in the glass. A steel rod 1 millimeter in diameter, if sealed to soft glass, would contract about 5 microns upon cooling from the annealing temperature of soft glass to room temperature. Although the seal would doubtless appear mechanically strong, the chances are great that the metal would pull away from the glass, a matter of no consequence in the case of a dissection needle. But a seal even slightly cracked could not be tolerated in an incandescent lamp bulb or other application involving high vacuum. The joint would leak. For sealing leads or other metal parts into vessels that must be exhausted and maintained at low pressure, the thermal coefficients of expansion of the metal and glass must match within about 1 part per million. Moreover, when

the seal is made, the molten glass must "wet" the metal. This is an easy requirement. The metal need only be oxidized slightly at its point of contact with the glass. The glass dissolves the oxide and in effect unites with the metal in a smooth chemical transition. The two materials are compatible because glass is composed largely of metallic oxides.

The thermal coefficients of expansion of only two metals approximately match those of common glasses. Platinum, which expands 90 parts per 10 million per degree Centigrade, is an excellent match with the soft glasses such as soda lime and lead that expand from about 87 to 92 parts per 10 million. Tungsten expands 48 parts per 10 million per degree Centigrade, compared with Corning 7740 Pyrex at 32.5 parts and 7720 Pyrex (better known as "Nonex") at 36 parts per 10 million per degree Centigrade. Uranium glass (Corning No. 3320) expands 40 parts per 10 million per degree Centigrade. As suggested by these data, platinum of any size can be sealed directly to the soft glasses to form a vacuum-tight joint. A similar seal can be made between tungsten and either 7720 glass or 3320 glass. These glasses, in turn, seal to 7740 Pyrex. Oddly enough, copper, which expands 168 parts per 10 million parts per degree Centigrade, can be sealed to any glass. This is made possible by the great ductility of copper. Plastic flow in the metal relieves the stress of the cooling seal before it reaches the breaking point of the glass. The technique of making such seals was developed in the early 1920's by William G. Housekeeper of the Western Electric Company.

Subsequently, a number of alloys with thermal coefficients of expansion that closely approximate those of specially compounded glasses, as well as those of conventional soft glasses, have been compounded. Most, such as Kovar, developed by the Westinghouse Electric Company, and Fernico, a product of the General Electric Company, are compounded principally of nickel, cobalt, and iron. They made possible the development of the "all-metal" electron tubes. Another is Sealmet, a product of the Higrade Sylvania Corporation. Unfortunately, these alloys require extended heat treatment at about 1000 degrees Centigrade (1832°F) in an atmosphere of hydrogen bubbled through water, and they must be used within a few hours of this degassing procedure. If the alloys are not so treated, fine bubbles appear in the seal that weaken the bond and cause leaks. Because few beginners, students, or small laboratories have access to thermostatically controlled hydrogen furnaces, we will not discuss the use of these alloys. Those who wish to pursue the topic are referred to the excellent professional reference, *Scientific and Industrial Glass Blowing and Laboratory Techniques*, by W. E. Barr and Victor J. Anhorn (Instruments Publishing Company, Pittsburgh, Pa. 1959).

Dumet seals

One alloy that is compatible with the soft glasses requires no degassing. This is a copper-coated composition of nickel and iron known as Dumet. The alloy is used for sealing leads into electric lamp bulbs, in electrodes of neon signs, and so on. Dumet comes in the form of wire in sizes ranging from about 20 to 28 gauge, precut to a length of about 6 centimeters. Normally, the wire is inserted through the end of a glass tube of appropriate diameter and sealed by softening the glass and squeezing the ends of the glass and the wire together. The result is known as a "press seal."

To make a seal using Dumet leads, first soften the end of a tube as in Figure 6-13, *a*. Crimp but do not comletely close the softened end (6-13, *b*). Insert the Dumet leads. (It should be noted at this point that some device will usually be connected to the inner ends of the leads—perhaps a cylindrical electrode, a filament, or a miniature metallic crucible containing a substance such as an alkali metal. If so, the metal assembly may be inserted in the open end of the tube with the Dumet leads facing the partially closed end.) Then incline the tube so the assembly slides to the partially closed end with the leads protruding (6-13, *c*). Soften the glass, squeeze into intimate contact with the metal, stretch about 3 millimeters, and then heat strongly to assure that it wets the metal (6-13, *d*). Surface tension will thicken the molten glass (6-13, *e*). Restore the seal to its former thickness by squeezing the end with a pair of tweezers (6-13, *f*). Anneal (6-13, *g*).

Sealing tungsten to borosilicate glass

Gas-tight seals between tungsten and borosilicate glass are not quite as easy to make as those between Dumet and the soft glasses. The metal itself tends to be leaky. Tungsten is reclaimed from its ore as a powder that is subsequently converted into billets by sintering. The billets tend to be slightly porous. Wire drawn from them may contain microscopic channels capable of conducting gases. To make the wire gas-tight another metal such as nickel may be butt-welded to the ends. Tungsten wire used for conducting electric current through glass is usually made by

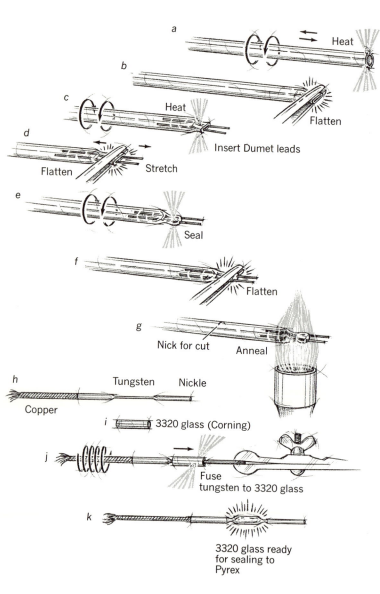

Figure 6-13.

welding a flexible copper lead to one end and a nickel wire to the other (Fig. 6-13, *h*). Such leads are available commercially.

Tungsten oxide does not enter into solution with molten glass as readily as does copper oxide. Yet, the glass must dissolve the oxide down to the metal if the seal is to be gas-tight. A thick, partially dissolved film of oxide may leak. In addition, tungsten must be degassed before it is sealed to glass, or bubbles will form at the interface between the glass and the metal. The bubbles weaken the seal and may encourage a leak. Finally, the thermal coefficient of expansion of tungsten differs so much from that of Pyrex glass that the two must be joined through a glass of intermediate expansion, a so-called "sealing" glass, if the metal is more than ½ millimeter thick.

We recommend the use of commercially prepared tungsten leads, those that have been plugged by butt-welding. The tungsten portion of the lead is degassed by bringing the metal to white heat in an oxygen-enriched fire. After the metal cools to a dull red, rub the tungsten against a lump of potassium nitrate and wash thoroughly in distilled water. This treatment should remove the oxide. If blotches of dark oxide remain, repeat the treatment until they disappear. Then reoxidize *lightly* by heating the tungsten to dull red for a few seconds. The thickness of the resulting oxide film varies with both the temperature and the heating time, quantities that must be determined by experiment. A film of correct thickness is easy to identify *after* the seal has cooled. The color of the interface between the metal and

the glass of a good seal ranges from yellow to reddish-brown. A film of oxide that is too thick causes a black interface. Such seals may occasionally be corrected by maintaining the glass in the molten state for a minute or so. If the treatment is successful, the black interface will turn reddish-brown. Conversely, oxide films of insufficient thickness do not make good seals. The glass does not adequately wet the metal. The interface has the color of the unoxidized tungsten.

The metal must always be coated by a glass that has a thermal coefficient of expansion intermediate between that of tungsten and that of Pyrex. If the thickness of the wire does not greatly exceed 1 millimeter, we use Corning 3320 (uranium glass) or Corning 7720 (Nonex). For thicker wires, we fuse 3320 glass to the metal, 7720 glass to the 3320, and Pyrex 7740 to the 7720—a structure known as a graded seal. (See the table at the end of Section I, page 18.)

To apply the sealing glass to the wire, first draw an 8-millimeter tube of 3320 glass to an inside diameter slightly larger than that of the metal. Cut the small tube to the same length as the tungsten to be covered (Fig. 6-13, *i*). Slip the tube over the *lightly* oxidized wire and fuse it in place by concentrating the heat on one end of the glass tubing. As the glass shrinks into contact with the metal, move the heat gradually to the other end (6-13, *j*). All air must be squeezed from the interface by the shrinking glass. Cool the seal slowly to minimize the development of strain (6-13, *k*).

Tungsten so coated may be used in a press seal, just as Dumet is sealed to soft glass. Alternatively, a single lead may be sealed through the wall of a bulb or other apparatus by applying the sealing glass to the metal in the form of a bead. The bead is then sealed into a hole of smaller diameter in the Pyrex. Incidentally, tungsten is a relatively brittle substance at room temperature. It may be bent if heated to a bright red.

Housekeeper seals

Copper in any one of four shapes— wire, thin sheet, tubes, or disks—may be sealed to either the soft or the borosilicate glasses. If you are using wire, first flatten the section that will come in contact with the glass to a thickness of not more than 0.5 millimeter and then file the edges to knife-sharpness (Fig. 6-14, *a, b, c*). As viewed in cross section, the flattened and sharpened portion may take the form of a parallelogram (6-14, *d*). Heat the piece until the color changes to a reddish-brown, indicating the formation of a light film of oxide, and immediately paint it with a concentrated solution of borax or drop it into the solution (6-14, *e*). For a solution, the Borateem variety used as a household detergent works nicely. When dry, the wire should be uniformly covered by a white film of borax. The metal may then be incorporated into a press seal. Confine the molten glass to the flattened portion of the wire and concentrate the fire more on the glass than on the metal (6-14, *f*). Heat converts the borax into a form of glass that not only helps to dissolve the oxide but shields the copper from excessive additional oxida-

tion, the property that accounts for the usefulness of the substance as a welding flux. Sheet copper up to 0.5 millimeter in thickness and 25 millimeters in width may be similarly sealed.

Copper tubing is prepared for sealing to glass tubing by filing or otherwise sharpening the end of the copper to a feather edge at an angle of approximately 10 degrees (6-14, *g*). A holder of some sort must be improvised that will plug the tubing and enable you to manipulate the hot metal. We use a tapered plug of Transite into which a handle of 8-millimeter glass rod is cemented with sodium silicate. Coat the heated tube with borax and then seal into a glass tube just large enough to slip over the end of the metal. The glass must not extend beyond the point at which the thickness of the copper exceeds 0.5 millimeter (6-14, *h*). Then burn off the glass just beyond the end of the metal and blow off the resulting bulb (6-14, *i*). Coat the inner surface of the metal by spinning the unattached portion of the glass over the edge by by means of a flaring tool (6-14, *j*). Promptly seal the glass coating to any desired tubing before the metal cools (6-14, *k*). Pyrex can be joined successfully to soft glass via a copper sleeve, and successful seals as large as 15 centimeters in diameter have been made. They are rather weak mechanically, but vacuum-tight. When joining Pyrex to soft glass by this technique, make the Pyrex-to-metal seal first.

Occasion also arises for closing the end of glass tubing with a metal disk in some types of gas discharge tubes and for sealing electrical conductors

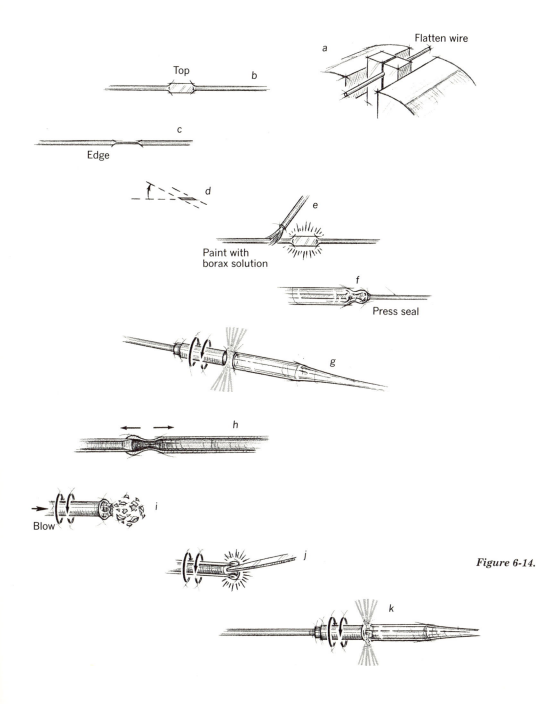

Flatten wire

Top

Edge

Paint with
borax solution

Press seal

Blow

Figure 6-14.

of large diameter into evacuated apparatus. Copper disks of any desired diameter and up to 0.5 millimeter in thickness seal readily to the flared ends of glass tubing. Just heat and lightly oxidize the disk, drop it while it is hot into the concentrated solution of borax, and dry (Fig. 6-15, *a*).

Place the disk on a hot block of carbon and bring the softened edge of the flare lightly into contact with the copper. The glass will melt the borax and adhere to the tacky film (6-15, *b*). Pick up the adhering disk with the glass and make a conventional butt seal to a second tube that has been flared to the same diameter (6-15, *c, d*). Pull a point in the second tube close to the disk (6-15, *e*). By blowing and simultaneously pulling, expand this point into a long, thin bulb (6-15, *f*). Strike off the bulb and remove the jagged edges by stroking with a piece of wire screening that has been tacked to a wooden paddle (6-15, *g*). Fire-polish the edges and anneal (6-15, *h*).

A conductor can be supported by the disk, of course. Simply drill the disk, insert a conductor of the desired size, and braze it in place with an alloy that melts at a reasonably high temperature, such as silver solder. Drop the hot brazed assembly into a pickling solution consisting of one part of sulfuric acid in nine parts of tap water. The pickling solution removes the excessive oxide formed by the brazing operation. Rinse the piece thoroughly to remove the acid. Then reheat to oxidize lightly and coat with borax (6-15, *i*). Support the metal assembly in the flared glass tube by means of a roll of asbestos tape, as illustrated (6-15, *j*). Make

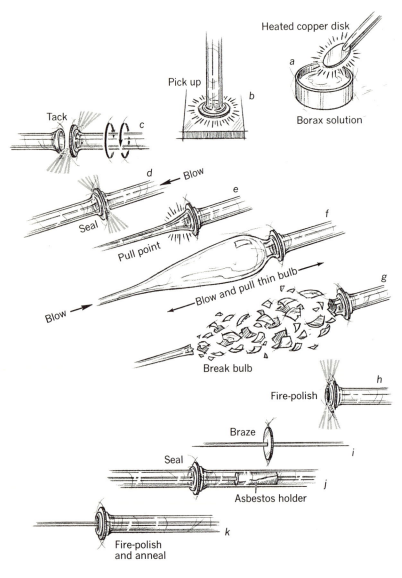

Figure 6-15.

the seal and form the glass ring on the outside of the disk as previously explained (6-15, *k*).

In general, Housekeeper seals are relatively weak, mechanically. They are also subject to attack by a number of chemicals as well as by Mercury. They may be electroplated easily, however, and thus protected against selected substances.

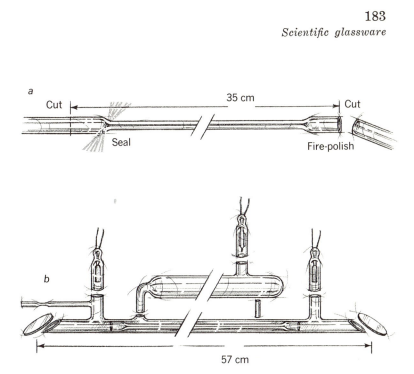

A helium-neon laser tube

One of the more important scientific advances of the middle twentieth century has been the development of the laser, actually a family of devices used for generating an intense beam of coherent light—light of a single frequency in which all waves travel in step. A detailed discussion of coherent light and laser technology is beyond the scope of this volume but the fabrication of an amplifier tube of the helium-neon type is a nice exercise for the beginner. When filled with a mixture of seven parts of helium and one part of neon, at a pressure of 2.7 torrs, and inserted between a pair of appropriate mirrors, this tube will, when energized, develop a beam of coherent light of 3-milliwatt intensity at a wavelength of 6328 Angstroms. The tube consists of a 2-millimeter capillary equipped with enlarged ends (short lengths of 10-millimeter tubing) that make a snug fit with an envelope of 13-millimeter tubing (Fig. 6-16, *a*).

The envelope of the tube, when used between spherical mirrors of 60-centimeter focal length (a typical size), may have an overall length of 57 centimeters (including the end windows) (6-16, *b*).

The capillary assembly may be made of borosilicate glass but the envelope should be of lead glass which, in contrast with the borosilicate glasses, is relatively impervious to helium. Short side arms are first sealed to the envelope tube, two for the subsequent attachment of electrodes at the ends and one for connecting a gas reservoir, as illustrated (6-16, *b*). The envelope must not be permitted to bend during the attachment of the side arms. If desired, the tube may be held in alignment during the sealing operation by means of a supporting fixture of the type previously described (see page 119). The reservoir should have a minimum length of 30 centimeters. A side arm of the reservoir supports a so-called

Figure 6-16.

"KIC getter" assembly, a pair of miniature crucibles of nickel-iron alloy that contain a few milligrams of metallic barium. (The getters are commercial items.) When heated by a current of 7 amperes, the vaporized barium condenses as a black film on the walls of the glass where it unites chemically with gaseous impurities in the helium-neon gas mixture and thus immobilizes the impurities.

Proceed in the following sequence when fabricating the tube: first add one of the side arms at the end, and equip it with a side arm of 6-millimeter tubing. Form a small dimple in the envelope on the inner side of the seal. The dimple serves as a stop for restricting the movement of the capillary assembly. Then add the side arm for the reservoir. After the work has cooled, insert the capillary assembly, add the third side arm, and form the second dimple. The edge of this dimple should not make contact with the enlarged end of the capillary. Allow a clearance of about 2 millimeters. Anneal the envelope assembly. Annealing will require the use of an oven. Next, cut the ends of the envelope tubing at an angle of 34 degrees, 34 minutes and precisely in the same plane of orientation. This may be accomplished with the use of either a carborundum wheel or a hacksaw equipped with a copper blade fed with a slurry of carborundum grit. (For comprehensive details on a simple and inexpensive technique of cutting laser tubes at this critical angle, see "The Amateur Scientist," *Scientific American,* December, 1964.) The electrodes of the laser may be made or purchased. Standard neon sign electrodes may be used. They consist of iron cylinders; the inner surface of each is coated lightly by a mixture of barium strontium carbonate suspended in collodion that has been diluted by 100 parts of acetone. (The solution may be applied with the end of a cotton swab, in case you make your own.) The coated electrodes are spot-welded to a pair of Dumet wires. (Two wires are used for good mechanical support.) The getters are connected in series with the Dumet leads. Seal the reservoir to the envelope, add the brace and then the electrodes. Finally, attach end windows of fused quartz, 1 millimeter in thickness, to the envelope by means of epoxy cement.

The Urey apparatus

An interesting apparatus, which involves sealing platinum directly to borosilicate glass and the fabrication of a heating unit as an integral part of the glasswork, is the tube devised by the chemist Harold Urey for simulating the origin of amino acids, the building blocks of life, in the earth's primordial seas. As the earth's early environment was reconstructed in theory by Urey and associates, the initial atmosphere consisted primarily of a mixture of hydrogen, methane, ammonia, carbon dioxide, and water vapor. The hot earth kept the seas near the boiling point. Lightning continuously ionized the gases, encouraging the molecules to recombine in new and increasingly complex compounds. Urey postulated that the amino acids would appear among the compounds thus synthesized. To test this contention a tube was constructed of borosilicate glass that contained some 200 millimeters of sterile water. The volume above the water was filled with the postulated mixture of gases. Spark discharges between platinum electrodes near the top of the envelope simulated lightning. The water was kept at the boiling point by a mantle of nichrome wire energized by an electric current. After the tube had operated continuously for a week, the water turned pink. Analysis proved that the solution now contained some eight of the twenty amino acids. Other experimenters have now synthesized the remaining acids, some of which have spontaneously combined into structures that may constitute the beginning of the living cell.

The construction involves in part sealing a 25-millimeter tube inside a 35-millimeter envelope. All parts are made of Corning 7740 Pyrex. The inner tube must be supported by a special holder when the seals are made. An adequate holder can be made by pulling a point on a 20-centimeter length of 20-millimeter tubing, removing the taper, blowing out the end, and sealing a convenient length of 8-millimeter tubing to the opening. A roll of asbestos tape on the 20-millimeter tube makes a snug fit with the interior wall of the envelope (Fig. 6-17, *a*). The electrodes (6-17, *b2*) consist of 20-gauge platinum wire with flattened zones filed to sharp edges for sealing by the Housekeeper (1923) technique. Platinum seals to Pyex by this technique as readily as does copper. Begin the assembly by inserting the holder and sealing one end of the 25-millimeter water jacket (6-17, *b5*) to the 35-millimeter enve-

lope (6-17, *b1*). While the seal is hot add the adacent hose connection (6-17, *b6*). In making these seals, stopper one end of the envelope and use the other end for blowing the seals to correct contour. A blowing hose fitted with an appropriate adapter may be employed if desired. The remaining ring seal is now made. Both sides of this seal must be blown, of course. This may be accomplished conveniently by coupling the blowing hose to both the open end of the envelope and the inlet of the water jacket by a Y fitting made of 8-millimeter tubing. While the seal is hot, add the second hose connection. The bottom of the envelope may now be closed. Add the stopcocks (6-17, *b3*, *b7*). Seal the brace to the inlet tube of the upper stopcock (6-17, *b3*) at a point about 2 centimeters from the shell. Seal the other end of the brace to the envelope. Finally, add the electrodes. Use an electrode holder when making the seals.

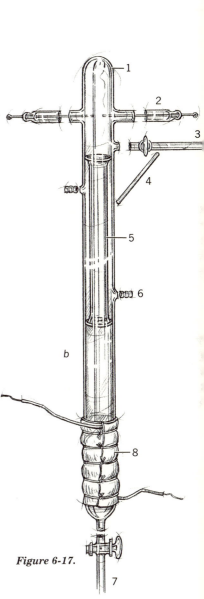

Figure 6-17.

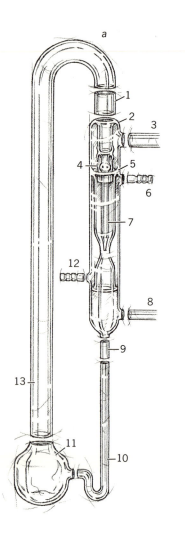

Figure 6-18.

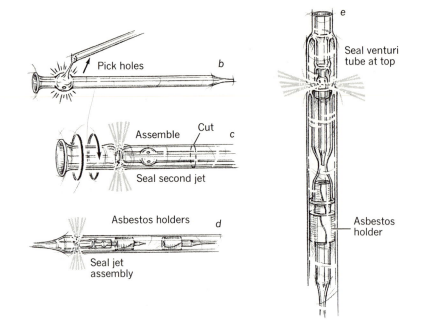

Table of dimensions for diffusion pump (*Fig. 6-18*)

Part number	Diameter in millimeters	Length in millimeters
1	25	30
2	35	240
3	18	60
4	15	65
5*	25	150
6	8	35
7**	8	96
8	10	60
9	8	30
10	8	210
11	60	60
12	8	35
13***	25	—

* Inner diameter of the constriction, 7 millimeters
** Inner diameter of the nozzle, 3 millimeters
*** Adjust for overall pump length of 480 millimeters

The heating mantle is made by wrapping the bottom of the envelope with two layers of asbestos paper 12 centimeters in width. Saturate the paper with sodium silicate (water glass) when the wrapping is made and tie it in place with a few turns of thread. Over the paper wind a single layer coil of nichrome wire. Space the turns at least 2 millimeters apart.

Suitable wire for the heater is available in the form of a 300-watt replacement unit at most hardware stores. The units come in the form of a helix. The wire can be straightened by slipping one end of the helix over a finishing nail clamped in a vise. Simply grasp the end of the wire with a pair of pliers and pull. The coil readily unwinds. Apply a second wrapping of asbestos paper over the heating coil, saturate the paper with sodium silicate, and bind it in place with four or five loops of tie wire. The heater is operated from a variable voltage transformer, such as a Variac. When the sodium silicate dries, the tube is ready for use.

A two-stage mercury diffusion pump

Few modern laboratories, particularly those concerned with the disciplines of physics or chemistry, are complete without a high vacuum system composed of at least a mechanical forepump and a two-stage diffusion pump. Adequate forepumps can be improvised from used refrigerator compressors by removing the check valve and using the former exhaust port as the inlet. Diffusion pumps, on the other hand, must be either pur-

chased or made. Currently, mercury diffusion pumps capable of exhausting gases at the rate of 3 liters per second are priced at about $100. The glass of which they are made is worth about $2. The artisan who has completed all the exercises in this volume will find that an adequate diffusion pump of this size is not difficult to make by hand. (See Fig. 6-8, *a* and Plate 9).

First make up the parts, the nozzle of the first-stage jet (6-18, *a4*, *a10*), the boiler (6-18, *a11*), the venturi (6-18, *a5*), the trap (6-18, *a10*), the boiler (6-18, *a11*), and the flue (6-18, *a13*), observing the dimensions listed in the table. In a pump of this type, mercury vapor from the boiler enters the second nozzle. Here the flow divides, and part of the vapor escapes through three equally spaced holes in the throat of the second-stage nozzle and enters the throat of the first-stage nozzle. The holes should have a diameter of about 3 millimeters and may be "picked" in the bulge (as drawn to scale in Fig. 6-18, *b*). The technique of picking holes is discussed on page 123 of Section IV.

This stage is assembled to the first-stage nozzle (6-18, *a4*) by a ring seal (6-18, *c*). Anneal. The subassembly is next sealed to the water jacket (6-18, *a2*). A point is first pulled on one end of the water jacket to serve as a handle. The second-stage nozzle is centered in the jacket by a holder of asbestos paper and a second holder fitted to the open end of the jacket to serve as a handle for making the ring seal, as illustrated (6-18, *d*). After this seal is complete, and the holders have been removed, anneal the work. After it cools, seal the upper end of the venturi (6-18, *25*) to the jacket (6-18, *e*). When making this seal support the venturi by a holder of the type suggested in the illustration. Carefully center the nozzle of the second stage in the venturi constriction before the glass hardens. Add the upper hose connection of the water jacket before the ring seal cools (6-18, *a6*). Next, seal on the side arm that serves as the inlet of the pump (6-18, *a3*). The lower end of the venturi is sealed to the jacket. The second hose connection (6-18, *a12*) and exhaust tube (6-18, *a8*) are added while the glass is hot. The remaining seals may be made in any desired sequence.

A final recommendation

The individual who becomes proficient in the simple arts discussed in this volume will discover that the fascinations of glass continue without limit. It is one thing to convert glass rod and tubing into attractive novelties or scientific apparatus and quite another to accomplish the same end by commencing with raw, white sand. Yet, with only modest facilities—a small crucible, a few fire bricks, some iron pipe, and a gas burner—the amateur can learn to make his own glass in any desired form or color. The raw ingredients may consist of such common materials as silica in the form of diatomaceous earth, lime and soda that are available in most communities from local suppliers of hardware, building materials, and poultry feed. A common mix would be the following: 50% cullet (broken glass), 34% silica, 11% soda, 5% lime. When these materials are combined and fired, the mixture becomes lime glass. (For titles of books on glass making, see the bibliography, page 191.)

The mass can be transformed into rod or tubing by means of two simple tools: a convenient length of iron pipe and an iron rod capped with a disk of iron. The latter tool, called a puntil (pronounced "punty"), may be made by welding an iron washer about 2 inches in diameter to the end of an iron rod $\frac{3}{8}$ inch in diameter. The molten glass is gathered on the iron pipe and partially blown as discussed (page 113). If tubing is desired, the disk of the puntil is first heated and attached to the outer end of the bulb by a helper. Tubing is formed by simultaneously blowing and stretching the bubble as the artisan and his helper move apart. A moist wooden board may be placed on the floor for catching the soft tubing. To make rod, a second puntil is substituted for the blowpipe. A gather is made, the second puntil is attached, and the rod is stretched to desired diameter.

Such procedures lie close to the historic beginnings of glass technology. At the other extreme are machines that accept molten glass from the pot and convert it into substantially every product known to commerce.

Arrange a visit to a glass factory and watch these machines in operation and, if possible, also the craftsmen who still make masterworks of glass by hand. A tour of the Corning Glass Center, Corning, New York, for example, where artists in glass work still create Steuben Ware by hand, can be an invaluable and unforgettable experience.

Sources of tools & materials

Glass tubing and rod
in all sizes, kinds, and colors.
Kits for beginners,
air compressors, and related supplies

Techno-Scientific Supply Company, Inc.
P.O. Box 191
Baldwin, New York 11510

Glass working tools

Arthur H. Thomas Company
Vine Street at Third
P.O. Box 779
Philadelphia, Pennsylvania 19105

Fisher Scientific Company
633 Greenwich Street
New York, New York 10014

Techno-Scientific Supply Company, Inc.
P.O. Box 191
Baldwin, New York 11510

Etching chemicals

Fisher Scientific Company
633 Greenwich Street
New York, New York 10014

Glass fires and gas burners

American Gas Furnace Company
Elizabeth, New Jersey 07207

Techno-Scientific Supply Company, Inc.
P.O. Box 191
Baldwin, New York 11510

Glass-to-metal seals

Associated Engineering, Inc.
Glen Ridge, New Jersey, 07028

Uranium glass

Houde Glass Company
Box 296
Keyport, New Jersey 07735

Kovar, Dumet

Westinghouse Electric Corporation
Blairsville, Pennsylvania 15717

Colored enamels

B. F. Drakenfeld & Company
45 Park Place
New York, New York 10007

Motion Pictures

W. H. Freeman and Company
660 Market Street
San Francisco, California 94104

Willard Pictures, Inc.
45 West 45th Street
New York, New York 10036

Motion picture films in full color (silent or with sound), in which James Hammesfahr demonstrates all of the basic operations of glass blowing described in this volume, are available. They are suitable for school or home showing. Write to W. H. Freeman and Company for illustrated brochure.

Bibliography

Barr, W. E., and J. Victor Anhorn. *Scientific and Industrial Glass Blowing*. Pittsburgh: Instruments Publishing Company, 1959.

Corning Glass Works. *This Is Glass*. New York: Corning, n.d.

Day, R. K. *Glass Research Methods*. Chicago: Industrial Publications, Inc., 1953.

Gunther, R. *Glass Tank Furnaces*. Sheffield, England: Thornton, Hallam, 1958.

Housekeeper, W. G. The Art of Sealing Base Metals Through Glass. *Journal of the American Institute of Electrical Engineers*, Vol. 42, 1923, pp. 954-960.

Morey, W. *The Properties of Glass*. New York: Reinhold Publishing Corp., 1954.

Park-Winder, William E. *Simple Glass Blowing for Laboratories and Schools*. London: Crosby, Lockwood & Son, Ltd., 1947.

Phillips, C. J. *Glass the Miracle Maker*. New York: Pittman Publishing Corp., 1941.

Right, R. W. *Manual of Laboratory Glass Blowing*. Brooklyn: Chemical Publishing Co., Inc., 1943.

Scholes, S. R. *Modern Glass Practice*. New York: Industrial Publications, Inc., 1952.

Sealing Glass to Kovar. Bulletin #145. Latrobe, Pa.: Stupakoff Ceramic and Manufacturing Co.

Shand, E. B. *Glass Engineering Handbook*. New York: McGraw-Hill Book Co., 1958.

Stanworth, J. E. *Physical Properties of Glass*. New York: Oxford University Press, 1938.

Stong, C. L. *The Scientific American Book of Projects for the Amateur Scientist*. New York: Simon and Schuster, Inc., 1960.

Strong, John, H. Victor Neher, Albert E. Whitford, C. Hawley Cartwright, and Roger Hayward. *Procedures in Experimental Physics*. Englewood Cliffs, N.J.: Prentice-Hall, Inc., 1938.

Tooley, F. V. *Handbook of Glass Manufacture*. New York: Glass Publishing Co., 1960.

Waugh, Sidney. *The Art of Glass Making*. New York: Dodd, Mead & Co., 1938.

Weyl, W. A. *Colored Glasses*. Cambridge, Mass.: Robert Bently, Inc., 1951.

Index